W9-BDF-805

VOCABULARY *in use*

UPPER INTERMEDIATE

Reference and practice for students
of North American English

**WITH
ANSWERS**

Michael McCarthy
Felicity O'Dell

with Ellen Shaw

CAMBRIDGE
UNIVERSITY PRESS

PUBLISHED BY THE PRESS SYNDICATE OF THE UNIVERSITY OF CAMBRIDGE
The Pitt Building, Trumpington Street, Cambridge CB2 1RP, United Kingdom

CAMBRIDGE UNIVERSITY PRESS
The Edinburgh Building, Cambridge CB2 2RU, United Kingdom
40 West 20th Street, New York, NY 10011-4211, USA
10 Stamford Road, Oakleigh, Melbourne 3166, Australia

© Cambridge University Press 1997

This book is in copyright. Subject to statutory exception
and to the provisions of relevant collective licensing agreements,
no reproduction of any part may take place without the written
permission of Cambridge University Press.

First published 1997
Second printing 1998

Printed in the United States of America

Typeset in Sabon

Library of Congress Cataloging-in-Publication Data

McCarthy, Michael (date).
Vocabulary in use upper intermediate / Michael McCarthy, Felicity O'Dell,
and Ellen Shaw.
p.   cm.
Includes index.
ISBN 0-521-57768-3 (with answers). – ISBN 0-521-57700-4 (without
answers)
1. Vocabulary – Problems, exercises, etc. 2. English language –
Textbooks for foreign speakers. I. O'Dell, Felicity (date).
II. Shaw, Ellen. III. Title.
PE1449.M28   1997
428.2'4–dc20   96-44820
                                                          CIP

A catalog record for this book is available from the British Library.

ISBN 0-521-57768-3 (with answers)
ISBN 0-521-57700-4 (without answers)

Contents

Topics

Notional concepts

Feelings and actions

Fixed expressions

Phrasal verbs and verb-based expressions

Special topics

Acknowledgments

The authors and publishers would like to thank the following for permission to reproduce copyright material in *Vocabulary in Use, Upper Intermediate.*

p. 2: extract from *The English Language* by David Crystal (London: Penguin Books Ltd.), p. 10, copyright © David Crystal 1988, reproduced by permission of Penguin Books Ltd.; pp. 10, 11: definitions of "subway," "hairy," and "slip" adapted and reprinted with permission from *Cambridge International Dictionary of English* (Cambridge: Cambridge University Press, 1995); p. 10: definition of "malignant" from *Longman Dictionary of Contemporary English,* 3rd ed., 1995, reprinted by permission of Addison Wesley Longman Ltd.; p. 12: extract from *Language Learning Strategies: What Every Teacher Should Know,* by Rebecca L. Oxford, p. 66 (Boston: Heinle & Heinle, 1990), reprinted by permission of Heinle & Heinle; p. 90: extract from *The Great Towns of the West,* by David Vokac (San Diego: West Press, 1985), p. 304, copyright © 1985 by David Vokac; p. 90: photograph by Liaison International / Michael J. Howell; pp. 93, 257: extracts from *The Cambridge Encyclopedia* by David Crystal (1991), Cambridge University Press; p. 103: cartoon from *The Wall Street Journal* – permission, Cartoon Features Syndicate; p. 108: photograph of Capitol by Jon Ortner © Tony Stone Images, photograph of Parliament by John Lamb © Tony Stone Images; p. 112: photograph by Mark Harwood © Tony Stone Images; p. 188: photograph courtesy of the Royal Canadian Mint.

Text composition by Don Williams.

Illustrations by Daisy De Puthod, Randy Jones, and Amanda MacPhail.

To the student

What is the purpose of this book?

Using this book will help you improve your English vocabulary. It will help you learn not only the meanings of words but also how they are used. It will also help you develop strategies for learning new vocabulary on your own after you have finished using the book. You can use the book either as a class text or for self-study.

How is the book organized?

The book has 100 two-page units. In most units the left-hand page explains new words and expressions that are studied in that unit. Where appropriate, there is information about how the words are used as well as their meaning. The right-hand page contains practice exercises to check that you have understood the information on the left-hand page. Occasionally the right-hand page will also teach you some more new words and phrases.

You can check your work by using the Answer Key at the back of the book. The key will sometimes give more than one answer or "suggested/possible answers" when the exercise is somewhat open ended. Sometimes the key provides comments that will help you learn even more about the words studied in the unit.

The index (which begins on page 203) lists the words and phrases covered in the book and the units in which they occur. The index also gives pronunciations for most single-word entries and many two-word compounds, using the symbols from the International Phonetic Alphabet. A key to those symbols is on page 202.

How should I use this book?

The introductory units in the first section should be completed first. These units will help you gain useful techniques and strategies for vocabulary learning, which you will be able to use throughout the book. After completing the introductory units (if you are studying on your own), you might want to work straight through the book, or you might prefer to do the units in a different order.

What else do I need in order to work with this book?

You will need a vocabulary notebook or file where you can write the new words you are learning. (See Unit 3 for advice on how to organize this.)

You will also need an English-English dictionary, preferably a learner's dictionary specifically for students whose first language is not English. Some good ones are the *Cambridge International Dictionary of English,* the *Longman Dictionary of Contemporary English,* and the *Longman Dictionary of American English.* (There are many other good learner's dictionaries.) It would be useful to find a good bilingual dictionary as well. If you can have only one dictionary, a learner's dictionary is probably the more useful of the two. (See Unit 5 for advice on using dictionaries.)

Learning vocabulary – general advice

What do you need to learn?

1. How many words are there in English? At least:
   a) 10,000   b) 100,000   c) 250,000   d) 500,000

2. How many words does the average English speaker use in everyday speech?
   a) 2,500   b) 5,000   c) 7,500   d) 10,000

3. How many words make up 45% of everything written in English?
   a) 50   b) 250   c) 1,000   d) 2,500

To summarize:

- There are many words in English that you don't need at all.
- There are other words you need simply to understand when you read or hear them.
- There are words that you need to be able to use yourself.

Clearly you need to spend the most time learning this last group.

In the text below underline the words you'd like to be able to use.

> English vocabulary has a remarkable range, flexibility and adaptability. Thanks to the periods of contact with foreign languages and its readiness to coin new words out of old elements, English seems to have far more words in its core vocabulary than other languages. For example, alongside *kingly* (from Anglo-Saxon) we find *royal* (from French) and *regal* (from Latin). There are many such sets of words which add greatly to our opportunities to express subtle shades of meaning at various levels of style.

To understand the text, you probably need only to understand, rather than to use, the verb *coin,* though there are many words above that you might like to be able to use.

What does knowing a new word mean?

It is not enough just to know the meaning of a word. You also need to know:

a) which words it is usually associated with
b) its grammatical characteristics
c) how it is pronounced (see also Unit 4)

Try to learn new words in phrases, not in isolation.

- Write down adjectives and nouns that are often associated, e.g., classical music, flying saucer, common sense.
- Write down verbs and nouns that form expressions, e.g., to express an opinion; to take sides.
- Write down nouns in appropriate phrases, e.g., in touch with; a sense of humor.
- Write down words with their prepositions, e.g., at a loss for words; thanks to you.
- Note special grammatical characteristics of new words. For example, note irregular verbs, e.g., *take, took, taken;* uncountable nouns, e.g., *luggage;* or nouns that are used only in the plural, e.g., *clothes.*
- Note any special pronunciation problems of new words.

1. How could you write these words in phrases to help you remember them?
   a) **chilly**   b) **dissuade**   c) **up to my neck**   d) **independent**
   e) **get married**
2. What would you write beside the following words?
   a) **scissors**   b) **weather**   c) **teach**   d) **advice**   e) **lose**   f) **pants**
3. What could you note beside the following words?
   a) **comb**   b) **catastrophe**   c) **photograph/photography**   d) **answer**

 Can you learn just by reading or listening to English?

You can help yourself learn English vocabulary by reading and listening to English as much as you can. Rank each item below from 0 to 4 to describe how important this way of learning vocabulary is for you personally. (4 is the most important.) You can add more items to the list if you like.

newspapers   TV (cable/subtitled)   movies   magazines   videos
radio   academic or professional readings   comics   fiction
cassettes or CDs (music or spoken word)   talking to English speakers

D **What should you do when you come across new words?**

- When you are reading something in English, don't stop to look up every new word or expression – this slows down your reading and your comprehension. Look up only those words that are really important for understanding the text. When you have finished reading, look back at what you have read and then perhaps look up some extra words and write down new expressions that interest you.
- Similarly, when you listen to English, don't panic when you hear words or expressions that you don't know. Keep listening for the overall meaning.
- When you read or listen to English, it is sometimes possible to guess the meaning of a word you don't know before you look it up or ask its meaning. Decide first which part of speech the word is, and then look for clues in its context or form.

Look at the following text. Before you read it, see if you know what the underlined words mean.

A <u>tortoise</u> is a <u>shelled</u> <u>reptile</u> <u>famed</u> for its slowness and <u>longevity</u>. The Giant Tortoise of the Galapagos may <u>attain</u> over 1.5 meters in length and have a <u>life span</u> of more than 150 years. Smaller tortoises from Southern Europe and North Africa make popular pets. They need to be <u>tended</u> carefully in cool climates and must have a warm place in which they can <u>hibernate</u>.

Which of the underlined words can you guess from the context or from the way the word is formed? First make a guess and then check by using a dictionary. Some words are impossible to guess from the context or from the form of the word. In those cases, go right to a dictionary for help.

Learning vocabulary – aids to learning

A   **Learning associated words together**

1. Learn words with associated meanings together.

Complete this bubble network for the word **CAT.** Add as many other bubbles as you like.

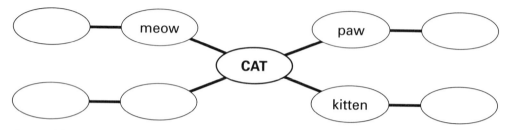

If possible, compare networks with your classmates. Add any of their ideas that you like to your own network.

2. Learn words with a grammatical association together.

Here are some groups of words, each of which has a grammatical connection. Can you see what the connection is? What other words could you add to these groups?

a) **child   tooth   foot**   c) **information   furniture   luggage**
b) **cut   split   put**

3. Learn words based on the same root together.

Can you add any words or expressions to these two groups?

a) **price   priceless   overpriced**
b) **handy   single-handed   give me a hand**

B   **Using pictures and diagrams**

Here are some ways that pictures can help you remember vocabulary.

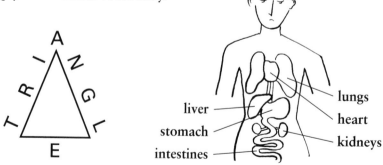

Can you draw any pictures that would help you remember the following vocabulary?

   a circle   to look a gift horse in the mouth   screwdriver

4

1. Word trees can be useful. Look at the word tree for **vacation.** Now complete a tree for **school.**

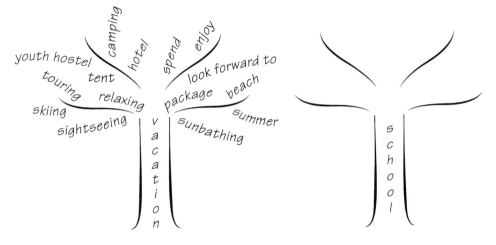

2. Word forks are a good way of learning adjectives and verbs. Look at the complete word forks below. Finish the others.

original		shoot		magnificent		kick	
brilliant		edit		breathtaking		hit	
unusual	idea	direct	a movie	superb	view	bounce	a ball
great		star in					
excellent		review					

3. A table can also help clarify collocations (words that are associated). Look at the following example of a table:

	a car	a motorcycle	a truck	a horse	a plane
to fly					+
to drive	+		+		
to ride		+		+	

Now complete the following sentences.

a) Her mother .... a truck for fifteen years, but now she's retired.
b) Have you ever .... a plane?
c) .... a motorcycle can be very dangerous.

You will do more practice with these and other ways of writing down vocabulary in Unit 3.

UNIT 3

Organizing a vocabulary notebook

There are many different ways to organize a vocabulary notebook. Here are some possibilities and examples.

A   Organizing words by meaning

Try dividing your notebook into different broad sections, with sections for **words for feelings, words to describe places, words for movement, words for thinking,** etc. In each section you can build families of words related in meaning.

B   Using various types of diagrams

1. Words can be grouped under a heading, or a more general word can be drawn as a tree diagram (see also Unit 2).

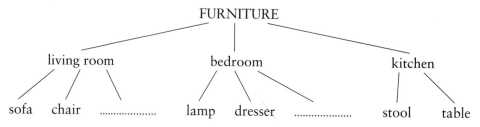

The dotted lines mean that you can add more words to the tree as you meet them.

2. A bubble network is also useful, since you can make it grow in whatever direction you want it to (see Unit 2).

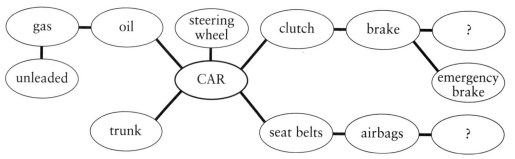

C   Organizing by word class

Here is how a Spanish learner of English marks word class in her notebook:

> I write phrases in red and also the definition. If they are verbs, in black, and blue if they are nouns . . . And if I write the Spanish translation I write it in another color. So it's very easy to see . . . I draw some pictures too.

D

When you find a synonym or an antonym of a word you already have in your book, enter it next to that word with a few notes:

> urban ≠ rural   stop = cease (more formal)

Exercises

3.1 Here is a list of words a Spanish learner of English made in her vocabulary notebook. How could she improve them and organize them better?

> clock - reloj
> tell the time - decir la hora
> office - despacho
> beneath
> under
> drowsy - The room was hot and I got drowsy.
> wristwatch - reloj de pulsera
> What time is it?
> next to - junto a/al lado de
> hands - the minute hand (minutero)
> wide awake (completely awake)

3.2 Here is a word map, a variation on the bubble network. What word do you think should go in the middle of the diagram?

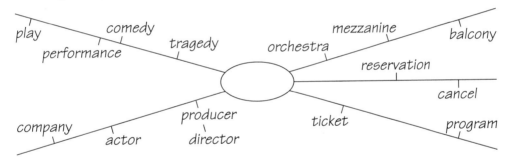

3.3 One learner tested himself regularly with his notebook, covering up the word and guessing it from his translation or from his other notes. Here is his system:

- If his translation and notes were clear, but he couldn't guess the word, he made a small red mark in the margin. Three red marks meant "needs extra effort."
- If his translation and notes couldn't help him guess the word, then he made a blue mark. This meant "need more information about this word."

What is your testing system? If you don't have a system, try to invent one, or ask other people what they do. Try out your system and decide if it works.

3.4 Making tables for word classes is a good idea, since you can fill in the blanks over time. What would you put in the remaining spaces in the table?

Noun	Verb	Adjective	Person
production	produce	....	producer
industry	....	industrial	....
export	....	....	....

The names of English language words

A   The names of basic parts of speech in English

article   noun   adverb   conjunction   gerund
↓   ↓   ↓   ↓   ↓
A   good student works hard at her studies, and she enjoys learning.
    ↑   ↑   ↑   ↑
    adjective   verb   preposition   pronoun

B   Words relating to nouns

Look at this sentence: *An artist loves beauty.* Artist is **countable** (i.e., it has a plural form: *artists*), but *beauty* is **uncountable**. Artist is the **subject** of the verb – it describes who does the verb; *beauty* is the **object** of the verb, i.e., what is affected by the verb.

C   Words relating to verbs

infinitive *(to go)*   **-ing form** *(going)*
past participle *(gone)*   **past tense** *(went)*

Go (go, went, gone) is an **irregular** verb, but *live* (live, lived, lived) is **regular.** *Go* is also **intransitive** because it does not need an **object** (e.g., Has Luis gone?). *Make* is **transitive** because it is followed by an **object** – you make something.

D   Words relating to the construction of words

In the word *irregularity,* *ir-* is a **prefix,** *regular* is a **root,** and *-ity* is a **suffix.** *Thin* is the **opposite** or **antonym** of *fat,* and *slim* is a **synonym** of *thin.* A **word family** is a set of words based on one **root,** e.g., *word, wordy, to reword.*

E   Words relating to pronunciation

A **syllable** is the minimum sound unit of a word, consisting of at least one vowel and any consonants on either side. There are three **syllables** (or beats) in the word *minimum,* and the **stress** is on the first **syllable.**

F   Words and their associations

There are different styles of speaking and writing appropriate to different situations. **Slang** is an extremely informal style; a **colloquial** style is suitable mainly for conversation (e.g., *a nice guy*). **Pejorative** words have a negative association. *Pigheaded* is **pejorative** whereas *determined,* which is very close in meaning, is not. **Collocation** refers to words that frequently occur together (e.g., *torrential rain*).

G   Words describing punctuation

.	period	,	comma	;	semicolon	’	apostrophe
-	hyphen	–	dash	!	exclamation point	?	question mark
( )	parentheses	" "	quotation marks	B	capital letter	:	colon

Exercises

4.1 Look at the paragraph about words and their associations in F opposite. Find at least three examples of each of the following:

1. nouns ....
2. verbs ....
3. adjectives ....
4. adverbs ....
5. prepositions ....

4.2 Mark the nouns in 4.1 with *C* (countable) or *UC* (uncountable). Mark the verbs *R* (regular) or *IR* (irregular), and *T* (transitive) or *IT* (intransitive).

4.3 Complete the following table.

Verb	Infinitive	-ing form	Past participle
define	....	....	....
mean	....	....	....
write	....	....	....

4.4 Think about the word *informal*.

1. What is its root, its prefix, and its suffix?
2. What is its opposite or antonym?
3. Does it have any synonyms?
4. Name some words that are included in its word family.

4.5 Look at all the words in bold in E, F, and G opposite. For each word with more than one syllable, mark which syllable is stressed.

4.6 The following pairs of words are close in meaning, but one word in each case is pejorative. Which?

1. terrorist / freedom fighter   3. fluent / wordy   5. cunning / shrewd
2. slim / skinny   4. stingy / thrifty   6. smug / confident

4.7 Can you form collocations with the words below?

night and .... chance
.... and gentlemen   savings ....

4.8 Cover the left-hand page and write the names of the punctuation marks.

( ) ....   ? ....   , ...
; ....   – ....   - ....
, ...   " " ....   ! ....

Using your dictionary

A

Good dictionaries in general, and learners' dictionaries in particular, can tell you a lot more about a word than just its meaning, including (among other things):

- Synonyms [words with the same or similar meaning], e.g., **mislay** and **misplace**
- Collocations [how words go together], e.g., **living** is often used in these phrases: **make a living / do something for a living; cost of living; standard of living; living things; living conditions; living daylights.**
- Pronunciation: This will mean learning some symbols that are different from the letters of the English alphabet. However, many symbols look just like ordinary letters and their pronunciation is easy to guess. For example: /ˈfren·zi/ for **frenzy** is fairly easy, but /θruˈɑʊt/ for **throughout** is more difficult. Be sure to check the pronunciation key.
- Word stress, often shown by a mark before the stressed syllable. For example: /ɪkˈspek·tən·si/ for **expectancy,** which is stressed on the second syllable.
- Syllable division, e.g., **reg·u·lar·ly**
- Differences between varieties of English, such as American, Australian, and British English. For example, look at these entries for **subway:**

sub•way UNDERGROUND PASSAGE /ˈsəb·weɪ/ *n* [C] *Br and Aus* an underground passage which allows people on foot to cross a busy road • *I walked through a graffiti-covered subway.*	**sub•way UNDERGROUND RAILWAY** /ˈsəb·weɪ/ *n* [C] *esp. Am* an underground electric railway; METRO; *We took the subway uptown.*

- Word class (usually abbreviations, e.g., **n:** noun, **adj:** adjective, etc.), whether a noun is countable or uncountable, and whether a verb is normally transitive (needs an object) or intransitive (doesn't need an object).
- Usage (how a word is used and any special grammatical pattern that goes with it): e.g., **suggest** + (that) + clause – "I suggest (that) you call her."
- Labels that give information about style and use in special situations (formal, informal, taboo, technical, dated). For example, look at this entry for **malignant:**

ma•lig•nant /məˈlɪg·nənt/ *adj* **1** *technical* a malignant TUMOUR, disease etc is one that develops uncontrollably and is likely to cause death –compare BENIGN (2) **2** *formal* showing hatred and a strong desire to harm someone: *He advanced towards them with a malignant look.* **–malignantly** *adv*

B

Don't forget that most words have more than one meaning. In this example, only the meaning on the right corresponds to the way **hairy** is used in this sentence:

It was a really **hairy** ride down the mountain road.

hair•y /ˈher·i/ *adj* **-ier, -iest** • Hairy means having a lot of hair, esp. on parts of the body other than the head; *hairy armpits/legs* • *He's very hairy, isn't he? Have you noticed his arms?*	**hair•y** /ˈher·i/ *adj* **-ier, -iest** *infml* frightening or dangerous, esp. in a way that is exciting • *I like going on the back of Lauren's motorbike, though it can get a bit hairy.*

Exercises

5.1 With a *bilingual* dictionary, try a double search: Look up a word in your language; the dictionary may give several possibilities in English. Look up each of those possibilities in the English section of the dictionary to see how they translate back into your language. This may help you to distinguish synonyms.

If you own a dictionary, make a little mark in the margin each time you look up a word. If a word gets three or more marks, it is worth an extra effort to learn it. What other learning techniques are there for dictionaries?

5.2 Some learners' dictionaries have *guide words,* which give core meanings, as in the examples below. For each sentence, identify which definition of *slip* is correct by writing the guide word beside the sentence.

1. **slip** SLIDE /slɪp/ *v* [I] **-pp-** to slide unintentionally • *Careful you don't slip – there's water on the floor.* • *She slipped while she was getting out of the bath.* • *A* **slipped disc** *is a medical condition in which one of the DISCS (= flat pieces of body tissue between the bones in the back) slides out of its usual place, causing pain in the back.*

2. **slip** *(obj)* DO QUICKLY /slɪp/ *v* [I] **-pp-** to go somewhere or carry out an action quickly, often so that you are not noticed • *Just slip out of the room while nobody's looking.*

3. **slip** GET WORSE /slɪp/ *v* [I] **-pp-** to go into a worse state, often because of lack of control or care • *Their standard of living has slipped steadily over the last ten years.* • *Productivity in the factory has slipped quite noticeably in the last year.*

4. **slip** PIECE OF PAPER /slɪp/ *n* [C] a small piece of paper • *She wrote my address on a slip of* **paper.** • *If you want to order a book fill in*

the green slip *(also* **form***).* • *Keep that slip (also* **receipt***) somewhere safe as proof of purchase.*

5. **slip** MISTAKE /slɪp/ *n* [C] a small mistake • *She's* **made** *one or two slips – mainly spelling errors – but it's basically well written.* • *I suffered the embarrassment of calling her new boyfriend by her previous boyfriend's name – it was just* **a slip of the tongue** *(= mistake made by using the wrong word).*

6. **slip** UNDERWEAR /slɪp/ *n* [C] a piece of underwear for a woman or girl which is like a dress or skirt

7. **slip** obj ESCAPE /slɪp/ *v* [T] **-pp-** to get free from, leave or escape (something) • *The ship slipped its moorings.* • *If you let an opportunity or a person* **slip through** *your* **fingers** *you lose it or them through lack of care or effort.* • *If something* **slips** *your* **memory/mind** *you forget it: I forgot I'd arranged to meet Richard last night – it completely slipped my mind.*

1. You can't wear that white dress with a black slip underneath. *underwear (6)*
2. He slipped on the ice and fell.
3. I meant to call you yesterday, but it slipped my mind.
4. Our profits are slowly slipping.
5. If you want to return something to a store, you need a sales slip.
6. I didn't mean to say that; it was just a slip.

5.3 Pronunciation. What English words are these and which syllable has the most stress in each one? Use the key on page 202.

1. /ˌedʒ·əˈkeɪ·ʃən/ ....
2. /ˈpæsˌpɔrt/ ....
3. /leŋkθ/ ....
4. /ˈlɪb·əɾ·i/ ....
5. /ˈrɪˈvɪ·ʒən/ ....
6. /ˈbrə·ðər/ ....

5.4 In the dictionary entry for *hairy* in B opposite, how many synonyms can you find?

UNIT
6 Reviewing vocabulary

A

Here is an extract from a book about language learning strategies on the importance of reviewing in an active way.

> Reviewing . . . is especially useful for remembering new material in the target language. It entails reviewing at different intervals, at first close together and then increasingly far apart. For instance, Misha is learning a set of vocabulary words in English. He practices them immediately, waits 15 minutes before practicing them again, and practices them an hour later, three hours later, the next day, two days later, four days later, the following week, two weeks later, and so on until the material becomes more or less automatic. In this way he keeps spiraling back to these particular vocabulary words, even though he might be encountering more material in class. Each time he practices these vocabulary words, Misha does it in a meaningful way, like putting them into a context or recombining them to make new sentences. Naturally, the amount of time needed to make new material automatic depends on the kind of material involved. (From *Language Learning Strategies: What Every Teacher Should Know,* by Rebecca L. Oxford)

B

Reviewing with this book

When you review a unit, first read it through. Next look at anything you wrote in your vocabulary notebook connected with the unit. Then, and most importantly, try to do something different with the new words and expressions in that unit in order to help fix them in your memory.

Here are some suggestions:

- Highlight (or underline) any words or expressions that you had forgotten or were not sure about.
- Look at the unit and choose ten words and expressions that you particularly want or need to learn. Write them down.
- Look up any words that you selected in an English-English dictionary. Do these words have any other uses or associations that might help you learn them? For example, looking up the verb **wish** might lead you to **wishbone** or **wishful thinking.** Write anything that appeals to you in an appropriate phrase or sentence.
- Perhaps the dictionary can also help you find some other words based on the same root. Looking up the noun **employment** will lead you to the verb **employ,** to the nouns **employer** and **employee,** and, perhaps, to the adjectives **employable, unemployed,** and **self-employed.**
- Note the pronunciation of the words and expressions you wish to learn. Use a dictionary to help you.
- In your notebook, write the words and phrases from a unit in a different way – put them into a network or a table, perhaps.
- The next day, ask yourself: How much can I remember?
- Test yourself. Cover part of a word or phrase. Can you remember the complete word or phrase?

C Making the new words active

One of the great advantages of reviewing vocabulary is that it should help you to make the step from having something in your receptive vocabulary to having it in your active vocabulary.

Encourage this process by:

- writing the words and expressions you are trying to learn in a sentence relating to your life and interests at the moment.
- making an effort to use the new words and expressions in your next class or homework or in some other way.
- keeping a learning diary in which you note down things that particularly interest you about the words you have learned.
- watching out for the words and expressions you are trying to learn in your general reading of English. If you come across any of them, write them down in their context in your diary or notebook.
- writing a paragraph or story linking the words and expressions you want to learn.

D What can you remember?

1. What do you remember now from the first six units in this book? Answer without looking back at the units.
2. Now read through the units again.
3. How much do you remember about the units now?
4. Choose at least one word and expression from each unit and work through all the suggestions made in B and C above. It may not always be appropriate in your future study to do all the steps in B, but try them now for practice.

E Some plans for your work with this book

1. How often are you going to review what you have done? (every week? every five units?)
2. Which techniques are you going to use for reviewing?
3. Now write yourself some notes to remind yourself of when you are going to review. For instance, you might like to write *review vocabulary* in your calendar for the next eight Fridays, if you decided to review every week. Alternatively, you could write REVIEW in capital letters after, say, every five units in the book.

Formal and informal words

Formality is about your relationship with the person you're speaking or writing to. If you use formal language, it may be because you want to show respect or politeness, or to put yourself at a distance (e.g., by using "official" language). Informal language can show friendliness, equality, or a feeling of closeness with someone. You should *never* use informal language just to sound fluent or witty.

A **Scales of formality**

Some groups of words can be put on a scale from (very) formal to (very) informal.

Very formal	Neutral	Very informal
abode/residence	house/apartment	place
alcoholic beverages	drinks	booze
offspring	children	kids

B **Short, monosyllabic informal words**

Informal versions of words are often short and monosyllabic, as we can see in the right-hand column in the table above. They include slang words.

It cost me ten **bucks.** [dollars]
My **bike** was stolen. [bicycle]
Come and meet my **mom** and **dad.** [mother and father]
Hi! Can't stop; see you, **bye!** [hello; goodbye]

C **Clipped words**

Shortening a word tends to make it less formal, as in **bye** in B.

I'll meet you in the **lab**(oratory).
We should put an **ad**(vertisement) in the (news)**paper.**
Are you still on the (tele)**phone?**
My sister's a **vet**(erinarian).

D **Formality in signs, instructions, etc.**

You will often see formal words in signs, notices, and directions. Here are some examples:

WE REGRET WE CANNOT ACCEPT CHECKS.

Smoking permitted in designated areas only

DO NOT LEAVE CHILDREN UNATTENDED

[Sorry, we don't take checks.]

[No smoking except in smoking sections.]

[Don't leave your children alone.]

(See also Unit 96 for more signs and notices.)

Exercises

7.1   If you look up an informal word in an English-English dictionary, you will often find a neutral synonym as part of the definition or explanation. For example, the *Cambridge Dictionary of International English* entry for *kid* says: "*infml* a child or young person."

Use an English-English dictionary to find neutral or more formal words for these:

1. snooze   3. a pal   5. brainy
2. a guy   4. a nerd   6. a cop

7.2   Make these conversations more *informal* by changing some of the words. Refer to the opposite page if necessary.

JIM: Ann, can you lend me fifty dollars?
ANN: What for?
JIM: To pay the rent on my abode.

MOM: Where's today's newspaper?
DAD: Mary might have it. She was looking at the advertisements.
MOM: Well, where is she?
DAD: In her room, talking on the telephone.

7.3   Say whether you think the following remarks/sentences are *okay, too formal,* or *too informal* for each situation described. If the remark/sentence is not quite right, suggest a different way to say it.

1. *(one classmate to another classmate)* Should we go to your residence or mine to work on our assignment?
2. *(parent to another parent at a school parents' meeting)* How many offspring do you have in school?
3. *(student to a university professor)* Will there be lab classes next week?
4. *(business letter to a customer)* Dear _____:
   Thank you for your inquiry regarding our new line of clothing for kids. . . .

7.4   Mini-quiz. Find words on the opposite page for the following:

1. the opposite of **prohibited**
2. a) **to be sorry**
   b) **selected**
3. informal versions of **Greetings!** and **Farewell!**

7.5   Explain these notices in less formal language. Where might you see them?

1.
> PAYMENT IS EXPECTED
> AT THE TIME SERVICES
> ARE RENDERED.

2.
> Carrier reserves the right to refuse carriage to any person who has acquired a ticket in violation of applicable law.

Suffixes

Suffixes can change the word class and the meaning of the word.

A Common noun suffixes

- -er is used for the person who does an activity, e.g., **writer, worker, consumer, teacher.** You can use -er with many verbs to make them into nouns.
- Sometimes, the -er suffix is written as -or, e.g., **doctor, sailor, supervisor.**
- -er/-or are also used for things that do a particular job, e.g., **pencil sharpener, computer, bottle opener, grater, projector.**
- -er and -ee can contrast with each other, -er meaning "person who does something" and -ee meaning "person who receives or experiences the action," e.g., **employer/employee, sender/addressee, payee** (e.g., of a check).
- -tion/-sion/-ion are used to form nouns from verbs, e.g., **complication, pollution, reduction, donation, promotion, admission.**
- -ism (an activity or ideology) and -ist (a person) are used for beliefs and ideologies, and sometimes professions (compare with -er/-or professions above), e.g., **liberalism, Buddhism, journalism, typist, physicist, terrorist, pianist.**
- -ness is used to form nouns from adjectives. Note what happens to adjectives that end in -y: **goodness, laziness, forgetfulness, happiness, sadness.**

B Adjective suffixes

-able/-ible combined with verbs often means "can be done," e.g., **washable** [can be washed] or **flexible** [can be bent].

drinkable	breakable	forgivable
readable	edible	

C Verbs

-ize forms verbs from adjectives, e.g., **modernize** [make modern], **commercialize, industrialize, popularize.**

D Other suffixes that can help you recognize the word class

-ment: (nouns) excitement   enjoyment   replacement
-ity: (nouns) flexibility   productivity   scarcity
-hood: (abstract nouns, especially family terms) childhood   motherhood
-ship: (abstract nouns, especially status) friendship   partnership   membership
-ive: (adjectives) passive   productive   active
-al: (adjectives) brutal   legal   (nouns) refusal   arrival
-ous: (adjectives) delicious   outrageous   furious
-ful: (adjectives) forgetful   hopeful   useful
-less: (adjectives) useless   harmless   homeless
-ify: (verbs) beautify   purify   terrify

Exercises

8.1 Use the suffixes *-er/-or*, *-ee*, and *-ist* to form the names of the following.

Example: A person who plays jazz on the piano.   *a jazz pianist*

1. The thing that wipes rain off your car windshield.
2. A person who plays classical piano.
3. A person who takes professional photographs.
4. A person who is employed by someone else.
5. An appliance for drying hair.
6. A person who donates his/her organs upon death.

8.2 Each picture is of an object ending in *-er* or *-or*. Can you name them?

8.3 List six jobs you would like to have in order of preference. How many different suffixes are there in your list? Which of the job names do not have a suffix? (e.g., pilot, movie star)

8.4 Do these words mean a thing, a person, or both?

1. a typewriter
2. a cleaner
3. a CD player
4. a dishwasher
5. a singer

8.5 Spelling changes. Rewrite each sentence by changing the underlined words, using a suffix from the opposite page. Make any necessary spelling changes.

1. Most of his crimes can be <u>forgiven</u>.
   Most of his crimes are ....
2. The club refuses to <u>admit</u> anyone not wearing shoes.
   The club refuses .... to anyone not wearing shoes.
3. Her only fault is that she is <u>lazy</u>.
   Her only fault is ....
4. This company has <u>produced</u> a lot in recent years.
   This company has been very .... in recent years.

8.6 Can you think of anything in your country that should be *nationalized* (e.g., airlines), *privatized*, *standardized*, *modernized*, or *computerized*?

8.7 Which word is the odd one out in each group and why?

1. brotherhood   neighborhood   manhood   priesthood
2. appointment   involvement   compliment   arrangement
3. tearful   spiteful   dreadful   handful
4. worship   kinship   friendship   partnership

9 Prefixes

A Prefixes are often used to give adjectives a negative or an opposite meaning. For example, comfortable/**un**comfortable, convenient/**in**convenient, and similar/**dis**similar are opposites. Other examples are **un**just, **in**edible, **dis**loyal. Unfortunately, there is no easy way of knowing which prefix any adjective will use to form its opposite.

Note:
- **in-** becomes **im-** before a root beginning with *m* or *p*, e.g., **im**mature, **im**patient, **im**partial, **im**probable. Similarly **in-** becomes **ir-** before a word beginning with *r*, e.g., **ir**replaceable, **ir**reversible, and **in-** becomes **il-** before a word beginning with *l*, e.g., **il**legal, **il**legible, **il**literate.
- The prefix **in-** (and its variations) does not always have a negative meaning – often it gives the idea of "inside" or "into," e.g., **in**ternal, **im**port, **in**sert, **in**come.

B The prefixes **un-** and **dis-** can also form the opposites of verbs, e.g., tie/**un**tie, appear/**dis**appear. These prefixes are used to reverse the action of the verb. Here are some more examples: **dis**agree, **dis**approve, **dis**believe, **dis**connect, **dis**credit, **dis**like, **dis**prove, **dis**qualify, **un**bend, **un**do, **un**dress, **un**earth, **un**fold, **un**load, **un**lock, **un**veil, **un**wrap.

C Here are examples of other prefixes in English. Some of these words are used with a hyphen. Check a dictionary if you're not sure.

Prefix	Meaning	Examples
anti	against	antisocial antibiotic antiwar
auto	of or by oneself	autograph autopilot autobiography
bi	two, twice	bicycle bilateral biannual bilingual
ex	former	ex-wife ex-smoker ex-boss
ex	out of	extract exhale excommunicate
micro	small	microcassette microwave microscopic
mis	badly/wrongly	misunderstand misspell misinform
mono	one/single	monotonous monologue monogamous
multi	many	multinational multipurpose multimedia
over	too much	overdo overqualified oversleep overeat
post	after	postwar postgraduate postimpressionist
pre	before	precede preconceived predict precaution
pro	in favor of	proponent pro-choice pro-labor
pseudo	false	pseudonym pseudo-intellectual
re	again or back	retype reread replace rewind
semi	half	semicircular semicolon semiconductor
sub	under	subway submarine subdivision
under	not enough	underworked underused undercooked

Exercises

9.1 Practice using words with negative prefixes. Contradict the following statements in the same way as the example. (Not all the words you need are on the opposite page.)

Example: He's a very honest man. *I don't agree. I think he's dishonest.*

1. I'm sure she's discreet.
2. I always find her very sensitive.
3. It's a convincing argument.
4. That's a very relevant point.
5. He's very efficient.
6. She's always seemed responsible.
7. He seems grateful for our help.
8. I'm sure she's loyal to the company.

9.2 Which negative adjective fits each of the following definitions?

1. .... means impossible to eat.
2. .... means unable to read or write.
3. .... means not having a job.
4. .... means spelled incorrectly.

9.3 Choose a negative verb from B opposite to fit each sentence below. Put it in the correct form.

Example: The runner was *disqualified* .... after a blood test.

1. I almost always find that I .... with her opinion.
2. I'm sure he's lying, but it's going to be hard to .... his story.
3. After a short speech the President .... the new statue.
4. It took the movers an hour to .... our things from the van.
5. Their telephone was .... because they didn't pay their last bill.

9.4 Answer the following questions. The answers are all in C opposite.

1. What kind of oven cooks things fast?
2. What kind of drug can help somebody with an infection?
3. What kind of company has branches in many countries?
4. What is a student who is studying for an advanced degree?
5. What is an *underground railroad* (U.S.) or an *underground passage* (U.K.)?

9.5 Construct English words to replace the underlined words.

Example: People often <u>pronounce</u> my name <u>incorrectly</u>. *They mispronounce it.*

1. Most people say they <u>have to work too hard and are paid too little</u>.
2. He dated his check with <u>a date that was later than the real date</u>.
3. She's still on good terms with <u>the man who used to be her husband</u>.
4. He made so many mistakes in the letter that he had to <u>write it again</u>.
5. I think the newspapers have <u>stated the facts incorrectly</u>.

9.6 Think of two more examples for each prefix in C opposite.

UNIT 10 Roots

A Many words in English are formed from Latin roots. These words are often considered fairly formal in English. Here are some examples of the more common Latin roots, with some of the English verbs derived from them.

spect: see, look
You should **respect** your parents / the laws of a country. [look up to]
The police **suspected** they were guilty but had no proof. [had a feeling]
Many American pioneers traveled west to **prospect** for gold. [search]

vert: turn
I tried a word processor but I soon **reverted** to my old typewriter. [went back]
Missionaries went to Africa to **convert** people to Christianity. [change the beliefs of]
The scandal **diverted** attention from the political crisis. [took away]

port: carry, take
How are you going to **transport** those boxes overseas? [send across]
The U.S. both **imports** and **exports** cars. [buys in, sells out]
The roof is **supported** by the old beams. [held up]

duc, duct: lead
She was **educated** abroad. [went to school]
He **conducted** the orchestra brilliantly. [led]
Japan **produces** a lot of electronic equipment. [makes]

press: press, push
I was **impressed** by your presentation. [full of admiration and respect]
This weather **depresses** me. [makes me feel miserable]
She always **expresses** herself articulately. [puts her thoughts into words]

pose, pone: place, put
The meeting has been **postponed** until next week. [changed to a later date]
The king was **deposed** by his own son. [put off the throne]
I don't want to **impose** my views on you. [force]

B The examples above are of verbs only. Note that for all the verbs listed, there is usually at least one noun and at least one adjective as well. Here are some examples.

Verb	Person noun	Abstract noun	Adjective
inspect	inspector	inspection	inspecting
advertise	advertiser	advertisement	advertising
deport	deportee	deportation	deported
introduce	introducer	introduction	introductory
oppress	oppressor	oppression	oppressive
compose	composer	composition	composite

Exercises

10.1 Complete as much of the table as possible with other forms of words in A opposite. Use a dictionary to help you if necessary.

Verb	Person noun	Adjective	Abstract noun
convert	*convert*	....	....
produce	....	....	....
conduct	....	....	....
impress	....	....	....
support	....	....	....
impose	....	....	....

10.2 Fill in the blanks in the sentences with words from B opposite.

1. He .... for having a forged passport.
2. This magazine has nothing in it but .... for cosmetics.
3. May I .... you to my boss?
4. The new take-out pizza place has a very good .... offer.
5. Before you buy a new home, be sure to .... it thoroughly.
6. Tchaikovsky .... some wonderful ballet music.

10.3 Can you figure out the meanings of the underlined words below? To help you, here are the meanings of their Latin prefixes:

intro: within, inward   **o, ob:** against   **re:** again, back
de: down, from   **ex:** out of   **sub, sup:** under

1. She's a very <u>introspective</u> person, and he's also very <u>introverted</u>.
2. He always seems to <u>oppose</u> everything I suggest.
3. I don't think it's healthy to <u>repress</u> one's emotions too much.
4. Perhaps you can <u>deduce</u> what the word means from the way it is formed.
5. The documentary <u>exposed</u> corruption in high places.
6. She tried hard to <u>suppress</u> a laugh.

10.4 Think of three other words based on each of the roots listed in A opposite. Put each into an appropriate phrase.

10.5 Match the verbs on the left with equivalent two-word verbs on the right. Which are more informal?

support	put off
postpone	turn away
oppose	look at
inspect	go against
deposit	cut down
reduce	hold up
divert	put down

Don't put off till tomorrow what you can do today.

UNIT 11 Abstract nouns

A An abstract noun represents an idea, experience, or quality, rather than an object that you can touch. **Happiness, intention,** and **shock** are abstract nouns, but **pen, bed,** and **clothes** are not.

B Suffixes are letters added to the ends of words to form new words. Certain suffixes are used frequently in abstract nouns. The most common are **-ment, -ion, -ness,** and **-ity.** The suffix **-ion** sometimes becomes **-tion, -sion, -ation,** or **-ition.** Here are some examples:

achievement	action	aggressiveness	absurdity
adjustment	collection	attractiveness	anonymity
amazement	combination	bitterness	complexity
discouragement	illusion	carelessness	curiosity
improvement	imagination	consciousness	generosity
investment	production	friendliness	hostility
replacement	recognition	permissiveness	prosperity
retirement	reduction	tenderness	sensitivity

Note: **-ment** and **-ion** are usually used to make verbs into abstract nouns. The suffixes **-ness** and **-ity** are often added to adjectives.

C Other suffixes that form abstract nouns are **-ship, -dom, -th,** and **-hood.** Here are some examples:

apprenticeship	boredom	breadth	adulthood
companionship	freedom	depth	brotherhood
membership	kingdom	length	childhood
ownership	martyrdom	strength	motherhood
partnership	stardom	warmth	neighborhood
relationship	wisdom	width	(wo)manhood

Note: The suffixes **-ship** and **-hood** are often added to nouns to form abstract nouns. The suffix **-th** is often added to adjectives, and the suffix **-dom** can combine with either nouns or adjectives.

D Many abstract nouns do not use any suffix at all. Here are some examples:

anger	faith	luck	sense
belief	fear	principle	sight
calm	humor	rage	speed
chance	idea	reason	thought

You can find more examples of suffixes in Units 8 and 10 and of abstract nouns in Units 68 and 69.

Exercises

11.1   Which abstract nouns are related to each of the following adjectives? (Some, but not all, of these nouns are listed on the opposite page.)

Example: happy   *happiness*

1. kind	5. amused	9. attentive	13. equal
2. secure	6. graceful	10. excited	14. hopeful
3. sensitive	7. original	11. popular	15. resentful
4. friendly	8. stupid	12. weak	16. wise

11.2   Which verbs are related to these abstract nouns?

Example: argument   *to argue*

1. collection	4. intensity	7. action	10. ownership
2. emptiness	5. strength	8. excitement	11. imagination
3. satisfaction	6. boredom	9. production	12. adjustment

11.3   Think of at least one more noun using each of the suffixes in B opposite (*-ment, -ion, -ness,* and *-ity*). Then think of at least one more noun using each of the suffixes in C opposite (*-ship, -dom, -th,* and *-hood*).

11.4   On the opposite page, find a synonym with the suffix in parentheses for each of the following nouns.

Example: animosity (-ness)   *aggressiveness*

1. astonishment (-ment)	5. substitution (-ment)	9. vision (no suffix)
2. inquisitiveness (-ity)	6. fame (-dom)	10. liberty (-dom)
3. fraternity (-hood)	7. decrease (-tion)	11. fury (no suffix)
4. possibility (no suffix)	8. community (-hood)	12. wealth (-ity)

11.5   Complete the quotations with these nouns.

imitation   advice   injustice   kingdom   darkness

1. "Better to light a candle than to curse the ...."
2. "Do not ask .... of the ignorant."
3. "Better to suffer .... than to commit it."
4. "... is the sincerest form of flattery."
5. "It is easy to govern a ...., but difficult to rule one's family."

11.6   Write your own quotations to describe the following abstract nouns.

1. freedom	3. life	5. imagination
2. friendship	4. curiosity	

Compound adjectives

A A compound adjective is made up of two parts. Sometimes it is written with a hyphen, e.g., **good-natured,** or as one word, e.g., **nearsighted.** Its meaning is usually clear from the words combined. The second part of the compound adjective is often a present or past participle. (*Note:* Some compound adjectives use a hyphen before a noun, e.g., a **well-known** singer, but not after a noun, e.g., That singer is **well known.**)

B A large number of compound adjectives describe personal appearance. Here is a somewhat **far-fetched** description of a person starting from the head down.

*Tom was a **curly-haired, suntanned, blue-eyed, rosy-cheeked, thin-lipped, broad-shouldered, left-handed, slim-hipped, long-legged, flatfooted** young man, wearing **brand-new, tight-fitting** jeans and **open-toed** sandals.*

C Other compound adjectives describe a person's character. Here is a **lighthearted** description of someone. The meanings are explained in parentheses.

*Melissa was **absent-minded** (forgetful), **easygoing** (relaxed), **good-natured** (cheerful), **warmhearted** (kind), and **quick-witted** (intelligent) if perhaps a little **pigheaded** (stubborn), **two-faced** (hypocritical), **self-centered** (egotistical), **quick-tempered** (easily angered), and **stuck-up** (conceited) at times.*

D Another special group of compound adjectives has a preposition in the second part. Some of these adjectives are listed below with a typical noun.

an **all-out** effort [total]   **built-in** furniture [can't be removed]
a **built-up** area [covered with buildings]   a **broken-down** car [it won't work]
a **burned-out** building [nothing left in it after a fire]
a **run-down** area [in poor condition]
worn-out shoes [can't be worn anymore]

E Here are some other useful compound adjectives:

air-conditioned	first-class	long-distance	so-called
bulletproof	handmade	longstanding	sugar-free
drip-dry	interest-free	off-peak	time-consuming
duty-free	last-minute	part-time	top-secret

F You can vary the compound adjectives listed by changing one part of the adjective. For example, **curly-haired, long-haired, red-haired,** and **straight-haired; first-class** (ticket), **firsthand** (knowledge), and **firstborn** (child).

Exercises

12.1 Fill in each of the blanks to form a new compound adjective. Use a dictionary if necessary.

1. ....
.... -eyed
....

2. ....
.... proof
....

3. ....
.... -minded
....

4. ....
.... -haired
....

5. ....
.... -made
....

6. ....
.... -free
....

7. ....
.... headed
....

8. ....
.... hearted
....

12.2 Put the words in E opposite into any categories that will help you learn them.

12.3 List as many compound adjectives beginning with *self* as you can. Mark them *P* or *N* for positive or negative characteristics, or write *neutral*.

12.4 Answer these questions with a compound adjective that is opposite in meaning. The answer may or may not have the same second part as the adjective in the question.

Example: Is he working full time? *No, part time.*

1. Isn't she a little nearsighted?
2. Is this vase mass produced?
3. Are her shoes high heeled?
4. Do you like tight-fitting clothes?

12.5 Think of two nouns that you could use with any ten compound adjectives listed in E opposite.

12.6 Add prepositions from the list below to form appropriate compound adjectives.

back   up   out   on   of

1. She's been working at the same low-paying job for so long that she's really fed .... with it.
2. The two cars were involved in a head-..................... collision.
3. He has a very casual, laid-..................... approach to life in general.
4. He's a big star here, but he's unheard .... in my country.
5. After working for two years without a vacation, she was completely worn-..................... .

12.7 Which of the adjectives from this unit could you use to describe yourself and your classmates or members of your family?

Compound nouns – combinations of two nouns

A A compound noun is a fixed expression, made up of two or more words that function as a noun. Compound nouns are usually combinations of two nouns, e.g., **address book, headache, science fiction.** A number of compound nouns are related to phrasal verbs; these are dealt with in Unit 14.

B If you understand both parts of the compound noun, the meaning will usually be clear. Compound nouns are often written as two words, e.g., **can opener, burglar alarm,** or as one word, e.g., **notebook, trademark.** Occasionally they may be written with a hyphen, e.g., **baby-sitter.**

C Usually the main stress is on the first part of the compound noun, but sometimes it is on the second part. The word with the main stress is underlined in the compound nouns below.

| answering machine | credit card | shoe horn | reference book |

Here are some examples of common countable compound nouns:

alarm clock	blood donor	heart attack	tea bag
answering machine	bus stop	phone book	windshield
assembly line	credit card	reference book	windshield wiper
bank account	handcuffs	shoe horn	youth hostel

D Compound nouns may be countable, uncountable, or used only in the singular or the plural. Part C (above) gives examples of countable compounds, and examples of the other types are listed below.

Here are some examples of common uncountable compound nouns:

air-traffic control	data processing	income tax
birth control	family planning	junk food
blood pressure	food poisoning	mail order
computer technology	hay fever [allergy to pollen]	pocket money

Here are some examples of common compound nouns used only in the singular:

death penalty	labor force
generation gap	mother tongue
global warming	sound barrier
greenhouse effect	brain drain [highly educated people leaving their country to work abroad]

Here are some examples of common compound nouns used only in the plural:

grass roots	luxury goods	race relations
kitchen scissors	public works	sunglasses

Exercises

13.1 Complete these bubble networks with any appropriate compound nouns from the opposite page. Add extra bubbles if you need them.

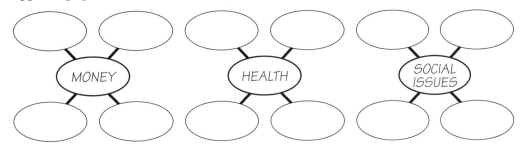

13.2 Sometimes more than one compound noun can be formed from a word. For example, what are the two compound nouns listed opposite with *blood* and what are the two based on *control*? Complete the following compound nouns with nouns other than the ones on the opposite page.

1. junk ....
2. computer ....
3. blood ....
4. tea ....
5. .... card
6. .... processing
7. .... tax
8. food ....
9. .... account

13.3 What are they talking about? All the answers are compound nouns on the opposite page.

Example: "I had it checked at the doctor's office this morning and it was a little high." *blood pressure*

1. "Whenever we're away from home, we leave it on."
2. "It's partly caused by such things as pollution and air conditioning."
3. "She always sneezes a lot in the early summer."
4. "That job is supposed to be much more stressful than being a pilot."
5. "Some people think it's justified for brutal crimes like murder. Do you agree?"
6. "It's much more convenient than paying by cash or check."
7. "He can't run away from the police with those on!"
8. "Sometimes I use it to shop from home. It's more convenient and less expensive than going to a store."

13.4 Now make up some sentences like the ones in exercise 13.3. Use some of the compound nouns from exercise 13.2 as the answers to your sentences.

13.5 Choose any article in a magazine or newspaper and write down all the compound nouns that you find.

13.6 Look at all the compound nouns you have worked with in this unit. Mark the ones that you would like to be able to use yourself rather than just understand when other people use them.

UNIT 14 Compound nouns – verb + preposition

A Some compound nouns are based on phrasal verbs, e.g., **takeover / to take over.** Nouns based on phrasal verbs often have an informal feel to them and are common in newspaper reporting. Here are examples of such nouns in use. (*Note:* To form the plural, -s is added to the end, e.g., **pinups.**)

> In response to the pay offer, there was a **walkout** at the factory. [strike]
> There will be a **crackdown** on wasteful government spending. [action against]
> There has been a **breakout** from the local prison. [escape]
> I never expected to see the **breakup** of the USSR. [collapse]
> Last month saw a big **shakeup** in personnel. [change]

B A number of these nouns have economic associations.

> The **takeover** of one of our leading hotel chains has just been announced.
>   [purchase by another company]
> We're trying to find some new **outlets** for our products. [places to sell]
> Take your things to the **checkout** to pay for them. [cashier's counter]
> **Cutbacks** will be essential until the company becomes profitable again.
>   [reductions]
> Management has begun a series of **layoffs** at the plant. [ending employment]
> There's been a **downturn** in the stock market recently. [decline]

C Some of these nouns are associated with technology and other aspects of contemporary life.

> What the computer produces depends on the quality of the **input.** [information
>   that is put in]
> **Output** has increased thanks to new technology. [production]
> We had heavy staff **turnover** last year. [change]
> He became a high school **dropout** at 16. [person who withdraws from school
>   early]
> I can easily get you a **printout** of the latest figures. [paper on which computer
>   information is printed]
> A **breakthrough** has been made in AIDS research. [important discovery]
> Do you have a **backup** for your computer data? [duplicate version or
>   substitute]

D Some of the words can be used in more general circumstances.

> Many of the problems were caused by a **breakdown** in communications.
>   [failure]
> The **outlook** for steel demand is good. [prospect]
> There are **drawbacks** as well as advantages to every situation. [negative
>   aspects]
> The **outcome** of the situation was not satisfactory. [conclusion]
> Some TV stations welcome **feedback** from viewers. [comments]
> It was clear from the **outset** that the **setup** would cause problems. [start/plan]
> New enterprises often suffer **setbacks** in the early stages. [circumstances that
>   delay progress]

Exercises

14.1 Here are some more compound nouns based on phrasal verbs. Guess the meaning of the underlined word from its context.

1. Cabin crew, please prepare for takeoff.
2. Police are warning of an increased number of break-ins in this area.
3. The news media are claiming the President ordered a cover-up.
4. She went to the tryouts for the tennis team.
5. There was a holdup at the bank. The robbers got away with $1 million.
6. The robbers made their getaway in a stolen car.

14.2 Which compound nouns studied on the opposite page would be most likely to follow the adjectives given below?

1. nervous ....
2. computer ....
3. final ....
4. retail ....
5. positive ....
6. drastic ....

14.3 Fill in the blanks with an appropriate word from the opposite page.

1. AtoZ Inc. has made a .... bid for XYZ Inc.
2. The President announced a .... in the Cabinet yesterday.
3. There's a long line at this .... Let's find another one.
4. She provided some very valuable .... to the discussion.
5. CIRCUS LION IN HORROR ....
6. The insides of their gym lockers were covered with ....

14.4 Create some more compound nouns. In each sentence the preposition is given but the other part is missing. Choose from the list of possibilities.

work   hand   hold   clean   write   turn   push

1. Their car was a ....-off after the accident.
2. The lecturer distributed ....outs before she started speaking.
3. Jack has a daily ....out at the gym, starting with 20 ....-ups.
4. I'm giving my office a major ....up this week.
5. Did you read about the ....up at our bank?
6. There was a surprisingly large ....out for the concert.

14.5 Can you explain the difference between these pairs? Use a dictionary if necessary.

1. outlook / lookout
2. setup / upset
3. outbreak / breakout
4. outlay / layout

14.6 Choose eight of the words in this unit that you particularly want to learn and write your own sentences using them.

Words with interesting origins – people and places

UNIT 15

A

A number of words in English have originated from the names of people.

boycott: [refuse to deal with or a refusal to deal with] a landlord in Ireland who made himself unpopular by his treatment of his tenants and was socially isolated

Braille: [name of a raised writing system used by blind people] from the name of its French inventor, Louis Braille

chauvinist: [strong belief that your country, race, or group is superior to others] after the Frenchman, Nicolas Chauvin, who was fanatically devoted to Napoleon

Machiavellian: [cunning, deceitful, unscrupulous in the pursuit of a goal] from Niccolo Machiavelli, the Italian statesman who died in 1527

mentor: [loyal and wise adviser] from Mentor, friend to Odysseus in Homer's *Odyssey*

nicotine: [chemical present in tobacco] from the 16th-century French diplomat, Jean Nicot, who introduced tobacco to France

pamphlet: [a small leaflet] from the character Pamphilus, in a 12th-century love poem

saxophone: [musical instrument] invented by Adolphe Sax, a Belgian

watt: [unit of power] from the 18th-century Scottish inventor James Watt

B

A number of other words in English come from place names.

bedlam: [chaos] from the name of a famous London mental hospital once situated where Liverpool Street Station now stands

hamburger: [famous American ground beef sandwich] named after the city Hamburg, Germany

Spartan: [severely simple] from the ancient Greek city of Sparta, famed for its austerity and discipline

gypsy: [member of a particular group of traveling people] from people who were once thought to have come from Egypt

A number of names of different kinds of cloth originate from place names. The place of origin is shown in parentheses.

denim (Nimes, France) **cashmere** (Kashmir) **suede** (Sweden)
satin (Qingjiang, China) **gauze** (Gaza) **tweed** (River Tweed, Scotland)

C

Some names of types of clothing, particularly hats, originate from the people who invented them or made them popular, or from places they are associated with.

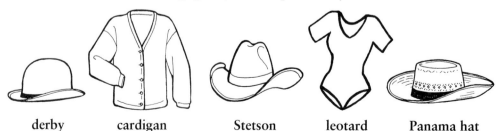

derby   cardigan   Stetson   leotard   Panama hat

Exercises

15.1 Which (if any) of the words listed on the opposite page are familiar to you because there are similar words in your own language?

15.2 Complete the bubble networks below with as many other words as you can from the words listed on the opposite page.

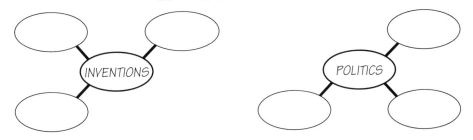

15.3 Complete the sentences with appropriate words from the opposite page.

1. I wish I could play the ....
2. It's like .... in here. Let's go somewhere quieter.
3. The farm workers' union urged consumers to .... lettuce.
4. What a beautiful .... sweater!
5. In the military, you learn to lead a .... life.

15.4 Choose at least one adjective to use with the following words.

Example: cardigan   *wool or light*

1. pamphlet   3. leotard
2. mentor   4. chauvinist

15.5 Now think of two nouns that you might expect to follow each adjective.

Example: suede   *jacket, boots*

1. denim   3. Spartan
2. Machiavellian   4. tweed

15.6 And now suggest how the following sentences could end.

1. She buttoned up her cardigan because . . .
2. It has been agreed to boycott . . .
3. Nicotine is the ingredient in cigarettes that . . .
4. You can see Stetson hats worn . . .
5. Despite their name, hamburgers are *not* made with . . .

15.7 Here are some more words of this type in English. Can you explain (a) their meaning and (b) their origin?

1. **Herculean** effort   4. **jersey**   7. bottle of **champagne**
2. **platonic** friendship   5. **Cesarean** section 8. **atlas**
3. **teddy bear**   6. **July**   9. **quixotic**

Words with interesting origins – from other languages

A English has borrowed words from most of the other languages with which it has had contact. It has taken many expressions from the ancient languages, Latin and Greek, and these borrowings often have academic or literary associations. European languages such as French, Spanish, Italian, and German have contributed lots of words related to cooking, the arts, politics, and more. Words loaned from other languages usually relate to things that English speakers experienced for the first time abroad.

B There are borrowings from a wide range of languages. For example, from Japanese, **tycoon, karate, origami, judo, futon,** and **bonsai;** and from Chinese, **tea, kumquat,** and **kung fu.** From Arabic, **mattress, cipher, alcove, carafe, algebra,** and **harem.** From Turkish, **yogurt, jackal, kiosk, tulip,** and **caftan;** from Farsi, **caravan, shawl, taffeta,** and **bazaar;** and from Eskimo, **kayak, igloo,** and **anorak.** India has given English the words **bungalow, pajamas, dungarees,** and **shampoo.**

C The map of Europe below shows the places of origin of some English words and expressions borrowed from some other European languages. Use a dictionary to check the meanings of any words you are not sure about.

Finland
sauna

Norway
fjord
lemming
ski
slalom

Sweden
ombudsman
verve

Russia
cosmonaut
mammoth
steppe
tsar
tundra

Netherlands
cruise
easel
landscape
yacht

Germany
blitz
dachshund
delicatessen
frankfurter
gimmick
hamburger
kindergarten
poodle
seminar
snorkel
waltz
wanderlust

France
avant-garde
boutique
chauffeur
coup
cuisine
cul-de-sac
elite
résumé
sauté

Spain
bonanza
embargo
guerrilla
junta
lasso
macho
mosquito
patio
siesta

Portugal
cobra
marmalade
molasses

Italy
balcony
ballerina
bandit
casino
confetti
fiasco
ghetto
piano
soprano
spaghetti
vendetta

Greece
catastrophe
dogma
drama
hippopotamus
lexicon
pseudonym
psychology
synonym
theory

Exercises

16.1   Which of the words listed opposite are also used in your language?

16.2   Is your native language represented on the opposite page? If so, can you add any words to the lists opposite? If not, do you know of any words that English has borrowed from your language? (There are almost sure to be some.) Do the words mean exactly the same in English as in your language? Are they pronounced in the same way?

16.3   Look at the words opposite in sections B and C and complete the following networks.

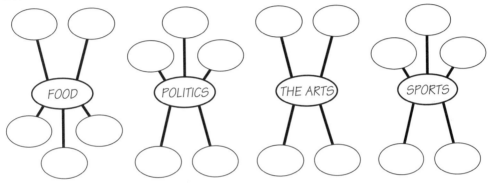

16.4   Make two or three other networks to help you to learn the words on the opposite page.

16.5   Match the words on the left with the nouns they are most likely to be associated with on the right.

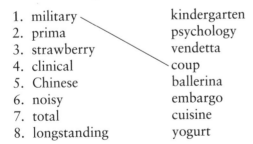

1. military
2. prima
3. strawberry
4. clinical
5. Chinese
6. noisy
7. total
8. longstanding

kindergarten
psychology
vendetta
coup
ballerina
embargo
cuisine
yogurt

16.6   Do you know which languages these words are borrowed from? Try to guess if you aren't sure.

Example: opera   *Italian*

1. guitar
2. garage
3. guru
4. litchi
5. intelligentsia
6. coffee
7. haiku
8. anonymous
9. taboo

16.7   Have any words or expressions been borrowed from English into your own language? Give some examples. Have they kept exactly the same meaning as they have in English? Are they pronounced in the same way?

Onomatopoeic words

A

Onomatopoeic words are words that seem to sound like their meaning. The most obvious examples are verbs relating to the noises that animals make, e.g., cows **moo** and cats **meow**. See Unit 73 for more about animal noises.

B

Certain combinations of letters have particular sound associations in English.

cl- at the beginning of a word can suggest something sharp and/or metallic, e.g., **click** [make a short, sharp sound], **clang** [make a loud ringing noise], **clank** [make a dull metallic noise, not as loud as a clang], **clash** [make a loud, broken, confused noise as when metal objects strike together], **clink** [make the sound of small bits of metal or glass knocking together]. Horses go **clip-clop** on the road.

gr- at the beginning of a word can suggest something unpleasant or miserable, e.g., **groan** [to make a deep sound forced out by pain or despair], **grumble** [to complain in a bad-tempered way], **grumpy** [bad tempered or moody], **grunt** [to make a low, rough sound like pigs do], **growl** [to make a deep, threatening sound].

sp- at the beginning of a word can have an association with water or other liquids or powders, e.g., **splash** [cause a liquid to fly up in the air in drops], **spit** [send liquid out from the mouth], **splutter** [make a series of spitting sounds], **spray** [send liquid through the air in a mist either by wind or some instrument], **sprinkle** [scatter small drops], **spurt** [come out in a sudden burst].

wh- at the beginning of a word often suggests the movement of air, e.g., **whistle** [a high-pitched noise made by forcing air or steam through a small opening], **whirr** [sound like a bird's wings moving rapidly], **whizz** [make the sound of something rushing through air], **wheeze** [breathe noisily, especially with a whistling sound in the chest], **whip** [long piece of rope or leather; or to hit with one of these].

-ash at the end of a word can suggest something fast and violent, e.g., **smash** [break violently into small pieces], **dash** [move or be moved quickly or violently], **crash** [suddenly strike violently and noisily], **mash** [make soft or pulpy by beating or crushing], **gash** [a long, deep cut or wound].

-ckle, -ggle, or **-zzle** at the end of a word can suggest something light and repeated, e.g., **trickle** [flow slowly in a thin stream or in drops], **crackle** [make a series of short, sharp sounds], **tinkle** [make a series of light ringing sounds], **giggle** [laugh lightly], **wriggle** [move with quick, short twistings], **sizzle** [make a hissing sound like something cooking in fat], **drizzle** [small, fine rain].

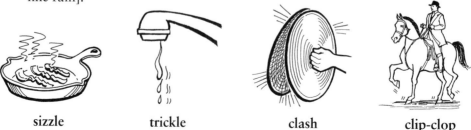

sizzle   trickle   clash   clip-clop

Exercises

17.1 Which of the consonant combinations listed in B opposite exist in your language? Do they ever have similar associations?

17.2 Look in your dictionary. Can you find any other examples of words beginning with *cl, gr, sp,* or *wh* with the associations described opposite?

17.3 Which of the words from B opposite fit best in the sentences below?

1. She heard the key .... as it turned in the lock.
2. The blades of the propeller .... noisily.
3. Do you like your potatoes baked, fried, or ....?
4. They .... glasses and drank to each other's health.
5. There was a terrible car .... on the freeway today.
6. Everyone .... with disappointment at the news.
7. The baby loves .... in its bath.
8. It's not raining hard yet; it's just ....

17.4 Almost all the words in B opposite can be both nouns and regular verbs. There is, however, one irregular verb; one word that is only an adjective; and one word that is both verb and noun, but the noun has a different meaning from the verb. What are these words? Choose from the alternatives offered below.

1. *The irregular verb:* whip, grunt, spurt, spit, or wriggle?
2. *The word that is only an adjective:* gash, grumpy, wheeze, or whirr?
3. *The verb that is both verb and noun, but the noun has a different meaning:* trickle, growl, splutter, spit, splash, or crash?

17.5 What words on the opposite page do these pictures represent?

1.   2.   3.   4.   5.

17.6 Pair the words below so that in each case there is a noun and a matching verb.

Example: schoolchildren giggle

1. schoolchildren   wriggles
2. a teakettle   crackles
3. a bored child   growls
4. a church bell   clanks
5. the bell on a cat's collar   wheezes
6. a fire   clangs
7. a bad-tempered person   giggle
8. a prisoner's chain   whistles
9. someone with asthma   tinkles

Words commonly mispronounced

This page looks at some of the words that cause pronunciation difficulties for learners of English. The phonetic transcription is provided for some of the words below. If you are not sure of the pronunciation of any of the other words, check the Index on page 203, and the list of phonetic symbols on page 202.

A

To master English pronunciation, it is helpful to learn the 15 phonetic symbols for English vowel sounds. It is not so important to learn the consonant symbols, because it is usually not difficult to know how consonants are pronounced. However vowel letters can be pronounced in many different ways. (*Note:* Some dictionaries may use a slightly different phonetic system.)

a	about /ə/	wander /ɑ/	last /æ/	late /eɪ/
i	alive /aɪ/	give /ɪ/		
u	put /ʊ/	cut /ə/	cupid /ju/	
ie	fiend /i/	friend /e/	science /aɪ·ə/	
ei	rein /eɪ/	receive /i/	reinforce /i·ə/	
e	met /e/	meter /i/		
o	hot /ɑ/	go /oʊ/	lost /ɔ/	to /u/
ea	head /e/	team /i/	react /i'æ/	
ou	out /aʊ/	soup /u/	would /ʊ/	
oo	cool /u/	cook /ʊ/	cooperate /o'ɑ/	

B

The letters below are silent in the examples:

p	psychic /'saɪ·kɪk/ psychiatry pneumatic receipt pseudonym psychology
b	comb /koʊm/ dumb numb tomb climb womb lamb
b	doubt /daʊt/ subtle debt debtor
l	could /kʊd/ should would half talk walk salmon chalk
h	honor /'ɑn·ər/ honorable honest hour hourly heir heiress
t	castle /'kæs·əl/ whistle fasten soften Christmas
k	knee /ni/ knife know knob knowledge knot knit

C

In two-syllable words in English, the stress is often on the first syllable if it is a noun and on the second syllable if it is a verb, e.g., "We gave her a **present**" (noun); "She's going to pre**sent** the award" (verb). Here are other words like this.

conduct	decrease	increase	protest	subject
conflict	desert	insult	record	suspect
contest	export	permit	reject	transport
contract	import	progress	reprint	upset

D

Here are some other words that are often mispronounced.

apostrophe /ə'pɑs·trə·fi/	catastrophe /kə'tæs·trə·fi/	cupboard /'kəb·ərd/
recipe /'res·ə·pi/	answer /'æn·sər/	muscle /'məs·əl/

Exercises

18.1 Mark all the silent letters in each of the following nonsense sentences.

1. They sang a psalm to honor the memory of the psychologist as she was laid to rest in the family tomb.
2. The psychiatrist was knifed in the knee as he was walking home.
3. You could have left me half of the Christmas cake.
4. He should have whistled as he fastened the knot.

18.2 Which word is the odd one out in each group? (Look at the vowel sounds.)

1. come   some   dome
2. head   plead   tread
3. land   wand   sand
4. took   boot   foot
5. could   doubt   would
6. though   rough   tough

18.3 What word could a poet use to rhyme with each of the words below?

1. laugh *staff* ....
2. bough ....
3. enough ....
4. though ....
5. through ....
6. cough ....

18.4 Circle or highlight the stressed syllable in each of the underlined words.

1. Although the police <u>suspected</u> several people, Jo was the main <u>suspect</u>.
2. I <u>object</u> to having that ugly <u>object</u> in our home. It is not art!
3. There are <u>conflicting</u> views as to the cause of the <u>conflict</u>.
4. All this <u>upset</u> over the wedding has really <u>upset</u> them.
5. The cost of living has <u>increased</u> while there has been no <u>increase</u> in wages.
6. A work <u>permit</u> will <u>permit</u> you to work for a period of six months.
7. If I make enough <u>progress</u>, I can <u>progress</u> to the next level.
8. Despite the obnoxious <u>conduct</u> of the audience, James went on <u>conducting</u> the orchestra.

18.5 Write the words below using the normal English alphabet.

1. /ˈməs·əl/
2. /kəˈtæs·trə·fi/
3. /ˈhæŋ·kər·tʃɪf/
4. /ˈkem·ɪ·kəl/
5. /ˈsət·ᵊl/
6. /ɪˈsit/
7. /haɪt/
8. /ˈres·ə·pi/

18.6 Underline the stressed syllable in each of the words.

1. photograph   photography   photographer   photographic
2. politics   political   politician
3. economy   economical   economics
4. psychology   psychologist   psychological
5. psychiatry   psychiatric   psychiatrist
6. mathematics   mathematician   mathematical

UNIT 19 Homonyms

A

Homonyms can be subdivided into **homographs** and **homophones**. **Homographs** are written in the same way but have different meanings and may be pronounced differently. Compare **bow** in "He took a **bow** /baʊ/ at the end of the concert" and "He was wearing a **bow** /boʊ/ tie." **Homophones** are words with different meanings that are pronounced the same way but spelled differently. Compare **sale** and **sail** /seɪl/ as in "We bought this TV on **sale**" and "I love to **sail** my boat."

B

Here are some more examples of homographs in English.

I **live** in California. /lɪv/
Your favorite rock group is performing **live** on TV tonight. /laɪv/

I **read** in bed every night. /rid/
I **read** *War and Peace* last year. /red/

The **lead** singer in the group is great. /lid/
Lead pipes are dangerous. /led/

The **wind** blew the tree down. /wɪnd/
Don't forget to **wind** your watch. /waɪnd/

I **wound** my watch last night. /waʊnd/
He suffered a terrible **wound** in the war. /wund/

This book is called *Vocabulary in* Use. /jus/
You need to know how to **use** words, as well as their meaning. /juz/

They lived in a large old **house**. /haʊs/
The buildings **house** a library and two concert halls as well as a theater. /haʊz/

The **sow** has five piglets. /saʊ/
The farmers **sow** the seeds in the spring. /soʊ/

C

Here are some of the many examples of homophones in English.

air/heir	hoarse/horse	pray/prey	steak/stake
aloud/allowed	its/it's	raise/rays	tea/tee
break/brake	mail/male	right/write	there/their/they're
dough/doe	mown/moan	scene/seen	through/threw
fare/fair	our/hour	sea/see	toe/tow
faze/phase	pair/pear/pare	sent/scent	waist/waste
flu/flew	pale/pail	sight/site	wait/weight
grate/great	pane/pain	sole/soul	weak/week
groan/grown	peal/peel	some/sum	wood/would

Exercises

19.1 Each underlined word rhymes with, or sounds similar to, one of the words in
parentheses; choose the matching word.

1. The woman I live with knows a good club with live music. (five/give)
2. The main house houses a collection of rare stamps. (mouse/browse)
3. You sow the seeds while I feed the sow. (cow/show)
4. The violinist in the bow tie took a bow. (now/go)
5. He's the lead singer in the heavy metal group "Lead Bullets." (head/deed)
6. Does he still suffer from his war wound? (found/mooned)
7. I wound the rope around the tree. (round/tuned)
8. It's no use! I can't use this gadget. (snooze/juice)

19.2 Write the word in phonetic transcription using the correct spelling for the
sentence.

Example: I should get some exercise or I'll never lose /weɪt/.   *weight*

1. Watching TV game shows is such a /weɪst/ of time.
2. There is a hole in the /soʊl/ of my shoe.
3. He broke a /peɪn/ of glass in the kitchen window.
4. You are not /əˈlaʊd/ to talk during the test.
5. She's going /θruː/ a rather difficult /feɪz/.
6. Don't throw away that orange /pil/. I need it for a recipe.

19.3 Many jokes in English are based on homophones and homographs. Match the
first part of each of these children's jokes with the second part, and then explain
the play on words.

1. What did the big chimney say to
   the little chimney?
2. Why did the man take his pencil to bed?
3. What's pale and trembles at the
   bottom of the sea?
4. Why is history the sweetest lesson?
5. What's black and white and red all over?

A nervous wreck.
Because it's full of dates.
A newspaper.
He wanted to draw the curtains.
You're too young to smoke.

19.4 Choose pairs of words from C opposite to describe the pictures below.

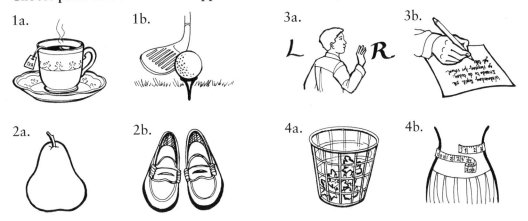

1a. 1b. 3a. 3b.

2a. 2b. 4a. 4b.

A **One thing before another**

Before I went to work, I fed the cat.
Before going to work, I ran a mile. [formal/written style]
It was nice to be in Mexico City. **Previously** I'd been to Cancun and
 Guadalajara. [fairly formal; less formal: **Before that, I** . . .]
I was in the office by 2:30. **Earlier** I was out. [less formal: **Before that, I** . . .]
The Dodgers are a Los Angeles baseball team. **Formerly** they were the
 Brooklyn Dodgers. [at an earlier time]

B **Things happening at the same time**

While I waited, I read the newspaper. [more formal: **While waiting,** I read . . .;
 the waiting and reading happened together]
As I was driving to work, I saw an accident. [**As** is about the same as **while.**]
I saw her **just as** she was turning the corner. [simultaneously; at that precise
 moment]
During the war, I lived in Canada. [does not specify how *long*]
Throughout the war, food was rationed. [from beginning to end]
Whenever I see a sentimental movie, I can't help crying. [every time]

C **One thing after another**

After I locked up, I went to bed. [more formal: **After locking** up . . .]
First we went to the movies. **After that,** we went out for coffee.
He had a stroke and was rushed to the hospital. He died soon **afterward.** [In
 these two examples, **after that** and **afterward** are interchangeable.]
Following my visit to Beijing, I bought lots of books about China. [fairly
 formal]

D **Time when**

When I'm rich, I'll buy a yacht. [*Note:* not "When I will be rich . . ."]
As soon as we finish packing, we can leave. [immediately after]
Once we finish packing, we can go get some coffee. [after, but less specific]
The moment / The minute I saw his face, I knew I'd met him before.

E **Connecting two periods or events**

Dinner will take about an hour. **In the meantime,** relax and have a drink.
 [between now and dinner]
The new computers are arriving soon. **Till then,** we'll just use the old ones.
 [informal for **Until then**]
By the time I retire, I will have worked here for 26 years. [*Note:* not ". . . I
 will work here for 26 years."]

Exercises

20.1   Look at these pages from the personal diary of Laura, a businesswoman who travels a lot. Then do the exercise.

Mon. 12 *Toronto – day 5 Eaton Centre, then concert.*	*Got up early. Said goodbye to Nick and left. Saw a bad accident on the highway.* **Fri. 16**
Tues. 13 *Been away 6 days! Toronto great, but miss home!*	*Answered the mail, then watched TV.* **Sat. 17**
Wed. 14 *Left Toronto 10 a.m. Huge pile of mail waiting at home!*	*Lots of phone calls! Sandy, Joyce, and Doug all in a row! Lazy day!* **Sun. 18**
Thur. 15 *Boston. Met Mary at Nick's.*	*Pick up tickets for trip to Korea – 30th!* **Notes**

Fill in the blanks with connectors from the opposite page.

1. ..*Before*........ going to Boston, Laura was in Toronto.
2. Her next trip after Boston is on the 30th. ...., she can spend some time at home.
3. She was in Toronto for over a week. .... she got home, there was a big pile of mail waiting for her.
4. .... she was at Nick's place on the 15th, she met Mary.
5. She went to a concert in Toronto on Monday. ...., she had been to Eaton Centre.
6. .... she said goodbye to Nick, she left.
7. .... she had answered all her letters, she watched TV for a while.
8. .... she hung up the phone, it rang again. This time it was Doug.

Make more sentences with connectors you haven't used, based on the diary.

20.2   Think of things that are true for you in these situations and complete the sentences. Add more sentences if you can.

1. While I'm asleep, *I usually dream a lot.*
2. After I eat too much, . . .
3. The minute I wake up, I . . .
4. Throughout my childhood, I . . .
5. I'm working on vocabulary right now. Earlier, I was . . .
6. Once I finish my language course, I'll . . .
7. Before I go on vacation, I always . . .
8. Following an argument with someone, I always feel . . .

UNIT 21 Condition

A

In addition to **if,** there are several other words and phrases for expressing condition in English.

1. You can't get in **unless** you have a ticket.

2. You can use this book **on condition that** you return it by 5:00.

3. **In case of** fire, dial 911.

4. You can stay **as long as** you don't mind sleeping on the sofa.

as long as: the least formal **on condition that:** the most formal
providing (that) /**provided (that):** a little more formal (it can also be used in 2 and 4 above)

In 3, don't confuse **in case of** with **in case,** e.g., "Take your umbrella in case it rains." [It isn't raining, but there's a chance of rain today.]

B

Possibility with *supposing/suppose* and *what if*

Supposing/Suppose and **What if** express possible situations in the future (usually in spoken language). For example:

Supposing/Suppose it rains tonight – will the baseball game be called off?
What if he doesn't turn up – what will we do then?

C

Conditions with *-ever*

However you do it, it will cost a lot of money.
You'll get to the train station, **whichever** bus you take.
Whoever wins the election, nothing will really change.
That box is so big, it will be in the way **wherever** you leave it.

These four sentences can also be expressed using **no matter,** e.g.:

No matter how you do it, it will cost a lot of money.
You'll get to the train station **no matter** which bus you take.

D

Some nouns that express condition

Certain **conditions** must be **met** before the peace talks can begin.
Proficiency in English is a **prerequisite** for admission to an American university.
    [absolutely necessary; a formal word]
What are the **requirements** for obtaining a driver's license? [official conditions]
I would not move to a big city **under any circumstances.** I hate big cities!

Exercises

21.1 Fill in the blanks with an appropriate word or phrase from A or B opposite.

1. You can come to the party .... you don't bring that awful friend of yours.
2. .... emergency in the factory, sound the alarm and notify the supervisor at once.
3. .... I hear from you, I'll assume you are coming.
4. Applicants may take the driving test again .... they have not already taken a test within the past fourteen days.
5. .... I lent you my car, would that help?

21.2 The pictures show conditions that must be met to do certain things. Make different sentences using words and phrases from the opposite page.

Example: You can have a passenger on a motorcycle provided the passenger wears a helmet. or Unless you wear a helmet, you can't ride on a motorcycle.

1.   2.   3.

21.3 Change the sentences with *-ever* to *no matter*, and vice versa.

1. Wherever she goes, she always takes that dog of hers.
2. If anyone calls, I don't want to speak to them, no matter who it is.
3. No matter what I do, I always seem to do the wrong thing.
4. No matter how I do it, that recipe never seems to work.

21.4 What would your answers be to these questions?

1. Are there any prerequisites for the job you do or would like to do in the future?
2. Under what circumstances would you move from where you're living now?
3. What are the normal admission requirements for universities in your country?
4. On what condition would you lend a friend your house/apartment?

Cause, reason, purpose, and result

A Cause and reason

You probably know how to use words like **because** and **since** to refer to the **cause** of or **reason** for something. Here are some other ways to express cause and reason.

> **Owing to / Because of** the icy conditions, the two trucks collided.
> The collision **was due to** the icy conditions.
> The collision **was caused by** ice on the road.
> **The cause of** the collision was ice on the road.

Here are some other "cause" words and typical contexts.

> The cuts in social services **sparked (off) / ignited** a new round of bitter protests. [often used for very strong, perhaps violent, reactions to events]
> The President's statement **gave rise to / provoked / generated** a lot of criticism. [not as strong as **spark** or **spark off**]
> The peace talks have **brought about / led to** a cease-fire. [often used for political/social change]
> Unemployment in the region **stems from** the steady decline in manufacturing jobs. [explaining the direct origins of events and states]
> The court case **arose from** allegations made in a newspaper. [the allegations started the process that led to the court case]

B Reasons for and purposes of doing things

> Her **reason for** leaving her job was that she was offered a better position at another company. *or* The reason she left her job was that . . . [reason/cause]
> I wonder what his **motives** were **in** sending that letter. [purpose]
> I wonder what **prompted** him to send that letter. [reason/cause]
> She wrote to the newspaper **with the aim of** exposing the scandal. [purpose]
> She refused to answer **on the grounds that** her lawyer wasn't present. [reason]
> **The purpose of** his visit was to establish goodwill.

C Results

> He didn't study. **As a result / Therefore / As a consequence / Consequently,** he failed his exams.
> **The result/consequence of** all these changes is that no one is happy. [The examples with **consequence/consequently** sound more formal than **result.**]
> His remarks **resulted in** an explosion of anger. [as a verb + **in**]
> The meeting had an **outcome** that no one could have predicted. [result of a process or events, or of meetings, discussions, etc.]
> The **upshot of** all these problems was that we had to start again. [less formal than **outcome**]

Exercises

22.1 Make complete sentences using "cause and reason" words from A opposite.

Example: decision to raise tuition ⟶ protests on campus *The decision to raise tuition sparked (off) protests on campus.*

1. the new law ⟶ changes in the tax system
2. a faulty signal ⟶ train crash
3. a violent storm ⟶ widespread flooding
4. food shortages ⟶ riots in several cities
5. declining profits ⟶ poor management of the company

22.2 Make two sentences into one, using the "reason and purpose" words in parentheses. Look at B opposite if you aren't sure.

Example: There was a controversial decision. She wrote to the local newspaper to protest. (prompt) *The controversial decision prompted her to write to the local newspaper to protest.*

1. I didn't call you. I'd lost your phone number. (reason)
2. I will not sign. This contract is illegal. (grounds)
3. Lawmakers passed a new bill. It was in order to balance the budget. (aim)
4. She sent everyone flowers. I wonder why. (motives)
5. The salary was high. She applied for the job. (prompt)

22.3 Use the pictures to describe the *causes* and *results* of events in different ways.

1. The road was blocked.

3. The customers got angry.

2. Everyone got a refund.

4. We had to take a taxi.

22.4 Fill in the missing words.

1. My reasons .... not joining the club are personal.
2. The purpose .... this pedal is to control the speed.
3. All this arose .... one small mistake we made.
4. It was done .... the aim .... lowering inflation.
5. That news article has .... rise .... a lot of criticism.

Concession and contrast

Concession means stating an idea or fact that seems to be the opposite of another idea or fact. For example:

Although they were poor, they were rich in spirit.
She is a little bit foolish. **Nevertheless/Nonetheless,** she's very kind.

A Verbs of concession

I **acknowledge/agree** that it was a bad idea, but it seemed sensible at the time. [**acknowledge** is more formal]
I **admit** I was wrong, but I still think there was reason to doubt her.
I **concede** that you are right about the goal, but not the method. [formal]

B Adverbs and other phrases showing contrast

I expected Mr. Widebody to be fat. **The reverse was true.**

A: Was the movie any good?
B: **Quite the contrary.** It was awful.

Even though / Although / Though I warned you about the dangers, you didn't listen.
You shouldn't seem so surprised. **After all,** I did warn you.
It's **all very well** saying you want a dog, but who'll take care of it?
He is boring, and he is rather cold and unfriendly, but **despite all that,** he *is* your uncle and we should invite him.
In spite of the bad weather, we had a great vacation.
Our old house was sunny and bright. **In contrast,** the new place is dark and gloomy.
Admittedly, she put in a lot of effort, but sadly it was all wasted.
It's not raining now. **On the other hand,** it may rain later, so take the umbrella.
John, quiet? **On the contrary,** he's the noisiest person I know.
[*Remember:* **On the other hand** shows that two contrasting facts are both true.
 On the contrary means that one statement is true and the other is not true.]

C Collocating phrases for contrast

When it comes to politics, Jim and Ann are **poles apart.**
There's a **world of difference** between being a friend and a lover.
There's a **great divide** between liberals and conservatives in general.
There's a **huge discrepancy** between his ideals and his actions.

Exercises

23.1 Rewrite these sentences using the most likely verb from A opposite (there is usually more than one possibility).

1. I know that you weren't entirely to blame, but you have to take *some* responsibility.
2. He didn't deny that we had tried our best, but he still wasn't content.
3. The company is prepared to say that you have experienced some delay, but we do not accept liability.
4. Okay, I was wrong and you were right; he *is* a nice guy.

23.2 Write a *beginning* for these sentences, as in the example.

1. <u>I expected Mary to be tall and dark.</u> The reverse was true; she was short, with blond hair.
2. .... On the other hand, it does have a great view, so I think we should rent it.
3. JIM: ....?
   MARY: On the contrary, it's one of the cheapest hotels in town.
4. .... In contrast, the traffic in Japan drives on the left.

23.3 Try to do this word puzzle from memory. If you can't, look at C opposite.

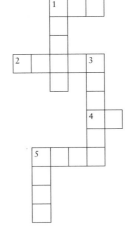

Across
1. despite .... that
2. a .... of difference
4. .... contrast
5. a .... discrepancy

Down
1. poles ....
3. a great ....
5. on the other ....

23.4 Complete the sentences with phrases from B and C opposite.

1. I'm not worried; ...., I feel quite calm.
2. It's expensive, but ...., we do need it.
3. There's a .... between what she says and what she does.
4. No need to rush. ...., the play doesn't start till six.
5. She's bossy and rude, but ...., she *is* a friend.
6. There's a .... between being a student and being a teacher.
7. .... saying you'll pay me back soon; *when* is what *I* want to know!
8. ...., I could have tried harder, but I don't think I deserve all this criticism.

UNIT 24 Addition

There are a number of ways of adding one idea to another in English. You probably already know words like **and, also,** and **too.**

A   Words for linking sentences/clauses

Sentence/Clause 1	And	Sentence/Clause 2
For this job you need a degree.	**In addition,**	you need some experience.
Video cameras are becoming easier to use.	**Furthermore, Moreover, What's more,***	they're becoming cheaper.
It'll take ages to get there and it'll cost a fortune.	**Besides, Anyway,****	I don't really want to go.
Children should respect their parents.	**Likewise, Similarly,**	they should respect their teachers.
We'll have all the trouble of going to court.	**On top of (all) that,*****	we'll have to pay the lawyers' fees.

*   **Furthermore** and **moreover** are normally interchangeable. **What's more** is less formal; **What is more** is more formal.
**   **Besides** and **Anyway** are more emphatic.
*** **On top of (all) that** is even more emphatic; usually informal.

Note also: To keep fit you need a good diet **plus** regular exercise. [**Plus** is normally used to connect noun phrases, but it can connect clauses in informal speech.]

B   Adding words at the end of clauses/sentences

They sell chairs, tables, beds, **and so on / etc.** [et cetera]
It'll go to the committee, then to the board, then to another committee, **and so forth (and so on).** [suggests a long continuation]
He was a good athlete and an excellent musician **to top it off / to boot.** [emphasizes the combination of items]

C   Adding words that begin or come in the middle of clauses/sentences

Pursuant to my letter of May first, I am writing to . . . [formal opening for a letter]
In addition to his B.A. in history, he has a Ph.D. in sociology.
He's on the school board, **as well as** being a volunteer firefighter.
Besides / Apart from having a full-time job, she also has a part-time job.
Jo Evans was there, **along with** a few other people I didn't know.

Note: This last group is followed by nouns, noun phrases, or **-ing.** *Don't say:* As well as she speaks French, she also speaks Japanese. (*Say:* As well as **speaking** French, she . . .)

Exercises

24.1 Fill in the blanks in this letter with words and phrases that express addition. Try to do it without looking at the opposite page.

> Dear Mr. Stoneheart:
>
> .... (1) my letter of April 10th, I would like to give you more information concerning my qualifications and experience. .... (2) holding a degree in hotel management, I also have an advanced certificate in catering. My hotel management studies covered the usual areas: finance, front services, publicity, space allocation, ... (3). I also wish to point out that .... (4) holding these qualifications, I have now been working in the hotel industry for five years. .... (5), my previous experience was also connected with tourism and hospitality.
>
> I hope you will give my application due consideration.
>
> Sincerely,
> *Laura Yuen*
> Laura Yuen

24.2 Rewrite the sentences using the word or phrase in parentheses at the end.

1. Physical labor can exhaust the body very quickly. Excessive study can rapidly reduce mental powers too. (similarly)
2. My cousin turned up and some classmates of his came with him. (along with)
3. He owns a big chemical factory and he runs an enormous oil business. (as well as)
4. She was my teacher and she was a good friend. (to boot)
5. I'm the scientific adviser and act as consultant to the director. (in addition to)

24.3 Correct the mistakes in the use of addition words and phrases in these sentences.

1. I work part time as well as I am a student, so I have a busy life.
2. Besides to have a good job, my ambition is to meet someone nice to share my life with.
3. Apart from I have many other responsibilities, I am now in charge of staff training.
4. In addition has a degree, she also has an advanced certificate.
5. My father won't agree. My mother's sure to find likewise something to object to.
6. He said he'd first have to consider the organization, then the system, then the finance, and so on so forth.

24.4 Which addition words/phrases can you associate with these pictures?

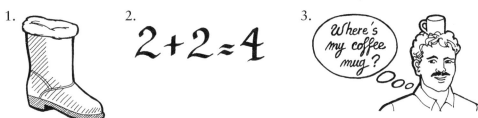

1.   2. $2+2=4$ 3. *Where's my coffee mug?*

Text-referring words

Text-referring words take their meaning from the surrounding text. For example, this sentence in isolation does not mean much:

> We decided to look at the problem again and try to find a solution.

What problem? We need to refer to some other sentence or to the context to find out. The words **problem** and **solution** help organize the argument of the text, but they do not tell us the topic of the text. They refer to something somewhere else.

Here are some examples. The word in bold refers to the underlined words.

> Pollution is increasing. The **problem** is getting worse each day.
> Should taxes be raised or lowered? This was the biggest **issue** in the election.
>   [topic causing argument and controversy]
> Whether the war could have been avoided is a **question** that continues to
>   interest historians.
> Let's discuss movies. That's always an interesting **topic.** [subject to argue
>   about or discuss, e.g., in a debate or in an essay]
> Punishment is only one **aspect** of crime. [part of the topic]

Problem-solution words

Text-referring words are often used with "problem-solution" types of text, where a problem is presented and ways of solving it are discussed. In the following example, the words in bold concern a problem or a solution. Try to learn these words as a family.

> The **situation** in our cities with regard to traffic is going from bad to worse. Congestion is a daily feature of urban life. The **problem** is now beginning to **affect** our national economy. Unless a new **approach** is found to control traffic, we will never find a **solution** to the **dilemma.**

Here are some more words associated with problem-solution texts. They are grouped in families associated with the key words in bold. The prepositions normally used with these words are given in parentheses.

situation: state of affairs   position   circumstance (with regard to)
problem: difficulty [more formal]   crisis   matter   dilemma
response: reaction (to)   attitude (toward)
solution: answer (to)   resolution (to)   key (to)   way out (of)   proposal (to)
evaluation (of the solution): assessment   judgment   appraisal

Exercises

25.1 Match each sentence in the left-hand column to a word in the right-hand column, joining each sentence with a corresponding label.

Example: The earth is in orbit around the sun. *(fact)*

1. The earth is in orbit around the sun.　　　　problem
2. World poverty and overpopulation.　　　　　evaluation
3. God exists and loves everybody.　　　　　　fact
4. I've run out of cash.　　　　　　　　　　　belief
5. It has proved to be most efficient.　　　　　view
6. They should get married, in my opinion.　　　issue

25.2 Fill in the blanks with an appropriate word to refer to the underlined parts of the sentences.

1. So you were talking about <u>animal rights</u>? That's quite a big .... nowadays.
2. We are <u>running out of funds</u>. How do you propose we deal with the ....?
3. <u>Is there life on other planets</u>? This is a .... nobody has yet been able to answer.
4. *(teacher to the class)* You can write your essay on "<u>My best vacation ever</u>." If you don't like that ...., I'll give you another one.
5. She thinks we should all <u>fly around in little helicopters</u>. This is a unique .... to the traffic problem in cities. I wonder if it's viable.

25.3 Match the newspaper headlines with extracts from their texts.

NEW APPROACH TO CANCER TREATMENT

PROPOSAL TO INCREASE TELEPHONE RATES DRAWS FIRE

NEW ARGUMENT OVER UNEMPLOYMENT

SCIENTIST REJECTS CLAIMS OVER FAST FOOD

SOLUTION TO AGE-OLD MYSTERY IN KENYA

SITUATION IN SAHEL WORSENING DAILY

1. she said if the world community failed to respond, thousands of children could die

2. The Secretary of Labor denied that this was true, pointing out evidence that

3. the response of some ratepayers and competitors is that the move is unfair

4. tests were being carried out to see if the new drug really did

5. there was no proof at all that such things were harmful, and in

6. the bones proved beyond doubt that human beings had inhabited the region during

Uncountable nouns

Countable nouns can be used with **a/an** and made plural (e.g., **a hat, two hats**). Uncountable nouns are not normally used with **a/an** or the plural (e.g., **information**, *not* "an information" or "some informations"). You can learn uncountable nouns in groups associated with the same subject or area. Here are some possible headings.

A   **Travel**

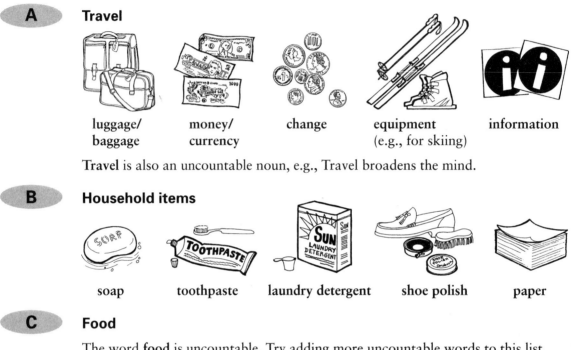

| luggage/ baggage | money/ currency | change | equipment (e.g., for skiing) | information |

Travel is also an uncountable noun, e.g., Travel broadens the mind.

B   **Household items**

soap   toothpaste   laundry detergent   shoe polish   paper

C   **Food**

The word **food** is uncountable. Try adding more uncountable words to this list.

sugar   rice   spaghetti   butter   flour   *soup* ....

D   **Abstract uncountable nouns**

She gave me some **advice** on how to study for the exam.
I have very little **knowledge** about English grammar.
He's made a lot of **progress** in a very short time.
She has done some **research** on marine life.
They've done a lot of **work** on the project.

E   **Materials and resources**

For making clothes, furniture, etc.: cloth (e.g., cotton, silk)   leather   wool
For buildings: stone   brick   plastic   wood/timber   concrete   glass
For energy: coal   oil   fuel   gas   electricity

F   **Common mistakes**

Don't say: What a terrible weather!   She has long hairs.   I have a news for you.
Say: What terrible weather!   She has long hair.   I have (some) news for you.

(See also Unit 27.)

Exercises

26.1 Decide whether these sentences need *a/an*. Not all of the nouns are on the opposite page. Use a dictionary that tells you whether the nouns are countable.

1. He gave us all .... advice on what to take with us.
2. I'm sorry. I can't go. I have .... homework to do.
3. She's doing .... study of teenage slang for her university project.
4. You'll need .... rice if you want to make a Chinese meal.
5. Paul getting divorced? That's .... interesting news!
6. I need .... change to make a telephone call. Do you have .... quarter?

26.2 List these words in two columns side by side, one for *uncountables* and one for *countables*. Then join the words with similar meanings.

clothing   tip   suitcase   information   job   advice   travel
garment   trip   work   baggage   fact

26.3 Imagine you are going away for a week's vacation and you pack a suitcase with a number of things. Make a list of what you would pack, and check off the items on your list that are *uncountable* nouns in English.

26.4 Correct the mistakes in these sentences.

1. We had such a terrible weather last night! The storm knocked out the electricities for hours.
2. I love antique furnitures, but I would need an advice from a specialist before I bought any. My knowledges in that area are very poor.
3. His researches are definitely making great progresses these days. He has done a lot of original works recently.
4. If you have your hairs cut at that salon, it will cost a lot of monies.

26.5 Personal qualities and skills use a lot of uncountable words. For example, we might say that a secretary should have *intelligence, reliability, charm,* and *enthusiasm* (all uncountable nouns). Choose from the list which qualities these people should have. Say whether they need *some, a lot,* or *a little bit* of the quality. Use a dictionary for any difficult words.

Jobs: soldier   nurse   teacher   actor   athlete   writer   receptionist
Qualities: patience   courage   determination   goodwill   charm   stamina
    reliability   loyalty   energy   experience   commitment   talent   creativity
    intelligence   training   discipline

26.6 Could I have . . . ? Practice asking for these household items and decide whether you should say *a* or *some*.

vinegar   broom   needle   thread   tape   tea bag   shoe polish

Nouns that are usually plural

A **Tools, instruments, pieces of equipment**

Some of these are always plural.

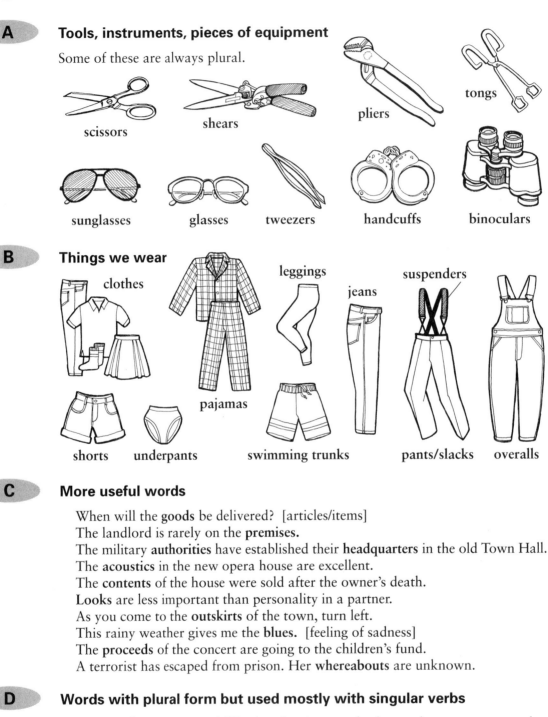

scissors

shears

pliers

tongs

sunglasses

glasses

tweezers

handcuffs

binoculars

B **Things we wear**

clothes

leggings

jeans

suspenders

shorts

underpants

pajamas

swimming trunks

pants/slacks

overalls

C **More useful words**

When will the **goods** be delivered? [articles/items]
The landlord is rarely on the **premises.**
The military **authorities** have established their **headquarters** in the old Town Hall.
The **acoustics** in the new opera house are excellent.
The **contents** of the house were sold after the owner's death.
Looks are less important than personality in a partner.
As you come to the **outskirts** of the town, turn left.
This rainy weather gives me the **blues.** [feeling of sadness]
The **proceeds** of the concert are going to the children's fund.
A terrorist has escaped from prison. Her **whereabouts** are unknown.

D **Words with plural form but used mostly with singular verbs**

Names of some games: billiards dominoes checkers darts craps cards
Names of subjects/activities: physics economics classics gymnastics
aerobics athletics

Note: Some words look plural but are not, e.g., **series, means, news, spaghetti:**
a **series** of programs on TV   a cheap **means** of transportation

Exercises

27.1 Make a list of (a) subjects you studied at school or elsewhere, and (b) your leisure interests. How many of the words are plural? Use a dictionary if necessary.

27.2 Which things listed on the opposite page can be used to . . .

1. cut a hedge?   *shears*
2. hold your pants up?
3. cut paper?
4. get a splinter out of your skin?
5. look at distant objects?
6. get a nail out of a piece of wood?

27.3 How many articles on the clothesline are plural nouns?

27.4 Fill in the blanks with an appropriate plural noun.

1. *(to a child)* Get your .... on! It's time to go to bed.
2. The .... of the rock concert are going to charity.
3. The escaped prisoner's .... are still unknown.
4. The .... have prohibited the import of all foreign
....

27.5 Odd one out. In each group, one noun is always used in the plural. Which?

1. sleeve   pant   slipper
2. billiard   squash   tennis
3. knife   scissor   razor
4. suit   costume   underpant

27.6 **In this silly story, change the singular nouns to plural where appropriate.**

After teaching gymnastic for years, I decided that I wanted to be a pop star and moved to Los Angeles. I got a room, but it was on the outskirt of the city. The owner didn't live on the premise, so I could make as much noise as I liked. The acoustic in the bathroom was fantastic, so I practiced playing rock music and rhythm & blue there. I went to the headquarter of the musicians' union, but a guy there said I just didn't have a good enough look to be famous. Oh well, forget it!

Countable and uncountable nouns with different meanings

UNIT 28

A When we use a countable noun, we are thinking of specific **things** that can be counted, e.g., two glasses. When we use it as an uncountable noun, we are thinking of **stuff** or **material** or the **idea of a thing in general**, e.g., "Glass is breakable."

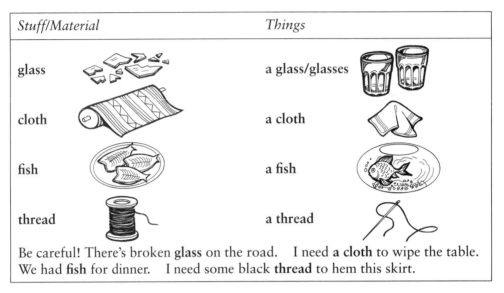

Stuff/Material	*Things*
glass	a glass/glasses
cloth	a cloth
fish	a fish
thread	a thread

Be careful! There's broken **glass** on the road.   I need **a cloth** to wipe the table.
We had **fish** for dinner.   I need some black **thread** to hem this skirt.

Here are some more nouns used in both ways. Make sure you know the difference between the uncountable and the countable meanings.

hair – a hair   paper – a paper   land – a land
people – a people   home – a home   work – a work

Waiter! There's **a hair** in my soup!
Did you buy **a paper** this morning? [a newspaper]
I love meeting **people** from different **lands**. [individuals/countries]
Her grandmother lives in a **home**. [an institution]
Hamlet is one of Shakespeare's most famous **works**.

B The names of food items often have a different meaning depending on whether they are used as countable or uncountable nouns (see **fish** above).

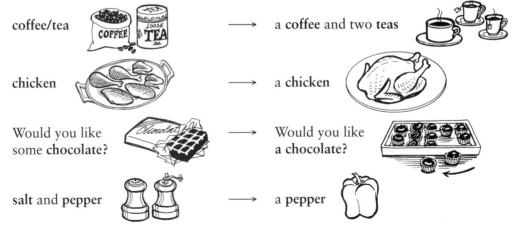

coffee/tea ⟶ a **coffee** and two **teas**

chicken ⟶ a chicken

Would you like some **chocolate?** ⟶ Would you like **a chocolate?**

salt and **pepper** ⟶ a pepper

56

Exercises

28.1 Would you expect to find these things in or near most people's homes? In which room or place? Answer for both meanings (countable and uncountable).

Example: iron   *Most people have an iron to iron their clothes, usually in the kitchen or laundry room. People don't normally keep iron (the metal) at home, but they may have things made of iron, such as a frying pan in the kitchen.*

1. cloth   2. pepper   3. tape   4. fish   5. glass

28.2 Which question would you ask? *Could I have/borrow a . . . ?* or *Could I have/borrow some . . . ?*

Example: wine   Could I have some wine?

1. iron

2. pepper

3. glass

4. chicken

28.3 Answer these remarks using the word in parentheses. Use *a/an* if the meaning is countable.

Example: Oh no! I spilled milk on the floor! (cloth)   *Don't worry. Here's a cloth; just wipe it up.*

1. How did you get that puncture in your tire? (glass)
2. This soup tastes a little bland. What can we sprinkle on it? (pepper)
3. Mommy, what's the *Mona Lisa*? (work)
4. There's something hanging from the bottom of your coat. (thread)

28.4 Explain the difference between (a) and (b) in each pair.

1. (a) I enjoy painting as a hobby.
   (b) Are these paintings by Picasso?
2. (a) Did you hear a noise coming from the basement?
   (b) Will you kids stop making so much noise?
3. (a) Can I have some light?
   (b) Can I have a light?

Collective nouns

Collective nouns are used to describe a **group** of the same things.

A ## People

a **group** of people
(small group)

a **crowd** of people
(large number)

a **gang** of thieves
(negative)

B ## Words associated with certain animals

A **flock** of sheep or birds, e.g., geese/pigeons; a **herd** of cattle, sheep, deer; a **school** of fish; a **swarm** of insects (or any particular insect, most typically flying ones), e.g., a **swarm** of bees/gnats. A **pack** of . . . can be used for dogs, hyenas, wolves, etc., as well as for (playing) cards. We also say a **deck** of cards.

C ## People involved in the same job/activity

These phrases are used as singular nouns.

A **team** of surgeons/doctors/experts/reporters/scientists/rescue workers/ detectives arrived at the scene of the disaster.
The **crew** was saved when the ship sank. [workers on a ship]
The **company** is rehearsing a new production. [group of actors]
The **cast** was composed entirely of amateurs. [actors in a particular production]
The **staff** arrives at 9:00 a.m. [general word for groups who share a place of work, e.g., teachers in a school, people in an office]
The **public** has a right to know the truth. [the people as a whole]
Note: The phrase **the people** takes a plural verb, e.g., **The people** are tired of taxes.

D ## Things in general

a **pile/heap**
of papers
(or clothes,
dishes, etc.)

a **set** of tools
(or pots and
pans, dishes,
etc.)

a **bunch** of
flowers (or
bananas,
grapes, etc.)

a **clump** of
trees (or
bushes, grass,
plants, etc.)

a **stack** of
chairs (or
tables,
boxes, etc.)

Exercises

29.1   Fill in each blank with an appropriate collective noun.

1. There are .... of mosquitoes in the forests in summer.
2. As we looked over the side of the boat, we saw a .... of brightly colored fish swimming just below the surface.
3. There was a .... of youths standing on the corner; they didn't look too friendly.
4. You'll see a .... of cards on the bookshelf. Will you get them for me, please?
5. A .... of biologists is studying marine life in this area.

29.2   Odd one out. In each case, one of the examples is wrong. Which one?

1. Company is often used for: actors   opera singers   swimmers
2. Cast is often used for: a play   a book   a movie
3. Crew is often used for: a yacht   a plane   a hospital
4. Pack is often used for: cats   dogs   wolves

29.3   Match collective words with appropriate nouns.

Example: a clump of bushes

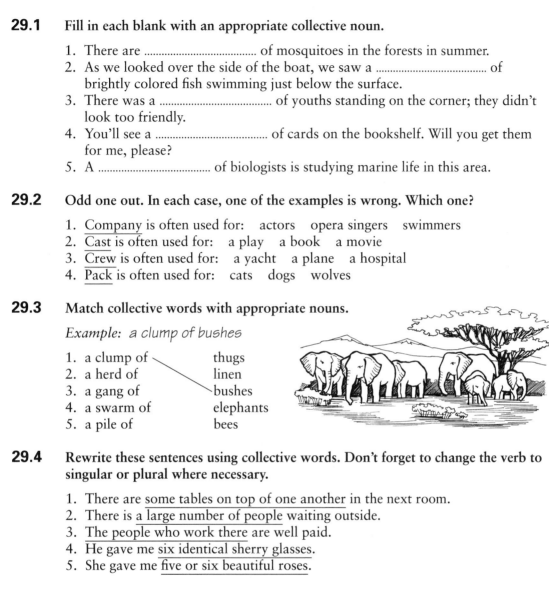

1. a clump of   thugs
2. a herd of   linen
3. a gang of   bushes
4. a swarm of   elephants
5. a pile of   bees

29.4   Rewrite these sentences using collective words. Don't forget to change the verb to singular or plural where necessary.

1. There are some tables on top of one another in the next room.
2. There is a large number of people waiting outside.
3. The people who work there are well paid.
4. He gave me six identical sherry glasses.
5. She gave me five or six beautiful roses.

29.5   Some collective nouns are associated with words about using language. Underline any you can see in this news text.

THE JOURNALISTS raised a whole host of questions about the actions of the police during the demonstration. There had been a barrage of complaints about police violence. The Chief of Police replied that he would not listen to a string of wild allegations without any evidence. Eventually he gave reporters a series of short answers that left everyone dissatisfied.

Making uncountable nouns countable

A

You can make many uncountable nouns singular by adding **a piece of** or **a (little) bit of.** Similarly, you can make such nouns plural with **pieces of** or (less frequently) **bits of.**

> She bought an attractive **piece of** furniture at an antique shop.
> I'll need a **little bit of** information before making a decision.
> Chopin wrote some wonderful **pieces of** music.
> Let me give you a **bit of** advice . . .

B

A number of other words go with specific uncountable nouns.

Weather

> We've had a long **spell of** hot weather this summer.
> Did you hear that **rumble of** thunder?
> Yes, I did. It came almost immediately after the **flash of** lightning.
> A sudden **gust of** wind turned my umbrella inside out.
> Did you feel a **drop of** rain just now?

(See also Unit 32 for more weather words.)

Groceries

two pieces/slices* of toast
a carton of milk
a loaf of bread
two bars of soap
a bar of chocolate
a package of cookies
a tube of toothpaste

*Slice can also be used with cake, bread, meat, and cheese.

Nature

> Look at the grasshopper on that **blade of** grass!
> What happened? Look at that **cloud of** smoke hanging over the city!
> Let's go out and get a **breath of** fresh air.

Other

> I had an incredible **stroke of** luck this morning.
> Your idea was a **stroke of** genius.
> The donkey is the basic **means of** transportation on the island.
> Pantyhose must be the most useful **article/item of** clothing ever invented.

C

The phrase **a state of** can serve to make uncountable nouns singular. Those nouns are usually abstract and include emergency, uncertainty, chaos, disrepair, confusion, poverty, health, mind, and flux, e.g., **a state of** emergency.

Exercises

30.1   Match the words in the list on the left with their partner on the right.

Example: *a rumble of thunder*

1. a stroke of	clothing
2. a rumble of	rain
3. a cloud of	thunder
4. an article of	transportation
5. a flash of	grass
6. a blade of	luck
7. a drop of	lightning
8. a means of	smoke

30.2   Change the uncountable nouns to countable nouns by using either *a piece of /
a bit of* or one of the more specific words listed in B opposite.

Example: Could you get me some bread, please?   *Could you get me a loaf of
bread, please?*

1. My mother gave me some advice that I have always remembered.
2. Suddenly the wind almost blew him off his feet.
3. Would you like some more toast?
4. Let's go to the park – I need some fresh air.
5. I can give you some important information about that.
6. I need to get some furniture for my apartment.

30.3   Use words from C opposite to fit the clues for the puzzle below.

1. My grandmother wouldn't be in such a poor state of .... now if she
   hadn't smoked all her life.
2. The government announced a state of .... after the earthquake.
3. We fell in love with the house,
   although it was in a terrible
   state of ....
4. We are still in a state
   of .... as to who
   has won the election.
5. Although this is supposed
   to be an affluent society,
   many people are living
   in a state of ....

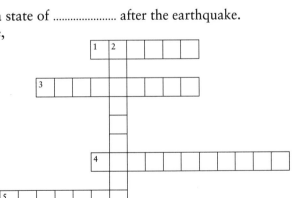

30.4   Make up a puzzle of your own like the one above using the language practiced in
this unit. If possible, test a friend.

30.5   Make up your own sentences using *a state of . . .* with these words.

1. chaos   2. flux   3. confusion   4. mind

Countries, nationalities, and languages

 A **Using *the***

Most names of countries are used without **the,** but some countries and other names have **the** before them, e.g., **the United States / the U.S., the United Kingdom / the U.K., the Philippines, the Netherlands.**

 B **Adjectives referring to countries and languages**

With **-ish:** Spanish British Irish Polish Danish Turkish
With **-(i)an:** Canadian Brazilian American Korean Venezuelan Mexican
With **-ese:** Japanese Chinese Vietnamese Portuguese Taiwanese
With **-i:** Israeli Iraqi Kuwaiti Pakistani Yemeni Bangladeshi
With **-ic:** Icelandic Arabic

Some adjectives are worth learning separately, e.g., **Swiss, Thai, Greek, Dutch.**

C **Nationalities**

Some nationalities have nouns for referring to people, e.g., **a Spaniard, a Filipino, a Turk, a Swede, a Dane, a Briton, an Arab.** For most nationalities we can use the adjective as a noun, e.g., **a Canadian, a German, an Italian, a Greek, an African.** Some need woman/man/person added to them (you can't say "a Dutch"), so if in doubt, use them, e.g., **a Dutch man, a Swiss woman, an Irish person.**

 D **World regions**

Here are the major regions.

E **Peoples and races**

People belong to **ethnic groups** and **regional groups** such as **African-Americans, Asians,** and **Latin Americans.** They speak **dialects** as well as languages. Everyone has a **native language,** or **first language;** many have **second** and **third languages.** Some people speak more than one language **fluently** and are **bilingual** or **multilingual.**

Exercises

31.1 Similar adjectives can typify regional groups, e.g., Latin American countries are almost all described by *-(i)an* adjectives.

1. Complete this list of Latin American adjectives. Look at a world map if you have to! Brazilian, Chilean, . . .
2. The same applies to some Eastern European countries and parts of the former Soviet Union. Complete the list. Hungarian, Armenian, . . .
3. What other regional groupings can you see on the left-hand page? (For example, many *-ish* adjectives are European.)

31.2 These nationality adjectives have a change in stress from the name of the country. Underline the stressed syllable in each word. Can you pronounce them?

Example: Panama → Panamanian

1. Egypt → Egyptian   4. Vietnam → Vietnamese
2. Italy → Italian   5. Jordan → Jordanian
3. Canada → Canadian   6. China → Chinese

31.3 Correct the mistakes in these newspaper headlines.

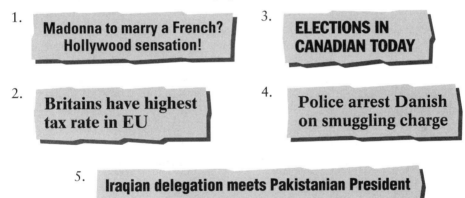

1. **Madonna to marry a French? Hollywood sensation!**

2. **Britains have highest tax rate in EU**

3. **ELECTIONS IN CANADIAN TODAY**

4. **Police arrest Danish on smuggling charge**

5. **Iraqian delegation meets Pakistanian President**

31.4 World quiz.

1. What are the five most widely spoken languages?
2. What are the five countries with the largest populations?
3. Which countries, strictly speaking, are in Scandinavia?
4. How many languages are there in the world?
5. Where do people speak Inuit?
6. What are the main ethnic groups in Malaysia?

Follow-up: Can you describe your nationality, country, region, ethnic group, language(s), etc., in English?

UNIT
32

The weather

Cold weather

> In Scandinavia, the **chilly** (1) days of autumn soon change to the cold days of winter. The first **frosts** (2) arrive and the roads become icy. Rain becomes **sleet** (3) and then snow, at first turning to **slush** (4) in the streets, with severe **blizzards** (5) and **snowdrifts** (6) in the far north. **Freezing** (7) weather often continues in the far north until May or even June, when the ground starts to **thaw** (8) and the ice **melts** (9) again.

(1) cold, but not extremely   (2) thin white coat of ice on everything
(3) frozen or partly frozen rain and snow mixed   (4) dirty, brownish, half-melted snow   (5) heavy snow blown by high winds   (6) deep banks of snow against walls, etc.   (7) extremely cold, with temperatures at or below the freezing point   (8) change from hard, frozen state to more liquid
(9) change from solid to liquid under heat

B   Warm/hot weather

stifling [hot, uncomfortable; you can hardly breathe]   **humid** [moist, damp air]   **muggy** [unpleasantly warm and extremely humid; makes you sweat]
scorching [burning heat]   **boiling** [excessively hot]   **sweltering** [oppressive heat]   **close** [uncomfortably warm and stuffy]   **mild** [moderate; not severe or extreme, e.g., a mild winter]   *Note also:* We had a **heat wave** last month. [a period of unusually hot weather]

C   Wet weather

This wet weather scale gets stronger from left to right.

damp → drizzle → pour/downpour → torrential rain → flood

Fall is usually **chilly** and **damp** with **rain** and **drizzle**.
It was absolutely **pouring.** / There was a real **downpour.**
In the tropics there is often **torrential rain,** and the roads get **flooded.**
This rain won't last long; it's only a **shower.** [short duration]
The **storm** damaged several houses. [high winds and rain together]
We got soaked in the **thunderstorm.** [thunder and heavy rain]
Hailstones battered the roof of our car. [small balls of ice falling from the sky]
The sky's **overcast;** I think it's going to rain. [very cloudy]
We had a **drought** last summer. It didn't rain for six weeks.
The air was **misty** after the light rain. [particles of moisture in the air]
It was so **foggy** that I could barely see ahead of me. [thick, heavy moisture in the air]

D   Wind

There was a gentle **breeze** on the beach, just enough to cool us.
It's a **blustery** day; the **gusts** of wind will just blow the umbrella away.
There's been a **gale** warning; it would be crazy to go sailing.
People boarded up their windows when they heard a **hurricane** was on the way.

Exercises

32.1   Match each word with a word from the box.

1. thunder   3. down   5. hail   7. gale
2. torrential   4. heat   6. snow

| stones | drift | storm | warning | rain | wave | pour |

32.2   Fill in the blanks with words from the left-hand page.

My first experience of real winter weather was when I went to Northern
Canada. I was used to the kind of snow that falls back home, which quickly
turns into brown .... (1) with all the people walking in it. In
fact, most of the time I was growing up, it didn't really snow at all – it was
mostly .... (2). Otherwise, our winters meant a little bit of
white .... (3) in my garden and occasionally having to drive
very carefully on icy roads early in the morning. I had never experienced the
.... (4) and .... (5) that can paralyze a whole
city in less than an hour and close roads completely. However, when the earth
finally .... (6) and all the snow .... (7) away
in spring, everything comes to life again and looks more beautiful than ever.

32.3   What kinds of weather do you think caused the following to happen? Write a
sentence that could go *before* each of these.

Example: The sweat was streaming down our backs.   *It was terribly muggy.*

1. We had to sit in the shade if we went outdoors.
2. I can hardly breathe; I wish it would rain to cool us down.
3. Even the mail carrier had to use a boat to get around.
4. They had to close the airport; it was three feet deep.
5. We were able to sit in the garden in the middle of winter.
6. The earth became rock-hard and a lot of plants died that summer.
7. It blew the newspaper completely out of my hands.
8. A row of big trees was uprooted like matchsticks.

32.4   What types of weather are bad and good for doing these things?

Example: skiing   *bad: mild weather that makes the snow melt; good: cold,
clear days*

1. planting flowers in a garden   4. a day of sightseeing in a big city
2. having an evening barbecue   5. camping out in a tent
3. going out in a small sailboat   6. looking at ships through binoculars

32.5   Describe the weather in your country or home region during different seasons of
the year. Which season has the best weather? the worst?

*Example: Summer is the best season. It's warm and sunny, with cool breezes
at night. In winter it is cold and damp . . .*

Describing people – appearance

A   **Hair, face, and complexion**

straight black hair and **thin-faced**

long **wavy** hair and **round-faced** with a **double chin**

Afro hairstyle and **dark-skinned** (or **black**)

a **crew cut** with **bushy eyebrows**

receding hair and a few **wrinkles**

bald with **freckles**

beard and **mustache**

curly blond hair with a **fair complexion**

He used to have **black** hair, but now it's gone **gray**, almost **white**.
How would you describe your hair color? **Blond, brunette, dark/dark-haired, black**, or **red-haired/a redhead**?

Fair and **dark** can be used for hair or complexion.

B   **Height and build**

a **plump** or **heavyset** man

a **slim** woman [positive]

an **obese** person [negative, very fat]

a **chubby** baby

Fat may sound impolite. Instead we might say **a bit overweight**. If someone is broad and solid, we say they are **stocky**. A person with good muscles can be **well built** or **muscular**. If someone is very thin and refuses to eat, they may be **anorexic**.

C   **General appearance and age**

She's a very **stylish** and **elegant** woman, always **well dressed;** her husband is
    just the opposite, very **scruffy** and **messy/sloppy looking**.
He's very **good looking**, but his friend's rather **unattractive**.
Do you think **beautiful** women are always attracted to **handsome** men, and
    vice versa? I don't. I think **personality** matters more.
He's **in his early/mid-/late fifties**. She's **fortyish**. They're **thirty-something**. He's
    a teenager / in his teens. She's **middle-aged**. They're **old/elderly**. He's an
    older gentleman. They are **senior citizens / seniors**.

Exercises

33.1 Answer these remarks with the *opposite* description.

Example: A: I thought you said he was the short, chubby one.
B: No, just the opposite. *He's the tall, thin one.*

1. A: Was he the dark-skinned, wavy-haired man?
   B: No, just the opposite. He's . . .
2. A: I've heard that she's always well dressed.
   B: What? Who told you that? Every time I see her, she's . . .
3. A: Is Mary that plump, blond-haired woman over there?
   B: No, you're looking at the wrong one. Mary's . . .
4. A: I don't know why, but I expected the tour guide to be middle-aged or elderly.
   B: No, apparently she's only . . .

33.2 Write one sentence to describe each of these people, giving information about their hair and face, height and build, age group, and general appearance.

1. you yourself   3. a neighbor
2. your best friend   4. your ideal of a handsome man / a beautiful woman

Now, in the same way, describe a famous person; give some extra clues, e.g.,
pop star / politician, and see if someone else can guess who you are describing.

33.3 WANTED! MISSING! Fill in the blanks in these posters.

WANTED FOR FORGERY

Will Prowse
height: 6 ft.

...................................-faced
.... hair
.... complexion

**WANTED FOR
ARMED ROBBERY**

Sandra King
height 5 ft., 3 in.

.... hair
.... build
...................................-faced

WANTED
DEAD OR ALIVE

**Jake "Dagger"
Flagstone**

5 ft., 9 in.

................................, with
.... and ....;
.... build.

MISSING

Louisa Yin
Age 10, Chinese

.... hair

33.4 Make a collection of descriptions of people from newspapers and magazines.
Court/crime reports, celebrity and gossip pages of magazines, and the "personal"
ads by people seeking partners are good places to start.

UNIT 34 Describing people – character

A   **Intellectual ability**

Ability: intelligent   bright   smart   able   gifted   clever   shrewd
    talented   brainy (colloquial)

Lacking ability: stupid   foolish   simple   silly   brainless   dumb   clueless
    (the last three are colloquial)

Clever, in a negative way, using brains to trick or deceive: cunning   crafty   sly

B   **Attitudes toward life**

Looking on the bright side or the dark side: optimistic   pessimistic

Outward-looking or inward-looking: extroverted   introverted

Calm or not calm: relaxed   tense/anxious

Practical, not dreamy: sensible   down to earth

Feeling things intensely: sensitive

C   **Attitudes toward other people**

Enjoying others' company: sociable   gregarious   congenial

Disagreeing with others: quarrelsome   argumentative

Taking pleasure in others' pain: cruel   sadistic

Relaxed in attitude toward self and others: easygoing   even-tempered   affable

Not polite to others: impolite   rude   ill-mannered   discourteous (formal)

Telling the truth/keeping promises: honest   trustworthy   reliable   sincere

Unhappy if others have what one does not: jealous   envious

D   **One person's meat is another one's poison**

Some characteristics can be either positive or negative depending on your point of view. The words in the right-hand column mean roughly the same as the words in the left-hand column except that they have negative rather than positive connotations.

Positive	Negative
determined	obstinate stubborn pigheaded
thrifty/economical	stingy tight-fisted miserly cheap (colloquial)
self-assured/confident	self-important arrogant smug
assertive	aggressive bossy (colloquial)
unconventional/original	peculiar weird eccentric odd flaky (colloquial)
frank/direct/open	blunt abrupt brusque curt
broad-minded	unprincipled permissive
inquiring	prying nosy
generous	extravagant excessive
innocent	naive
ambitious	pushy (colloquial)

(See also Units 12, 73, and 78.)

Exercises

34.1   Match these words with their opposites.

1. bright   introverted
2. extroverted   tight-fisted
3. rude   courteous
4. cruel   gregarious
5. generous   kindhearted
6. unsociable   stupid

34.2   Do you think that the speaker likes or dislikes the people in these sentences?

1. Diane's very thrifty.   5. Dick is awfully pushy.
2. Nancy's usually frank.   6. I find Annemarie arrogant.
3. Jim's really determined.   7. Molly is somewhat nosy.
4. Paul can be bossy.   8. Jack is kind of unconventional.

34.3   Reword the sentences above to give the opposite impression.

Example: *Diane's very stingy.*

34.4   Magazines often publish questionnaires that are supposed to analyze your
character. Look at the words below and match them to the corresponding
question.

Example: If you arrange to meet someone at 7 p.m., do you arrive at 7 p.m.?
Reliable

pessimistic   argumentative   sensitive   sociable
extravagant   assertive   inquiring   reliable

1. Do you prefer to be in the company of other people?
2. Look at the picture. Do you think, "My glass is half empty"?
3. Do you find it easy to tell your boss if you feel he/she has
   treated you badly?
4. Do you always look out the window if you hear a car pull up?
5. Do you buy lots of things that you don't really need?
6. Do you frequently disagree with what other people say?
7. Do you lie awake at night if someone has said something unkind to you?

34.5   What questions like those in 34.4 could you ask to try to find out whether a
person is the following:

1. thrifty   3. sensible   5. even-tempered   7. obstinate
2. blunt   4. naive   6. unconventional   8. confident

34.6   Choose at least five adjectives from the opposite page that you think best describe
either your own or a friend's character. How do you or your friend demonstrate
these characteristics?

Example: *Sociable – I am sociable because I love being with other people.*

Relationships

A

Types of relationships

Here is a scale showing closeness and distance in relationships in different contexts.

	CLOSER ←		→ MORE DISTANT
friendship:	best friend good/old friend	friend	acquaintance
work:	close colleague	colleague/coworker	
love/romance:	lover boyfriend/girlfriend		ex-*
marriage:	wife/husband/spouse/partner		ex-*

*ex- can be used with or without another word: That's my **ex-boyfriend** *or* She's my **ex** (informal).

Mate is used as a suffix to describe a person you share something with, e.g., **classmate, roommate, shipmate.**

Coworker is used in most work contexts, **colleague** among professional people. English has no universally accepted word for "person I live with but am not married to," but **companion, partner,** and (sometimes) **lover** are fairly common.

B

Liking and not liking someone

Core verb	Positive		Negative	
like	love adore		dislike hate	
	worship idolize		can't stand loathe	
respect	look up to admire		look down on despise	
	honor esteem		detest put down	
attract	be attracted to turn someone on		repel turn someone off	

Put down, turn on, and **turn off** are informal. **Esteem** and **repel** are fairly formal.

> She doesn't just like Bob; she **idolizes** him! **I can't stand** him.
> I used to **look down on** my teachers; now I've begun to **admire** them.

C

Phrases and idioms for relationships

> Jane and I **get along** well. / I **get along** (well) with Jane. [have a good relationship]
> Paul and Liz don't **see eye to eye.** [often argue/disagree]
> I've had **a falling out** with my parents again. [argument]
> Tony and Sue have **broken up / split up.** [ended their marriage or relationship]
> George is **having an affair** with his boss. [a sexual relationship, usually secret]
> Children should respect their **elders.** [adults/parents, etc.]
> Let's try and **make up.** [be friends again after an argument]
> She's **my junior** / I'm **her senior** / **I'm senior to her,** so she does what she's told.
>   [refers to position/length of service at work]

(See Unit 69 for more words relating to likes and dislikes.)

Exercises

35.1 Change these sentences using words with the suffix -*mate*.

1. This is Jack. He and I share a room in the dormitory.
2. My grandfather still writes to his old friends from his seafaring days.
3. We were in the same class at Lincoln High School, weren't we?
4. She and I played on the softball team together.

35.2 How many relationships can you find between the people in column A and column B, using words from the left-hand page?

Example: John Silver and Laura Fine were once colleagues.

A

John Silver: Works at a language school for business people in Toronto. Worked at the Sun School, Ottawa, 1992–1994.

Josh Yates: Politician, was once married to Helen Cobb. Met Bill Nash a couple of times.

Sue Watts: Divorced from Bill Nash. Swam for Canada in the 1988 Olympics.

Ana Wood: Has been married to Bill Nash for the past five years.

B

Nora Costa: Was on the Canadian Olympic swimming team in 1988. Was in the same class at school as Sue Watts.

Bill Nash: Works every day with John Silver. Has known Helen Cobb for years.

Fred Parks: Politician. Knew Sue Watts years ago, but not very well.

Laura Fine: Taught at Sun School in Ottawa, 1991–1996. Lives with Josh Yates.

35.3 Liking and disliking. What kind of relationship do you think the people on the left might have with the people on the right? Use the words and phrases opposite.

1. teenage pop music fan

parents	pop star
strict teacher	best friend

2. secretary

another secretary	boss
very attractive coworker	

3. 45-year-old

teenagers	ex-companion

35.4 Correct the errors below.

1. Dave and Phil don't get along eye to eye.
2. I had a falling down with my parents last night. It wasn't my fault.
3. We had an argument but now we've made well.
4. Do you think those two are making an affair? I do.
5. She should learn to respect her olders.

UNIT 36 At home

A **Places in the home**

master bedroom: the largest, most important bedroom
den: an informal room for resting, watching TV, studying (sometimes called a study)
attic: the room just below the roof, often used for storage
basement: the room below ground level used for storage, play, or living
laundry room: a room with a clothes washer and dryer; in an apartment building a large room with coin-operated washers and dryers for tenants' use
hall/hallway: open area as you come into a house or a long corridor between rooms
landing: the floor at the top of a staircase
walk-in closet: a clothes closet large enough to walk into, attached to a bedroom
porch: a covered area outside the entrance door, used for sitting if large enough
patio/terrace: an uncovered area adjoining a house or an apartment and used for sitting
driveway: a (short) road leading from the street to a house, building, or garage

B **Small objects in the home**

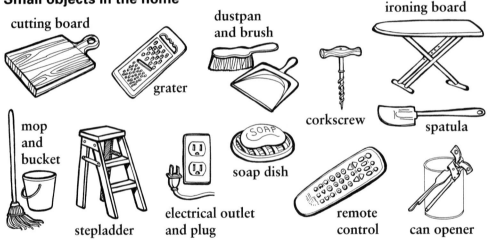

cutting board
grater
dustpan and brush
ironing board
corkscrew
spatula
mop and bucket
stepladder
electrical outlet and plug
soap dish
remote control
can opener

C **Types of houses/places where people live**

single-family home: a home for one family
apartment: a unit of one or more rooms in an apartment building or complex
studio apartment / studio: a single room for both living and sleeping
apartment building: a building with individual apartments but a common entrance
apartment complex: a large group of similar apartments, usually with separate entrances, sharing common grounds and managed by one company or group
townhouse: a house in a city, at least two stories high, often attached to similar units
mobile home / trailer: a manufactured home designed to be transported to a site
condominium/condo: a unit or apartment, owned by an individual, in a building or on land that is owned in common by all the holders

Exercises

36.1 Fill in the labels showing parts of a house.

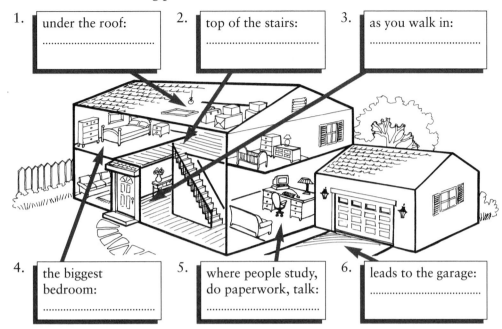

1. under the roof:
....

2. top of the stairs:
....

3. as you walk in:
....

4. the biggest bedroom:
....

5. where people study, do paperwork, talk:
....

6. leads to the garage:
....

36.2 Fill in the blanks.

1. I have a darkroom in the .... where I develop film. It's perfect because there are no windows down there.
2. Is there an .... where I can plug in this radio?
3. We keep our skis up in the .... during the summer. They're out of the way up there.
4. Let's have a cold drink outside on the .... and watch the sunset.
5. The light switch is on the .... at the top of the stairs.
6. I've moved into a .... It's much easier with only one room to clean!
7. We bought a .... It's just like an apartment, except we're the owners!

36.3 Where in a typical home would you usually find these things?

1. forks and spoons
2. dental floss
3. coat hangers
4. a grater
5. a clothes dryer
6. a videocassette recorder
7. outdoor furniture
8. a computer
9. an electrical outlet

36.4 Answer these questions yourself. Then ask a friend or classmate the same questions.

1. Do you live in a house, an apartment, or some other type of residence?
2. Have you ever been in a mobile home? What was it like?
3. Is it common to rent studio apartments in your country? If so, what kinds of people rent them?
4. Would you rather rent a home or own one, if you had a choice?

Everyday problems

A   **Things that go wrong in houses and apartments**

The lights are not **working.** There must be a **power failure / power outage.**

Oh no! The bathroom's **flooded!** Get a mop, quick!

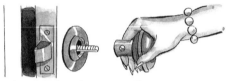

The doorknob **came off.**

The batteries are **dead** / have **run out.** I'll have to get some more / recharge them.

The washing machine **broke down.** We'll have to do the laundry by hand.

Oh no! This chair's **broken.** I wonder how that happened.

This pipe's **leaking.**

Your cup's **chipped.** I'll get you another one.

B   **Minor injuries**

Maria **fell down** and **cut** her knee.

I **bumped/banged** my head against the door and got a **bruise.**

She **twisted/sprained her ankle** coming down the stairs.

C   **Other everyday problems**

I **misplaced** Bob's letter. Have you seen it anywhere? [put it somewhere and can't find it]

She **spilled** coffee on the carpet. I hope it doesn't **stain.** [leave a permanent mark]

I **locked myself out.** Can I use your phone to call my wife?

The car **won't start.** I hope the battery isn't dead.

The clock's **slow/fast/stopped.** What time do you have?

Exercises

37.1 **What do you think happened to make these people do/say what they did?**

Example: We had to send for a plumber. *A pipe was leaking. / Our basement was flooded.*

1. I had to call the local mechanic.
2. Our neighbors let us use their washing machine.
3. Don't worry, it does that all the time; I'll just screw it back on.
4. Come here and I'll put a Band-Aid on it.
5. How many batteries does it take? I'll get some for you.
6. I don't know where you put them. Try the bedside table.

37.2 **Odd one out.**

Example: spill   flood   chip   *chip – the other two involve liquids.*

1. break down   smash   break   3. leak   come off   chip
2. fall down   bump   stain   4. cut   bruise   flood

37.3 **What would you do if . . .**

1. you misplaced your credit card?   4. your TV set broke down?
2. you noticed your guest's mug was chipped? 5. you bruised your chin?
3. one of your coat buttons came off?   6. your watch was slow?

37.4 **Match the pictures with the things that can go wrong with them. Not all of the words are on the opposite page.**

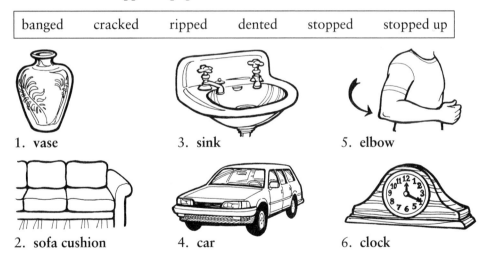

| banged | cracked | ripped | dented | stopped | stopped up |

1. vase   3. sink   5. elbow

2. sofa cushion 4. car   6. clock

37.5 **Complete these sentences using words and phrases from the opposite page.**

Example: There was a power outage, so we *had to use flashlights.*

1. The wind blew the door shut, and I realized I'd . . .
2. I would call her, but I'm afraid I've . . .
3. I can't take a picture; my camera's . . .
4. When I tried to run over the rocks, I . . .

Worldwide problems

A   **Disasters/tragedies**

earthquakes
[the earth moves/trembles]

explosions
[e.g., a bomb]

major accidents
[e.g., a plane crash,
a fire]

hurricanes/tornadoes/
typhoons [violent
winds/storms]

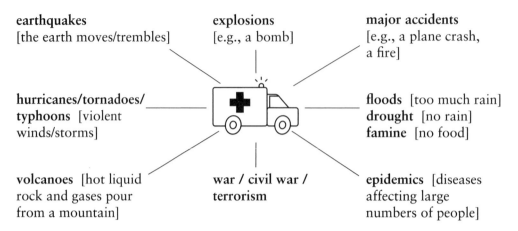

floods [too much rain]
drought [no rain]
famine [no food]

volcanoes [hot liquid
rock and gases pour
from a mountain]

war / civil war /
terrorism

epidemics [diseases
affecting large
numbers of people]

Verbs connected with these words

A volcano has **erupted** in Indonesia. Hundreds are feared dead.
The flu epidemic **spread** rapidly throughout the country.
Millions are **starving** as a result of the famine.
A big earthquake **shook** the city at noon today.
The area is **suffering** its worst drought for many years.
Civil war has **broken out** in the north of the country.
A tornado **swept** through the islands yesterday.
Remember: **injure** (people), **damage** (things):
Many people were **injured** and dozens of buildings were **damaged** in the hurricane.

B   **Words for people involved in disasters/tragedies**

The explosion/typhoon/flood resulted in 300 **casualties.** [dead and injured
people]
The real **victims** of the civil war are the children left without parents. [those
who suffer the results of the disaster]
There were only three **survivors.** All the other passengers were reported dead.
[people who live through a disaster]
Thousands of **refugees** have crossed the border looking for food and shelter.

C   **Headlines**

These headlines from newspapers are all connected with diseases and epidemics.

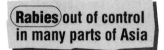

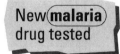

Cholera and **typhoid**
injections not needed,
says Tourism Minister

disease that can be
caused by bite from
a dog, raccoon, etc.

disease caught from
certain mosquitoes,
causing fever

diseases caused by
infected food and water

Exercises

38.1 What type of disasters from A opposite are these sentences about? Why?

Example: The lava flow destroyed three villages.   *volcano; lava is hot liquid rock that comes from a volcano.*

1. The earth is cracked and vegetation has withered.
2. The tremor struck at 3:35 p.m. local time.
3. People had boarded up stores and houses and stayed indoors.
4. Shelling and mortar fire could be heard all over the town.
5. Witnesses said they saw a fireball fall out of the sky.

38.2 Complete this word-class table, using a dictionary if necessary. Where there is a dash, you do not need to write anything.

Verb	Noun: thing or idea	Noun: person/people
....	explosion	–
injure	....	the injured
....	survival	....
starve	....	....
erupt	....	–

38.3 In these headlines, say whether the situation seems to be getting *worse* or *better,* or whether a disaster has *happened* or has been *avoided.*

1.
POISON GAS CLOUD SPREADS

2.
AIDS time bomb ticking away

3.
POLICE DEFUSE TERRORIST BOMB

4.
All survive jumbo emergency landing

5.
Oil slick recedes

6.
FLOOD WARNINGS NOT HEEDED IN TIME

38.4 Fill in the blanks with words from B opposite. Try to work from memory.

1. Another 50 people died today, all .... of the famine.
2. The government has agreed to allow 3,000 .... trying to escape the civil war to enter the country.
3. It was a tragic highway accident, with over 120 ....
4. A: Were there any .... from the ship that sank?
   B: I'm afraid not.

38.5 Which diseases are described below? Try to do this from memory.

1. One that can be caused by a mosquito bite
2. One you can get by drinking infected water
3. One you can get from an animal bite

Education

A Stages of compulsory education in the United States

Level (different names)	Grades	Approximate age range
preschool nursery school		2–5 years
elementary school primary school	kindergarten, 1–6	5–12 years
junior high school middle school	7–9	12–14 years
high school secondary school	10–12	15–18 years

School attendance is **compulsory** [required] between the ages of 6 and 16 in most states in the U.S. **Public schools** are free, tax-supported schools, controlled by state and local governments. They usually cover the span of **K–12** [kindergarten through 12th grade]. Students have the option of attending **private schools** or **parochial** [religious] **schools** (neither is free). These nonpublic schools teach the same core subjects as local public schools, and often teach additional subjects as well.

B Higher education in the United States

Universities provide teaching and research and normally have an **undergraduate** division that confers **bachelor's degrees**, e.g., **Bachelor of Arts (BA)** or **Bachelor of Science (BS)**, and a **graduate** (or **postgraduate**) division that confers advanced degrees such as **Master of Arts (MA)** and **Doctor of Philosophy (Ph.D.)**. (*Note:* A Ph.D. applies to most academic subjects, not only to philosophy.) A student's main area of study is called a **major** subject.

Undergraduate study normally lasts four years, and postgraduate study can last from one year to an indefinite length. **Community/junior colleges** [2 years] and **state colleges** [2 or 4 years] are tax-supported and usually charge low **tuition** [payment]. Private universities and colleges are more expensive, though some **scholarships** or **grants** [financial aid] are offered. Certain **professional schools**, such as **medical, dental,** or **law schools,** are attended after one has earned a bachelor's degree.

C Tests and exams

take a test

pass / do well on / ace *(colloquial)* a test

fail / do miserably on / flunk *(colloquial)* a test

If you want to get a **high mark/score** on a test, **review** the material beforehand. Some students **cram** [prepare in a short period] for tests.

Exercises

39.1 Find out about another country's education system by asking friends, classmates, coworkers, or teachers these questions and other questions of your own.

1. At what age do children start school?
2. How long must students remain in school (until what age)?
3. Are there evening classes for adults?
4. Do you have state colleges and private universities? Are there any entrance requirements?
5. Can students get scholarships or grants for higher education?

39.2 Make a table for the stages of compulsory education in your country or region, like the table in A opposite. How does it compare with the system in the U.S. or with systems in other countries that you know of? Also, compare higher education in your country or region, as described in B opposite, with that of the U.S. and other countries.

39.3 Correct the errors in these sentences.

1. I can't go out. I'm studying. I'm passing a test tomorrow.
2. Congratulations! I hear you succeeded your exams!
3. After she finished high school, she went on to law school.
4. I got very good notes on my tests this term.
5. Public schools in the U.S. charge tuition.

39.4 Fill in the blanks in this account of an American woman's education.

> Sue Washington started her education at age 3, when her mother enrolled her in .... (1). She "graduated" to .... (2) at age 5. After Sue completed .... (3) and .... (4) school, her family decided to send her to a .... (5) high school, rather than a public school. She got good .... (6) on her college admissions tests and entered a two-year community .... (7). She later transferred to a four-year college, where her .... (8) was economics. Upon receiving her .... (9) degree, she went on to .... (10) school, where she is now working toward a master's degree.

39.5 What questions could you ask to get these answers?

1. No, I had to finance my own studies.
2. In most states, it's sixteen, but a lot of kids stay on until eighteen.
3. Well, I was up all night cramming for an exam.
4. No, just the opposite: I flunked it!
5. No, both our kids started school in kindergarten. They didn't go to school before that.

UNIT 40 Work

A

Here are some job titles that are common to a wide range of different workplaces. Check the general meanings in a dictionary.

boss supervisor manager executive director chief executive officer (CEO) accountant secretary skilled worker unskilled worker entry-level employee blue-collar worker white-collar worker union official

B

Here are some **fields** of employment and a few of the **occupations** in them.

Health care	*Journalism*	*Construction / Home improvement*
physician (doctor)	reporter	construction worker
registered/practical nurse	camera operator	carpenter
physical therapist	correspondent	plumber
lab technician	editor	electrician
dietitian	photographer	
Mechanics/Repair	*Arts/Entertainment*	*Engineering*
auto mechanic	actor/actress	aerospace engineer
farm-equipment mechanic	writer	chemical engineer
air-conditioning technician	painter/artist	civil engineer
computer technician	director	mining engineer
telephone installer	choreographer	industrial engineer

C

Collocations of words connected with work

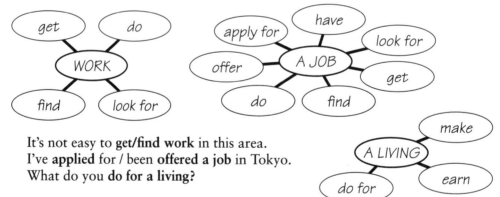

It's not easy to **get/find** work in this area.
I've **applied** for / been **offered a job** in Tokyo.
What do you **do for a living?**

D

Expressions connected with work

to work the night/day shift [period of time for work, either day or night]
to be on flextime [employee chooses work hours within guidelines]
to go/be on strike [dispute between management and workers]
to be fired [dismissed from a job, usually for a negative reason]
to be laid off / made redundant [dismissed; no longer needed]
to be unemployed [without a job]
to resign/quit [to leave a job because you want to; *quit* is less formal]
to give notice [formally notify of intent to leave a job or to dismiss an employee]
to be promoted / to get a promotion [get a higher position]
to be a workaholic [love work too much]
to moonlight [hold both a full-time job and a second, part-time job]

Exercises

40.1 **Which of the job titles in A opposite would best describe the following?**

1. A person who has a high position in a company, whose job is to make important decisions.
2. The person who represents the workers' interests in disputes with the management of a workplace.
3. A worker whose job requires no special training.
4. A person who works in an office, bank, etc., as opposed to a factory.
5. A person who keeps an eye on the day-to-day work of other workers.
6. The person who keeps and checks financial records.

40.2 **In which fields in B opposite would you list these occupations?**

1. bricklayer
2. dental hygienist
3. electrical engineer
4. ballet dancer
5. TV news anchorperson
6. vending machine servicer

Now think of at least one more occupation for each field in B opposite.

40.3 **Think of five people you know who work for a living. Can you name their jobs in English and the fields they are in? You can look them up in a bilingual dictionary or in a thesaurus.**

40.4 **Using the expressions in D opposite, imagine what has happened / is happening.**

Example: Most employees work nine to five, but he comes in at ten and leaves at six.   *He's on flextime.*

1. I lost my job. They had to make cutbacks.
2. I work from midnight until 8 a.m.
3. They've made her Personnel Manager as of next month!
4. I was late so often, I lost my job.
5. He hasn't had a job for six months.
6. Your trouble is that you are obsessed with work!

Now make a sentence for each of the verbs in D that you have not used.

40.5 **Fill in the blanks.**

I'd love to .... (1) a job in journalism, but it's not easy without qualifications. Since I have to make a .... (2) somehow, I'll have to get .... (3) wherever I can find it. I've .... (4) for a full-time job doing word processing, but it doesn't pay very well. Even if the job is .... (5) to me, the salary may not be enough to pay the bills. I might just have to find a second job and .... (6).

UNIT
41 Sports

A Some popular sports

in-line skating windsurfing bowling

pool/billiards horseback riding auto racing

B Equipment – what you hold in your hand

golf – **club**   squash/tennis/badminton – **racquet**   archery – **bow**
table tennis (Ping-Pong) – **paddle**   baseball – **bat**   fishing – **rod/line**
hockey – **stick**   pool/billiards – **cue**   canoeing – **paddle**   rowing – **oar**

C Athletics – some track and field events

discus   javelin   high jump   long jump   pole vault

She's a good **sprinter.** [fast over short distances]
He's a great **long-distance** runner. [e.g., 5000 meters, marathon]
Jogging around the park every Saturday is enough exercise for me.

D Verbs and their collocations in the context of sports

Our team **won/lost by** three **goals/points/runs.**
She **broke** the Olympic **record** last year. / She **set a** new Olympic **record.**
He **holds the record** for the 100-meter breaststroke.
Toronto **beat** New York 4–2 yesterday.
I'm planning to **take up** tennis.

E People who play particular sports

-**er** can be used for many sports, e.g., **swimmer, surfer, skater, golfer,** etc. **Player** is
often necessary, e.g., **tennis player, baseball player, pool player.** Some names must
be learned separately, e.g., **cyclist, mountaineer, jockey, gymnast.**

Exercises

41.1 Which of the sports opposite are these people probably talking about?

1. "The ball has a natural curve so it doesn't go down the lane in a straight line."
2. "It's all a matter of balance, really."
3. "I like the noise, the speed, and the danger – there's nothing more exciting to watch."
4. "You need a good eye and a lot of concentration."
5. "At first you get sore and can hardly sit down, but that wears off."

41.2 Look at the sports page of a newspaper (either in English or in your own language). Can you find some sports that are not listed in A opposite? What are their English names? Use a bilingual dictionary if necessary.

41.3 Name at least two sports in each of these categories. Some may overlap.

1. target sports *archery, shooting*
2. net games
3. water sports
4. animal racing
5. combat sports
6. stick and ball games
7. racquet and ball games
8. sports on wheels

Can you add some more sports categories, with examples?

41.4 Collocations. Fill in the blanks with appropriate verbs.

1. Were many records .... at the Olympics?
2. We've been .... so often that we're at the bottom of the league!
3. Congratulations! How many points did you .... by?
4. Who .... the world record for the 1000 meters? Is it a Russian?
5. You should .... jogging. You'd feel more energetic!

41.5 What do you call a person who . . . ?

1. does the long jump? *a long jumper*
2. rides horses in races?
3. drives cars in races?
4. throws the discus/javelin?
5. does gymnastics?
6. plays hockey?
7. runs long distance?
8. does the pole vault?

41.6 Make sure you know which sports these places are associated with, as in the example. Use a dictionary if necessary.

1. court *tennis, squash, etc.*
2. course
3. ring
4. field
5. rink
6. alley
7. slope
8. track

The arts

A **General branches of the arts**

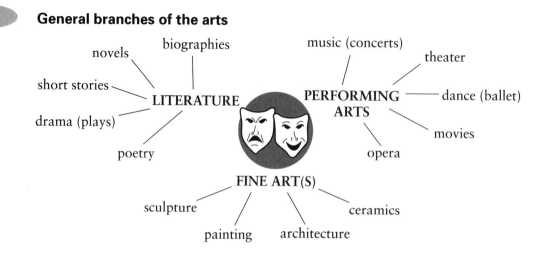

The **arts** (plural) covers everything in the network. **Art** (singular/uncountable) usually means **fine art,** but it can also refer to technique and creativity.

Have you read the **arts page** in the paper today? [covers everything in the network]
She's a great **art lover.** [loves painting and sculpture]
Shakespeare was skilled in **the art of** poetry. [creative ability]

Dance refers to the art of dancing, especially **modern dance** or more traditional **ballet. A novel** is a long story; a short work of prose fiction is a **short story.**

When we talk about a performing art in general, we can omit the definite article, e.g., I love **(the) opera/ballet/theater/movies.** For a particular performance we say: Would you like to go to **the opera/ballet/theater/movies** tonight?

B **Describing a performance**

We went to see a new **production** (1) of *Hamlet* last night. The **sets** (2) were incredibly realistic and the **costumes** (3) were wonderful. It was a good **cast** (4) and I thought the **direction** (5) was excellent. Anthony O'Donnell **gave** a **marvelous performance** (6). It **got rave reviews** (7) in the papers today.

(1) the presentation of a work, especially a play or movie
(2) scenery, buildings, furniture on the stage or in a studio
(3) clothes the actors wear in the performance
(4) all the actors in it
(5) the way the director organizes the performance
(6) and (7) are typical collocations; (7) means "got very enthusiastic comments"

C **Words connected with events in the arts**

There's an **exhibit/exhibition** of paintings by Manet at the National Gallery.
They're going to **publish** a new **edition** of the **works** of Cervantes next year.
The Opera Society is doing a **performance** of *Don Giovanni.*
Bergman's *Persona* is **playing at** the Paradise Theater next week.

Exercises

42.1 Which branch of the arts do you think these people are talking about?

Example: "It was a strong cast, but the play itself was weak." *theater*

1. "It's called *Peace*. It stands in the main square."
2. "It was so dull that I fell asleep during the second act."
3. "It was just pure movement, with very exciting rhythms."
4. "It doesn't have to rhyme to be good."
5. "Oils to me don't have the delicacy of watercolors."
6. "Her design for the new city hall won an award."
7. "I like to read them and imagine what they'd be like on stage."
8. "The first chapter was boring, but it got better later."
9. "The acting was marvelous, and I enjoyed seeing it on the big screen."
10. "Overall, the performance was good, though the tenor wasn't at his best."

42.2 Each of these sentences contains a mistake of usage. Find the mistake and correct it. You may need a dictionary.

Example: The scene in this theater projects right out into the audience.
not "scene" but "stage" [the place where the actors perform]

1. What's the name of the editorial of that book you recommended? Was it Cambridge University Press?
2. "Do I dare to eat a peach?" is my favorite stanza of poetry in English.
3. He's a very famous sculpture; he did that statue in the park, you know, the one with the soldiers.
4. Most of the novels in this collection are only five or six pages long. They're great for reading on short trips.
5. When will the President's biography be performed?
6. The cast wore beautiful sets in the new production of the play.

42.3 Ask *questions* for which these remarks would be appropriate answers.

Example: It's an oil on canvas. *What kind of painting is it?*

1. Yes, it got rave reviews.
2. No, I'm not really a concertgoer, but thanks anyway.
3. Oh, some beautiful old buildings and some ugly new ones.
4. The cast was fine, but the direction was weak.
5. A new Canadian film; would you like to see it?
6. It's OK, but I usually prefer modern dance.

42.4 Think of your favorites in the arts. Name at least five, using the following categories or your own categories. Then compare with a classmate or friend.

play   movie   novel   short story   sculpture   painting   poem
building   song   opera   ballet

Follow-up: See if you can name all the parts of a typical theater in English. A picture dictionary might help you.

Food

vegetables: cauliflower broccoli spinach cucumber lettuce squash
fruit: apple orange grapefruit pear strawberry banana pineapple kiwi
meat: ribs liver steak veal prime rib leg of lamb venison kidneys
fish: cod sole flounder haddock salmon herring sardines trout catfish
seafood: shrimp crab lobster crawfish squid clams oysters scallops
herbs: parsley rosemary thyme chives oregano tarragon sage basil

Flavors, tastes, and quality – adjectives and some opposites (≠)

sweet ≠ **bitter** [sharp/unpleasant]   **sour** [acid taste]
hot, spicy [e.g., curry] ≠ **mild**   **bland** [very little taste]
salty [a lot of salt]   **sugary** [a lot of sugar]
tasty [has a good taste/flavor] ≠ **tasteless** [has no flavor at all]
greasy/oily [too much oil/fat] ≠ **dry, dried out** [no moisture or juice]
lean [has little or no fat] ≠ **fatty** [has a lot of fat]

This meat is **overcooked / overdone / undercooked / underdone.**
Do you like your steak cooked **rare / medium-rare / medium / well-done?**

Ways of cooking food

boil   fry/sauté   bake   roast

broil/grill   barbecue   steam   stir-fry

Courses, dishes, servings

a helping/portion   a main dish / an entree   a side dish

more please

a stew   a casserole   a dessert   seconds

Exercises

43.1 To learn long lists of words, try dividing them up into groups. You could divide these vegetable names into groups in any way you like, e.g., "vegetables that grow underground" (potatoes, carrots, etc.). There are some words not given opposite.

leeks   cucumbers   spinach   carrots   potatoes   cauliflower
zucchini   green/red peppers   asparagus   corn   lettuce   onions
rice   peas   cabbage   eggplant   radishes   beans   shallots
turnips   beets   celery

43.2 Use words from B opposite to describe the following.

1. Indian curry
2. seawater
3. an unripe apple
4. a cup of coffee with five spoonfuls of sugar
5. strong black coffee with no sugar
6. factory-made white bread

43.3 What might you say to the person/people with you in a restaurant if . . .

1. your french fries had too much oil/fat on them?
2. your steak had obviously been cooked too much / too long?
3. your stew had too much salt in it?
4. your dish seemed to have no flavor at all?
5. your roast beef sandwich was half fat?

43.4 How do you like the following foods prepared? Use words from C opposite and any others. What do you like to put on these foods, from the list in the box?

chicken   eggs   potatoes   hamburger   filet of sole
shrimp   bacon   vegetables   coffee/tea   roast beef

salt   pepper   vinegar   mustard   gravy   ketchup   hot sauce
salad dressing   oil   mayonnaise   lemon juice   salsa

43.5　1. What do we call the *meat* of these animals?

calf   deer   sheep (two names)   pig (three names)

2. Which of these fruits normally grow in your country/region? Are there others not listed here?

peach   plum   grapefruit   grape   nectarine   fig
black currant   raspberry   melon   lime   kiwi   mango
date   litchi

3. Name your favorite fruit, vegetable, main dish, side dish, and dessert. Do you like big portions or small ones? When you are a dinner guest at someone's home, do you ever ask for seconds? Do you take seconds if offered? Compare your answers with a classmate or friend if possible.

UNIT 44 The environment

A There are many different words referring to features of the environment. Here are some arranged on a scale of small to large.

brook → stream → river   mound → hill → mountain
cove → bay → gulf   grove → woods → forest
puddle → pond → lake   footpath → lane → road

B You have to be careful about the use of **the** with features of the environment.

	Use with **the**?	*Examples*
cities, countries, continents	no	Paris, Peru, Asia
countries that are in a plural form	yes	the Philippines
individual mountains	no	Mount Fuji
mountain ranges	yes	the Rockies
islands	no	Easter Island
groups of islands	yes	the West Indies
rivers	yes	the Nile
oceans, seas	yes	the Pacific, the Caspian
gulfs, bays, and straits	yes	the Gulf of Mexico
lakes	no	Lake Michigan
general areas by compass direction	yes	the north, the southwest

C Read this encyclopedia entry about Iceland and note any words that refer to particular features of the environment.

> **Iceland** An island republic in the North Atlantic. The landscape consists largely of barren plains and mountains, with large ice fields, particularly in the southwest. The island has active volcanoes and is known for its thermal springs and geysers. With less than 1% of the land suitable for growing crops, the nation's economy is based on fishing, and fish products account for 80% of the exports. Area: 103,000 km². Population: 227,000. Capital: Reykjavik.

D Here are some other nouns that are useful when talking about the environment. Check their meanings with a dictionary if necessary.

Where land meets water: coast   shoreline   beach   estuary   cliff   peninsula
Words connected with rivers: source   tributary   waterfall   mouth   gorge
Words connected with mountains: foot   ridge   peak   summit   glacier

E Here are some words to describe environmental problems in the world today. Check a dictionary if necessary.

air, water, and sea pollution   overfishing   the greenhouse effect
global warming   destruction of the ozone layer
oil spills   toxic waste   overpopulation

Exercises

44.1 Label the pictures below.

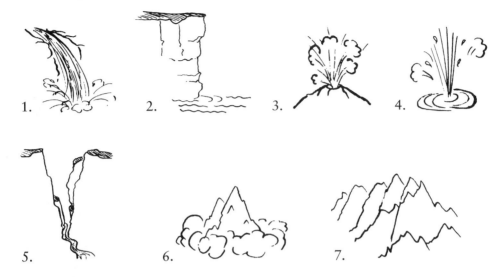

1. 2. 3. 4.

5. 6. 7.

44.2 In the paragraph below, all the instances of *the* have been omitted. Insert them wherever they are necessary.

> Brazil is fifth largest country in world. In north, densely forested basin of Amazon River covers half country. In east, country is washed by Atlantic. Highest mountain range in South America, Andes, does not lie in Brazil. Brazil's most famous city is Rio de Janeiro, former capital. Capital of Brazil is now Brasilia.

44.3 Give two nouns from the opposite page to go with the adjectives below. Try not to repeat any of the nouns you choose.

Example: sandy   *beach/shore*

1. sandy   2. steep   3. shallow   4. rocky   5. turbulent   6. dangerous

44.4 Complete the paragraph below about your own country, or any other country that interests you. Remember to use *the* whenever it is necessary.

.... (1) is a .... (2) in .... (3). The country's economy is based on .... (4). The best-known river in .... (5) is .... (6). The most famous mountain range is .... (7), and the highest mountain in that range is .... (8). .... (9) is a major environmental problem in .... (10) today.

44.5 Why do environmentalists say we should use unleaded gas and recycle paper, cans, and bottles? What else are they in favor of?

Towns

A

Read this description of Santa Fe, one of the oldest towns in the Southwestern United States. Underline any words or phrases that might be useful for describing your own or any other town.

Santa Fe is the most unusual town in America. Here is the only significant community that has existed through the entire recorded history of the American West. For well over three centuries, Santa Fe has been the regional capital of a succession of nations. Today, it is the capital of the state of New Mexico, a peerless repository of Southwestern lore, and a wonderfully cosmopolitan showcase for all of the arts. An astonishing assortment of museums, theaters, studios, galleries, restaurants, and nightclubs display the artistry of residents in adobe structures that reflect the timeless beauty of Santa Fe-style architecture. Today, Santa Fe is a perfectly scaled walking town centered around the splendid centuries-old Plaza. Churches, public buildings, and historic businesses offer a picturesque treasury of Pueblo and Spanish-colonial architecture through the ages.

The town is located at the edge of the vast Rio Grande basin amid gentle pine-covered foothills of the southernmost Rocky Mountains. Although it is one of the highest towns in the country, there is a pleasant four-season climate because of the southern location and sheltering peaks. (Adapted from *The Great Towns of the West* by David Vokac.)

B

Here are some of the facilities that you might find in a town.

Sports: swimming pool   sports center   golf course   tennis courts
   skating rink
Cultural: theater   opera house   concert hall   art gallery   museum
Educational: school   university   library   adult/continuing education
Dining, lodging, and nightlife: restaurant   coffee shop   nightclub   bar
   hotel   bed & breakfast   youth hostel   disco   casino   real estate agency
Transportation: subway   railroad station   bus service   taxi   car rental
Religion: church   synagogue   mosque   temple   cathedral
Other: hospital   clinic   law courts   city hall   police station
   shopping mall   department store   childcare center   supermarket

C

Here are some typical problems in modern towns:

Traffic jams: Traffic is very slow or even comes to a standstill.
Slums: certain parts of the city that are poor and in a very bad condition
Vandalism: pointless destruction of other people's property
Overcrowding: Too many people live in too small a place.
Pollution: The air and the water are no longer as pure as they were.
Homelessness: People without homes live on the streets or in temporary shelters.
Crime: See Unit 55.

Exercises

45.1 Check that you understand the text about Santa Fe by answering the questions.

1. Where is Santa Fe?
2. How long ago was Santa Fe founded?
3. Name some of the attractions you can find in Santa Fe.
4. What building material is commonly used in Santa Fe-style architecture?
5. For sightseeing, what's the best way to get around?
6. What is the central point of the town?
7. What famous river and mountain range touch Santa Fe?
8. How is the climate?

45.2 The description of Santa Fe comes from a travel book. Write sentences about a town of your choice. If you wish, follow this outline and use any expressions you noted in A opposite.

- Why is the town special?
- Where is it located?
- What features can you find in the town and nearby?
- What historic features does the town have?
- How can sightseers get around?
- What is the natural environment like?
- How is the climate?

45.3 Look at the facilities listed in B opposite. Check the ones that your town, or any town you know well, has.

45.4 Suggest three words that would combine well with each of the nouns below, as in the examples.

1. ....
   .... museum
   ....

3. _higher_ ....
   .... education
   ....

5. ....
   .... club
   ....

2. _sports_ ....
   .... center
   ....

4. ....
   .... court
   ....

6. ....
   .... agency
   ....

45.5 What facilities would your ideal town have? Name the most important facilities for you in each of the categories listed in B opposite. You may choose facilities other than those listed, if you wish.

45.6 Are any of the problems mentioned in C opposite found in your town or a town you know well? Could you suggest a solution to these problems?

The natural world

A Animals

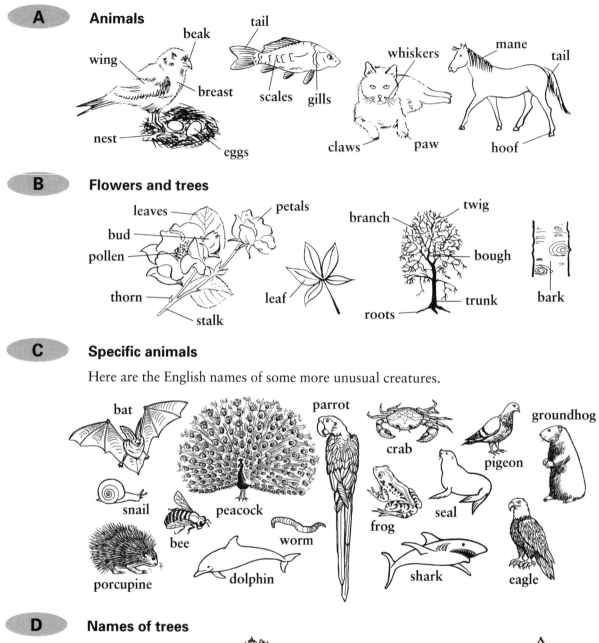

tail
beak
wing
breast
scales   gills
nest
eggs
whiskers
mane
tail
claws   paw
hoof

B Flowers and trees

leaves
petals
bud
pollen
thorn
stalk
leaf
branch
twig
bough
trunk
roots
bark

C Specific animals

Here are the English names of some more unusual creatures.

bat
parrot
groundhog
crab
pigeon
snail
peacock
bee
worm
frog
seal
porcupine
dolphin
shark
eagle

D Names of trees

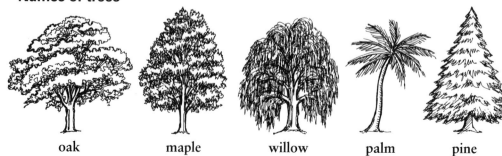

oak   maple   willow   palm   pine

Exercises

46.1 Can you answer the following general knowledge questions?

1. Is the whale a fish or a mammal?
2. What does the bee take from flowers to make honey?
3. Name three animals that hibernate in winter.
4. February 2nd is called Groundhog Day in the U.S. and Canada. Why?
5. Which is the fastest of all land animals?
6. Which bird symbolizes peace?
7. What do fish use their gills for?
8. Can you name an endangered species of plant or animal?
9. Which of these creatures is extinct – emu, dinosaur, phoenix?
10. Name three flowers and three birds in English.
11. What plants or animals are the symbols (or emblems) of Canada, the United States, Scotland, England, and New Zealand?
12. What plant or animal is the symbol of your country?

46.2 Write an appropriate adjective to go with each of the following nouns:

Example: flowing mane

mane   porcupine   petals   eagle   oak   willow   worm   bark

46.3 Fill in the blanks using words from the opposite page.

1. A tree's .... go a long way under ground.
2. A cat sharpens its .... against the .... of a tree.
3. The horse is limping. It must have hurt its ....
4. A flower that is just about to open is called a ....
5. If we pick up those ...., we can use them to start the fire.
6. Jane's as blind as a ...., and Pete eats like a ....
7. Anne's as busy as a ...., but Chris works at a ....'s pace.

46.4 Read this description of a camel from an encyclopedia. Underline any words that you think would be found frequently in such descriptions of animals.

> **camel** A mammal of the family Camelidae (2 species): the **Bactrian,** from cold deserts in Central Asia and domesticated elsewhere, and the **dromedary;** eats any vegetation; drinks salt water if necessary; closes slit-like nostrils to exclude sand; humps are stores of energy-rich fats. The two species may interbreed: the offspring has one hump; the males are usually sterile, while the females are fertile.

46.5 Write a similar description for an encyclopedia of an elephant, or any other animal of your own choice. Use reference books to help you if necessary.

Clothes

A   **Clothing and parts of clothing**

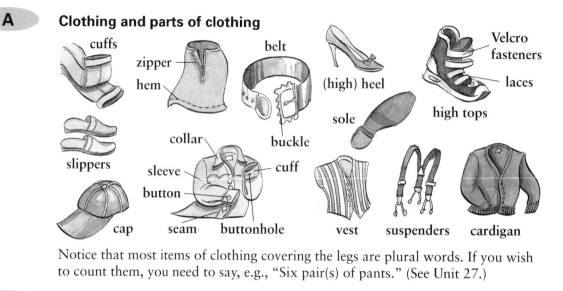

Notice that most items of clothing covering the legs are plural words. If you wish to count them, you need to say, e.g., "Six pair(s) of pants." (See Unit 27.)

B   Words for materials and fabrics can be either nouns or adjectives.

Natural: silk   cotton   velvet   corduroy   denim   leather   wool   suede
Synthetic: rayon   nylon   polyester   acrylic   acetate

C   **Patterns**

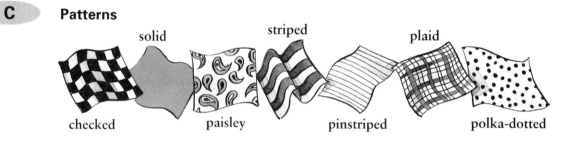

D   Here are some verbs and phrases associated with clothing.

He **undressed/got undressed,** throwing all his clothes on the floor.
I usually wear jeans, but I also like to **dress up/get dressed up** for parties.
Can I **try on** those red shoes in the window?
She **took off** her shoes and **put on** her slippers.
He **changed out of** his sports clothes and **into** his uniform.
That black bag **matches** your shoes.
Those shoes don't **fit** my son anymore. He's **grown out of** them.

E   Here are some adjectives for describing people's clothing or their appearance.

How things fit: baggy   loose   tight
Style: short-sleeved / long-sleeved   sleeveless   V-neck   turtleneck   pleated
   double-breasted
General: elegant   trendy   well dressed   old-fashioned   messy
   grungy (informal)

Exercises

47.1 Which of the words illustrated in A fit best in the following sentences?

1. I need to get my black shoes repaired. One .... is broken and both the .... have holes in them.
2. Tie your .... or you'll trip!
3. Put your .... on – this floor is very cold.
4. I ate too much! I have to loosen my ....
5. I'm almost finished making my dress for the party, but I still have to sew up the .... and sew on some ....

47.2 Fill in the blanks with any appropriate word. Use *pair* where necessary.

1. Blue .... are a kind of international uniform for young people.
2. People with ugly knees shouldn't wear ....
3. I need some new underwear. I'm going to buy three new .... today.
4. Oh no! There's a hole in my pantyhose. I'll have to get a new ....
5. Oh no! There's a hole in my pantyhose. I'll have to get some new ....

47.3 Match the following materials with the item they are most likely to be associated with from the box.

Example: satin *ribbon*

1. satin   2. cashmere   3. leather   4. corduroy   5. nylon   6. cotton

| boots | pants | T-shirt | sweater | ribbon | jogging suit |

47.4 Describe in detail what these people are wearing and their general appearance.

47.5 Describe how you like to dress at work, in class, on weekends, at parties.

(See Unit 33 for additional useful vocabulary for describing someone's appearance.)

Illness and medicine

A **What are your symptoms?**

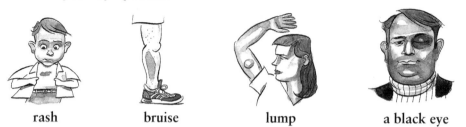

| rash | bruise | lump | a black eye |

I have a cold / a cough / a sore throat / a temperature / a stomachache /
  a headache / chest pains / an earache / a pain in my side / a rash on my chest /
  a bruise on my leg / a black eye / a lump on my arm / indigestion / diarrhea /
  insomnia / hives / sunburn.
I feel sick to my stomach / nauseous / dizzy / breathless / shivery / weak /
  stuffed up.
I am depressed / constipated / tense / hyper [colloquial] / tired all the time.
I've lost my appetite / voice. I can't sleep, my nose itches, and my leg hurts.

B **Some medical tests and measures**

(take your) temperature   (take your) pulse   (take your) blood pressure
blood test(s)   X-ray   mammogram   Pap test   urine analysis
MRI scan

C Doctors who **specialize** in particular fields are called **specialists.**

allergist	gastroenterologist	ophthalmologist	psychiatrist
cardiologist	gynecologist	osteopath	surgeon
chiropractor	internist	podiatrist	urologist
dermatologist	obstetrician	proctologist	

The doctor you see regularly, who treats you for all health matters, is usually
called a **general practitioner (GP)** or a **family doctor.**

D **What's the diagnosis?**

You have the flu / pneumonia / bronchitis / rheumatism / arthritis / hepatitis /
  an ulcer / hypertension / acne / a virus / an infection / a bug / something
  that's going around.
You've broken your wrist and sprained/dislocated your ankle.
You're pregnant / HIV positive / a hypochondriac.
He died of lung cancer / a heart attack / a brain hemorrhage / a stroke / AIDS.

E **What does the doctor prescribe?**

a) Take one pill/capsule/tablet three times a day after meals.
b) Take a teaspoonful every morning on an empty stomach.
c) Rub a little on before going to bed at night.
d) You'll have to have your leg put in a cast.
e) Get plenty of bed rest.

Exercises

48.1   Match the diseases with their symptoms.

1. hepatitis   swollen, painful joints or muscles, extreme stiffness
2. pneumonia   burning pain in abdomen, pain or nausea after eating
3. rheumatism   headache, aching muscles, fever, cough, sneezing
4. an ulcer   dry cough, high fever, chest pain, rapid breathing
5. the flu   fever, weakened condition, yellow color of skin

48.2   What does a doctor or nurse use the following things for?

Example: stethoscope   *for listening to a patient's chest*

1. thermometer   2. hypodermic needle   3. tongue depressor   4. scalpel

48.3   Which type of specialist might each of these people see for treatment?

1. someone with a skin rash that won't go away
2. someone who might have a heart condition
3. someone who suffers from chronic depression
4. someone who sneezes constantly in spring or summer
5. a woman who thinks she might be pregnant
6. someone who suffers from frequent back pain
7. someone who has a painful ingrown toenail
8. someone who has blurry vision

48.4   Complete the table.

Noun	Adjective	Verb
....	breathless	....
....	weak	....
....	shivery	....
....	dislocated	....
ache	....	....
treatment	treatable	....
....	swollen	....

48.5   What medical problems might you have or might you get if . . .

1. you eat too fast?
2. you smoke a lot?
3. you play soccer or football?
4. you go skiing?
5. you stay out in the sun too long?
6. you eat food you're allergic to?
7. you run unusually fast for a bus?
8. a mosquito bites you?
9. you eat food that has gone bad?
10. you think you're sick all the time?

48.6   Think of illnesses that you (or members of your family or friends) have had.
What were the symptoms and what did the doctor prescribe?

UNIT
49 **Transportation**

A **Types of transportation**

Transportation type	Kinds of vehicle	Parts of vehicle	People working with it	Associated facilities
automotive	car, bus, taxi, truck, van, recreational vehicle (RV)	trunk, engine, transmission, tires, brakes, horn, hood	driver, motorist, chauffeur, mechanic	gas station, service station, garage, bus terminal
rail	commuter train, freight train, local train, express	passenger car, dining car, sleeping car, freight car	engineer, conductor, porter, ticket agent	train station, waiting room, signal, railroad crossing
water	rowboat, ferry, cruise ship, yacht, barge, containership	deck, bridge, mast, porthole, anchor, gangplank	captain, skipper, purser, docker, first officer	dock, wharf, landing, port, lighthouse, shipyard
air	airplane, helicopter, (jumbo) jet, supersonic aircraft	cockpit, nose, tail, wings, fuselage, overhead bins, emergency exit	pilot, flight attendant, ground crew, air-traffic controller	departure lounge, duty-free shop, hangar, runway

B **Words at sea**

Traditionally sailors use different words at sea – a bedroom is a **cabin,** a bed is a **bunk,** the kitchen is a **galley,** right is **starboard** and left is **port,** and the group of people who work on the ship is called the **crew.** Many of these terms are now used in the context of an aircraft. Sailors also refer to their vessels as *she* rather than *it.*

C **Some road signs**

There are curves in the road ahead.   There's going to be a steep hill downward.   No U turn.   There's a railroad crossing ahead.

D **Some words and expressions connected with travel**

Last week she **flew** to Montreal. She was **booked** on an evening **flight.** The **plane** was **scheduled** to **take off** at 6 p.m. and **land** at 7 p.m. local time. The **plane** was **delayed** by fog, and she was **stranded** at the **airport** overnight. Trains usually **run on time** here. You have to **change** trains in Philadelphia. Our **car gets 35 miles to the gallon.** It **has good pickup** and **handles** well.

Exercises

49.1 Label the diagrams with these words. Use a dictionary to help you if necessary.

deck   engine   gangplank   hood   mast   nose   porthole
steering wheel   tail   tire   trunk   wharf   wing

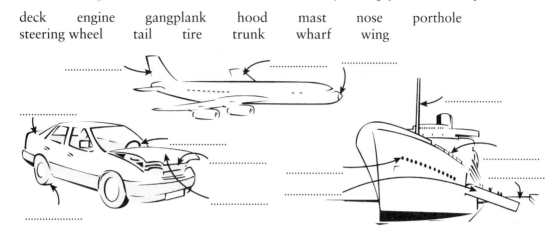

49.2 Where would these words fit into the table in A opposite?

fender	balloon	deck chair	metal detector
sail	gas pump	bus driver	funnel
glider	oar	rudder	baggage claim
check-in counter	rear view mirror	canoe	freeway

49.3 Here are some more road signs. Write an explanation of their meaning similar to the explanations in C opposite.

1.   2.   3.   4.

49.4 Fill in the blanks with words from the opposite page or from 49.2.

Yesterday John was supposed to take a .... (1) from Washington, D.C., to New York. He got up very early, put his luggage in the .... (2) of his car, and tried to start the engine. It wouldn't start. John lifted the .... (3), but he couldn't find anything wrong. He immediately called his local .... (4) to ask them to send a .... (5). Fortunately, the garage had someone available, and he got to John's car within ten minutes. He quickly saw what the matter was. "You're .... (6) of gas," he said. John felt very foolish. Despite all this, he got to the airport, checked in early, and then went straight to the .... (7) to read a newspaper while he waited. Soon he heard an announcement: "All flights to and from New York are .... (8) because of the weather." "If only I had decided to take the .... (9)," John thought. "It would probably have been faster, and it could have been quite pleasant having lunch in the .... (10) car, watching the scenery go by."

UNIT
50 Vacations

A

Here are some different places where you can spend a vacation.

resort: a hotel (usually large and expensive), with leisure facilities such as tennis courts, golf course, health spa, swimming pools, beach, etc.

motel: a hotel for motorists, with parking spaces directly outside the rooms

bed & breakfast (B&B): a small hotel, inn, or private home, providing a room and breakfast the next morning for one price

campsite: an outdoor area where you can pitch a tent or park a van or an RV

summer camp: a summer recreation area in the country, usually for children

youth hostel: cheap lodging, mainly for young people, who share facilities

time-share: a house or an apartment, usually in a resort area, owned by many people and used by each owner for a specified time period (e.g., 1–2 weeks a year for vacations)

B

Here are some things that people like to do on vacation.

sunbathe

swim *or* go swimming

do some sightseeing *or* go sightseeing

cycle *or* go cycling

go to an amusement park

hike *or* go hiking

go shopping

climb *or* go climbing

camp *or* go camping

C

Here are some useful expressions for when you are staying in a hotel or motel.

I'd like to book a single/double room with two beds / twin beds / a queen-size bed / a king-size bed.

Do you have a nonsmoking room with an ocean view / a river view available?

I'd like to guarantee my reservation with a credit card.

I'd like a wake-up call at 7 a.m., please.

We'd like room service, please.

The remote control for my TV isn't working.

Could I get some extra towels / blankets / clothes hangers, please?

I'd like to make a long-distance / an overseas call.

Is there a charge for local calls made from my room?

What time is check-in/check-out? Is late check-out available?

What time does the pool / health club / coffee shop open/close?

Exercises

50.1   Which of the vacation places in A have you or any of your friends stayed at? What are the advantages and disadvantages of each? Try to think of at least one advantage and one disadvantage for each even if you have no experience with them.

50.2   List the nine activities shown in B opposite according to your personal preferences. Can you think of others?

50.3   Look at B opposite again. Note the way you can say either "We *camped* in Yosemite Park this year" or "We *went camping* in Yosemite Park this year." Write the sentences below in an alternative form, either with or without *go* or *be*.

1. We like to go jogging around the lake.
2. I love going sailing.
3. He spends too much time fishing.
4. It's pretty expensive to shop in Rome.
5. I enjoy horseback riding on weekends.

50.4   What would you say in a hotel when . . .

1. you want to reserve a room for a couple?
2. you have to wake up at 6 a.m. for an important meeting?
3. your TV screen suddenly goes blank?
4. it's early in the morning and you want to go for a swim in the pool?
5. you'd rather not go to the restaurant for dinner?

50.5   There are five typical language mistakes in the paragraph below. Underline them and then write the corrections.

> The Wongs stayed at a camping last summer because all other
>
> kinds of vacations resorts were too expensive. Every day Mrs.
>
> Wong took a sunbath, Mr. Wong made a sightseeing, and the
>
> children did cycling around the island.

50.6   To find useful language about vacations, get some brochures or other tourist information in English. You could try the embassies or tourist offices of English-speaking countries, or a travel agency. When you receive the information, note down any useful new words and expressions that you find.

50.7   Where would you spend your ideal vacation? What kind of place would you stay in? How would you spend your time? Write a paragraph.

Numbers and shapes

Notice how the following are said in English.

28%	twenty-eight percent	5'8"	five feet, eight inches (*or*
10.3	ten point three		five-foot-eight, common in spoken
⁴⁄₉	four-ninths		English when giving height)
4^2	four squared	4 ft. × 6 ft.	four feet by six feet
⁹⁄₁₃	nine-thirteenths *or*	5 m. × 10 m.	five meters by ten meters
	nine over thirteen		(*or* five by ten meters)
8^4	eight to the fourth	1⅔	one and two-thirds
	power	7^3	seven cubed

0° C *or* 32° F   zero degrees centigrade/Celsius *or* thirty-two degrees Fahrenheit
1,623,400   one million, six hundred (and) twenty-three thousand, four hundred

Two-dimensional shapes

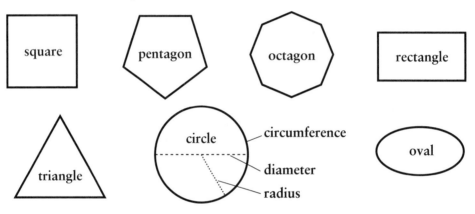

square   pentagon   octagon   rectangle

triangle   circle   circumference   diameter   radius   oval

A **rectangle** has four **right angles**.
A **circle** is cut in half by its **diameter**. Its two halves can be called **semicircles**.
The **radius** of a circle is the distance from its center to the **circumference**.

Three-dimensional shapes

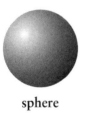   

sphere   cube   pyramid   spiral

Here are the four basic processes of arithmetic.

+ addition   − subtraction   × multiplication   ÷ division

$6 \times 7 = 42$ Six times seven is forty-two. *or* Six times seven equals forty-two.

$2x + 3y - z = \dfrac{3z}{4x}$ Two *x* plus three *y* minus *z* equals three *z* divided by
four *x* (*or* three *z* over four *x*).

Exercises

51.1   Try this numbers quiz. Say the answers aloud.

1. Name the first four odd numbers.
2. Name the first four even numbers.
3. How much is 4^3?
4. Give an example of a decimal fraction.
5. How do you read this formula and what does it represent? $e = mc^2$
6. How do you read this and what does it represent? $2\pi r$

THE WALL STREET JOURNAL

"**Actually, being married to a pollster isn't 50% bad, 83% of the time.**"

51.2   Write the following in words rather than in figures or symbols.

1. 79% of American women diet each year, yet 95% of those diets fail.
2. 0° C = 32° F.
3. About 15% of children under age 10 are left-handed.
4. ⅔ + ¼ × 4^2 = 14⅔.
5. 2,769,425 people live here.
6. The inflation rate was 3.5% last year and .4% last month.

51.3   Look at the shapes in B and C opposite. What is the adjective relating to each one? Use a dictionary if necessary.

Example: triangle – triangular

51.4   Read the following records aloud.

1. Oxygen accounts for 46.6% of the earth's crust.
2. The highest waterfall in the world is Angel Falls, Venezuela, with a drop of 979 m.
3. The top coffee-drinking country in the world is Finland, where 1892 cups per annum are consumed per head of the population.
4. The longest known strike lasted 33 years. It was a strike of barbers' assistants in Copenhagen, Denmark, and it ended in 1961.
5. The smallest country in the world is Vatican City, with an area of 0.4 sq. km.

Write at least two sentences like the ones above, with interesting facts or statistics about any places or topics that interest you. Read them aloud.

51.5   Draw the following.

1. A right-angled triangle with two equal sides of about one inch in length. Draw a small circle in the center of the triangle and then draw lines from the circumference of the circle to each of the angles of the triangle.
2. A rectangle with diagonal lines joining opposite angles.
3. An octagon with equal sides. Draw an oval in the middle of the octagon.
4. A cube of roughly 2 cm. by 2 cm. by 2 cm.

Science and technology

A

You are probably familiar with the traditional branches of science, e.g., biology, chemistry, physics, botany, and zoology. But what about these newer fields?

genetic engineering: the manipulation of genetic material (DNA) of living things to alter hereditary traits

ergonomics / human engineering: the study of the design of physical working spaces and how people interact with them

molecular biology: the study of organic molecules

cybernetics: the study of the way information is moved and controlled by the brain and the nervous system or by machinery

bioclimatology: the study of how climate affects living things

geopolitics: the study of how geographical factors influence the politics of nations

cryogenics: the study of physical systems at extremely low temperatures

astrophysics: the application of physical laws and theories to stars and galaxies

B

Here are some fairly recent inventions that we are now becoming used to.

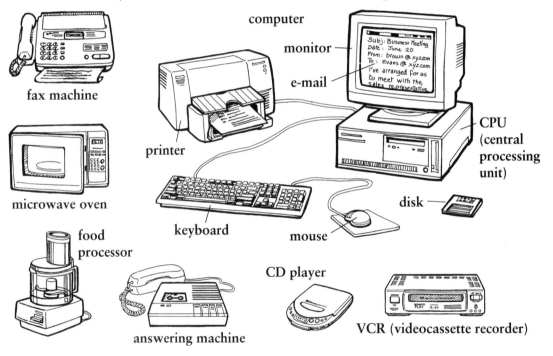

fax machine

computer

monitor

e-mail

CPU (central processing unit)

printer

microwave oven

disk

food processor

keyboard

mouse

CD player

answering machine

VCR (videocassette recorder)

C

The verbs in the sentences below are all useful in scientific contexts.

He **experimented** with many different materials before **finding** the right one.
The zoologist **dissected** the animal.
When they were **combined,** the two chemicals **reacted** violently with each other.
After **analyzing** the problem, the physicist **concluded** that there was a flaw in her initial **hypothesis.**
James Watt **invented** the steam engine; Alexander Fleming **discovered** penicillin.
You should **patent** your invention as quickly as possible.

Exercises

52.1 Complete the list with the name of the specialist in each field.

Science	*Scientist*
chemistry	....
physics	....
zoology	....
genetics	....
computer technology	....
civil engineering	....

52.2 Below are some of the amazing achievements of modern technology. Match the names on the left with the definitions on the right.

1. VCR
2. photocopier
3. fax machine
4. tape recorder
5. modem
6. camcorder
7. word processor
8. food processor

a kind of sophisticated typewriter using a computer
a machine that records and plays back sound
a machine that records and plays back sound and pictures
a camera that records moving pictures and sound
a machine for chopping, slicing, blending, etc.
a machine that makes copies of documents
a machine that makes copies of documents and sends
   them along telephone lines to another machine
a piece of equipment that sends information along
   telephone lines from one computer to another computer

52.3 Write descriptions like those in exercise 52.2 for the following objects.

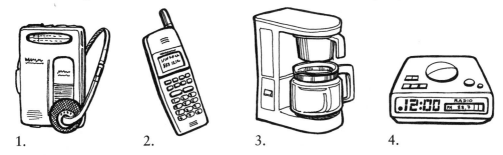

1.   2.   3.   4.

52.4 What are the nouns connected with the following verbs?

1. discover	3. combine	5. patent	7. dissect
2. invent	4. conclude	6. analyze	8. experiment

52.5 Increase your knowledge of scientific vocabulary by reading articles of general scientific interest in English language newspapers or magazines. If possible, find a textbook in English for schoolchildren studying a branch of science that you have studied. The science should be relatively easy for you so that you can concentrate on the English used.

UNIT 53

The media and the press

A

A

The term **media** usually refers to TV, radio, newspapers, and magazines: means of communication that reach the public.

B

Radio and television

Types of TV programs: documentaries   news   current events shows / news specials   soap operas   situation comedies / sitcoms   movies talk shows   detective shows   mysteries   nature shows   dramas sports   weather   game shows   variety shows   commercials

Types of TV broadcasting: network/commercial TV   public TV cable TV   pay per view (*Note:* In the U.S., network and public TV are free; cable and pay per view carry fees.)

Types of radio broadcasting: AM and FM are the most common.

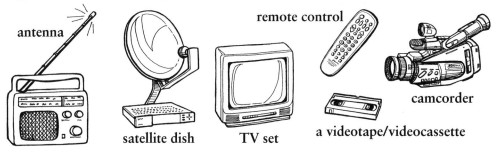

antenna   remote control   satellite dish   TV set   a videotape/videocassette   camcorder

C

Newspapers and publishing

Parts of a newspaper: headlines   news reports   editorials feature articles (e.g., about fashion or social trends)   horoscope cartoons/comics   crossword puzzle   classified ads   business news sports   entertainment   letters to the editor   advice columns

The **Sunday edition** of many newspapers contains additional **sections** and **supplements,** e.g., a weekly magazine, a book review section, a travel section, etc. **Tabloid newspapers / tabloids** focus more on sensation than serious news; they have large headlines, and stories are frequently about celebrities, crimes, and UFO sightings.

A **magazine** may be published weekly or monthly; it may be concerned with a particular topic such as fashion, music, computers, etc., or it may review the week's news. A **journal** is usually an academic magazine. A **comic book** is a magazine with cartoon stories, often (though not always) for children or teenagers.

D

The verbs in the sentences below are useful in the context of the media.

That book was **published** by Cambridge, but it was **printed** in Hong Kong.
The **documentary** was **shot/made** on location in Spain.
They **cut/edited** the movie before showing it on TV.

(See Unit 92 for the language of newspaper headlines.)

Exercises

53.1   What kind of TV programs do you think these are?

1. Murder on Her Mind
2. The Amazing Underwater World
3. World Cup Special
4. The $10,000 Question
5. Last Week in Washington
6. Late Night Talk with Joan Waters

53.2   Give the name of one program you know for each type listed in B opposite. It can be in English or in your native language.

53.3   Write definitions explaining what jobs these people do.

Example: A makeup artist puts makeup on the faces of people who appear on TV.

1. a foreign correspondent
2. a copy editor
3. an editor
4. a librarian
5. a bookseller
6. a publisher
7. a columnist
8. a critic

53.4   Fill in the blanks with the most appropriate word from the opposite page.

1. He never even gets up from the sofa to change channels; he just presses the buttons on the ....
2. Although our .... was expensive, we've taken some priceless movies of our children.
3. That movie on TV was .... so heavily, it didn't make sense!
4. I can't stand reading .... There's no real news, just gossip.
5. You won't find classical music on .... radio; try FM instead.
6. We subscribe to an excellent .... about gardening. It comes out once a month.

53.5   Choose any newspaper (it could be in your native language if you don't have one in English) and complete the following sentences.

1. The main story today is about ....
2. The editorial is about ....
3. The most interesting feature article is about ....
4. There is an advice column on page ...., a crossword puzzle on page ...., a cartoon on page ...., and classified ads (starting) on page ....
5. The most interesting business article is about ....,
   and the biggest sports story is about ....
6. The most striking photograph shows ....

53.6   Look at the TV page of an English language paper and/or watch an English language news broadcast on TV. Note any useful vocabulary on this theme.

UNIT 54 Politics and public institutions

A Types of government

democracy: a government elected by the people of the country
monarchy: a country ruled by a king or queen (sometimes in name only)
dictatorship: a government run by one person with complete power (a dictator)
federation: a union of political units (e.g., provinces) under a central government
independence: freedom from outside control; self-governing

B Presidential government and parliamentary government: U.S. and U.K.

United States

United Kingdom

Presidential government: The powers of the **President** and the **legislature** (**Congress**) are separate. These **branches** of government are elected **separately.**

The **President** is elected for a four-year term and can **appoint** or **nominate** high officials in government, including **cabinet** members (who advise) and federal **judges.** The President leads a major party, usually (but not always) the **majority party** in Congress.

Congress consists of two **houses,** the **House of Representatives** and the **Senate. Congressmen/women** and **Senators** are elected for fixed terms.

The **judiciary** is a separate branch. The **Supreme Court,** the highest court, can **overrule** the President and Congress.

Parliamentary government: The government consists of a **legislature** (**Parliament**) and a **Cabinet,** chosen from the majority party in Parliament.

The **Prime Minister** is the head of government and the leader of the **majority party** in the **House of Commons,** holding office while the party holds a **majority.** The Prime Minister selects high officials and heads the Cabinet.

Parliament consists of two **chambers,** the **House of Lords** and the **House of Commons.** MPs are **Members of Parliament** elected to the House of Commons.

The **judiciary** is independent, but it cannot **overrule** the Prime Minister or Parliament. The **Highest Court** consists of a group of Lords.

C Elections

vote: choose in a formal way, e.g., by marking/casting a ballot in an election
elect: choose someone or something by voting
candidate: someone who runs (for office) in an election
politician: someone for whom politics is a career, who may run for office
majority party: the political party with the most representatives elected
referendum: a direct vote by the people on an important public issue

Exercises

54.1 Choose the correct word.

1. India gained **monarchy/independence/democracy** from the U.K. in 1948.
2. The Supreme Court recently **elected/appointed/overruled** the President.
3. She's **running/sitting/nominating** for the Senate in the next election.
4. He was **voted/run/elected** Congressman for this district.
5. The U.S. is a **monarchy/federation/referendum** of fifty states.

54.2 Fill in the missing words in this text about government in the U.S.

The federal government in the U.S. is made up of three .... (1):
the legislature, the .... (2), and the executive branch. The
legislature, or Congress, has two .... (3), the Senate and the
House of Representatives. Congressmen and Congresswomen in the House are
.... (4) for a term of two years and Senators for six years. A
presidential .... (5) takes place every four years. The President
is not always a member of the .... (6) party in the Senate or
the House. The highest court is the .... (7). Justices are
.... (8) by the President, and they may serve for life.

54.3 Complete the table.

Abstract noun	Person noun	Verb	Adjective
revolution	revolutionary	revolutionize	revolutionary
representation	....	....	....
election	....	....	....
dictatorship	....	....	....
presidency	....	....	....
politics	....	....	....

54.4 Try this political quiz.

1. Name three monarchies.
2. Name two countries with a presidential system and two with a parliamentary
   system (not including the U.S. and the U.K.).
3. What is the oldest parliament in the world?
4. Name the President of the U.S., the Prime Minister of the U.K., and the Prime
   Minister of Canada.
5. Who represents you in local and national government?
6. What are the main political parties in the country where you are now?

54.5 Write a paragraph about the political system in your country, using as much of
the vocabulary on the opposite page as you can.

(You will find words dealing with types of political belief in Unit 67.)

Crime

This table gives information about some types of crimes.

Crime	Definition	Criminal	Verb
murder/homicide	killing someone by plan	murderer	murder
shoplifting	stealing something from a store	shoplifter	shoplift
burglary	breaking into a place to steal	burglar	burgle
robbery	stealing with (the threat of) violence	robber	rob
smuggling	taking something illegally into another country	smuggler	smuggle
arson	setting fire to something in a criminal way	arsonist	set fire to
kidnapping	taking a person hostage in exchange for money	kidnapper	kidnap

Note the difference between the verbs **steal** and **rob.** An object is stolen (e.g., "They stole my bike"), whereas a person or place is robbed (e.g., "I was robbed last night." "A masked man robbed the bank.").

Here are some verbs connected with crime and law. Note the prepositions.

to **commit** a crime or an offense: to do something illegal
to **accuse** someone **of** a crime: to blame someone for a crime
to **charge** someone **with** a crime: to bring someone to court
to **plead guilty** or **not guilty:** to swear in court that one is guilty or innocent
to **defend/prosecute** someone in court: to argue for or against someone in a trial
to **sentence** someone **to** a punishment: what the judge does after a guilty verdict
to **serve** a **sentence** / to **serve time:** to go through a time of imprisonment
to **acquit** an accused person **of** a charge: to decide in court that someone is not guilty
to **fine** someone: to punish someone by making them pay a sum of money
to **be tried:** to have a case judged in court

Here are some nouns associated with criminal courts and the law.

trial: a formal examination in a court of law to decide whether an accused person is guilty or not guilty
felony: a very serious crime, such as murder or robbery
misdemeanor: a crime that is less serious than a felony, such as vandalism
evidence: information presented during a trial
testimony: statements of a witness under oath during a trial
jury: group of impartial citizens who decide whether the accused is guilty or not
verdict: the decision: guilty or not guilty
judge: the person who leads a trial and decides on the sentence if there is one

Exercises

55.1 Here are some more crimes. Complete a table like the one in A opposite.

Crime	Criminal	Verb / verb phrase	Definition
terrorism	....	....	....
blackmail	....	....	....
drug trafficking	....	....	....
forgery	....	....	....
assault	....	....	....
pickpocketing	....	....	....
mugging	....	....	....

55.2 Put the right form of either *rob* or *steal* in the sentences below.

1. Last night an armed gang .... the post office. They .... $2000.
2. My handbag .... at the theater yesterday.
3. Every year large numbers of banks ....

55.3 Fill in the blanks with verbs from B opposite.

One of the two accused men .... (1) at yesterday's trial. Although his lawyer .... (2) him very well, he was still found guilty by the jury. Because the crime was serious, a .... (3), the judge .... (4) him to ten years in prison. He'll probably .... (5) less than five years of the sentence. The other accused man was luckier. He .... (6) and left the courtroom smiling.

55.4 Here are some words connected with law and crime. Divide them into three groups, in whatever seems the most logical way. If necessary, use a dictionary.

lawyer	member of a jury	judge	probation
prison	fine	bribery	drunken driving
detective	hijacking	lethal injection	witness
smuggling	death penalty	rape	theft

55.5 Write a paragraph to fit this newspaper headline. Give some details about the crime and the court case, using as many words from this unit as is appropriate.

> **Local girl's testimony gets mugger five-year sentence**

Follow-up: If possible, look at an English language newspaper. List all the words connected with crime and the law that you can find.

Money and finances

A

Banking and making purchases

When you buy something in a store, you may be asked: "How do you want to pay?" You can answer: **"Cash. / Check. / With a credit card."**

In a **bank** you usually have a **checking account.** You **make deposits** (put money in) and **withdrawals** (take money out). You **write checks** on the account to **pay bills.** You may also have a **savings account,** which usually pays you **interest** – money paid for keeping your savings there. The bank sends you a regular **bank statement** showing the activity in your account. If you take out more money from an account than you have in it (usually by writing checks), your account is **overdrawn,** a situation to be avoided! If you write a check but your account has **insufficient funds** to cover it, the check may **bounce** (colloquial use); that is, the bank refuses payment. Banks also offer **certificates of deposit (CDs),** which pay you higher interest rates than savings accounts. However, money can't be withdrawn from a CD for a specified time without a **penalty,** a fee charged for early withdrawals.

Sometimes the bank may **lend** you money – this is called a **bank loan.** If a bank (or a savings & loan institution) lends you money to buy a home, it is called a **mortgage.** You pay back the amount of the loan – the **principal** – with **interest.** Banks have higher **interest rates** for borrowers than for savers.

When you use a **credit card** to make purchases, you receive a **monthly statement** from the credit card company. The **billing date** is the date the statement was prepared, the **balance** is the amount you owe, and the **due date** is the date by which you must pay. However, you can pay a part of the balance and owe the rest, but you'll incur a **finance charge,** which is usually rather high.

Money that you pay for services (e.g., to a lawyer) is usually called a **fee** or **fees.** Money paid for student courses (e.g., at a university) is called **tuition;** other costs paid by students are called **fees** (e.g., registration/laboratory fee). Money paid for a trip is a **fare.**

B

Public finance

National and local governments collect money from residents through **taxes. Income tax** is collected on **wages** and **salaries. Inheritance tax** is collected on what people inherit from others upon death. **Customs duties** or **excise duties** are paid on certain goods imported from other countries. **Sales tax** is a percentage of the price of goods and services, added to the total cost. **Value added tax (VAT)** (found in the U.K. and other countries, but not in the U.S.) is a tax based on value, added to a product at each stage of production. Companies pay **corporate taxes** on their profits.

Every country has its own **currency.** The **rates of exchange** are published daily, and you can check, for example, how many yen there are currently to the dollar.

Exercises

56.1 Answer the following money quiz.

1. What currencies are used in Japan, Australia, India, and Russia?
2. What does the expression "hard currency" mean?
3. Name two credit cards that are usable worldwide.
4. Give two examples of imports that most countries impose customs duties on.
5. Give three examples of types of income that are not from salaries.
6. Name the coins and banknotes used in your country and one other country.

56.2 Match the words on the left with their definitions.

1. interest
2. mortgage
3. an overdrawn account
4. savings account
5. checking account
6. tuition
7. sales tax
8. insufficient funds

an account that checks are drawn on for
   day-to-day use
money chargeable on a loan or paid to savers
tax paid at the time of a purchase
money paid for education
a bank account with a negative balance
the reason a check bounces
a loan to purchase a home or property
an account that is used mainly for
   keeping money

56.3 Is the ordinary "person on the street" happy to see these headlines or not?

56.4 Complete the sentences with words from the opposite page.

1. Money that has to be paid on what you inherit is known as
   ....
2. If the bank lends you money, you have a bank ....
3. How much is the plane .... between Bangkok and Seoul?
4. If you can't pay the entire .... on your credit card each month,
   you have to pay a ....
5. If you hire a lawyer, you have to pay a ....
6. If you take out a six-month CD but decide you need the money after three
   months, you have to pay a ....

56.5 To improve your financial vocabulary, read articles on business in any English
magazine or newspaper. Write down any new words or expressions that you find.

UNIT 57

Number, quantity, degree, and intensity

A   Number and quantity

Number is used for countable nouns, e.g., **a large number** of people; **amount** is used for uncountables, e.g., **a large amount** of money.

Scale of adjectives useful for expressing number and quantity:

| tiny | small | average | large/considerable | gigantic/huge/vast |

Add just a **tiny amount** of chili pepper, or else it may get too hot.
A **considerable number** of people failed to get tickets. [formal]
Huge amounts of money have been wasted on this project.
"Were there many people at the airport?" "Oh, about **average**, I'd say."

Much/many, a lot, lots, plenty, a number of, a good/great deal of

Is there **much** work to do?
No, not **much.**
You were making **a lot of** noise last night. [less formal]
There are **lots of** nice stores on this street.
Don't worry, there's **plenty of** time.
There are **a number of / many** mistakes in this report. [more formal]
There's **a good deal of / a great deal of** work to be done. [more formal]
Note: **Much** + uncountable noun is used mostly in questions and negatives.

B   Informal and colloquial words for number/quantity

I have **dozens of** nails in my toolbox. Why buy more? [countable]
There's **loads** of time, so slow down! [countable or uncountable; informal]
Just **a drop of** wine for me, please. [tiny amount of any liquid]

Tons of can be countable or uncountable and is used mainly with things, rarely with abstract nouns:

There are **tons of** apples on this tree this year; last year there were hardly any. [countable]
There was **tons of** food at the party – way too much. [uncountable]

C   Degree and intensity

Some adjectives, such as **tired, worried, weak, hot,** can be described on a scale from weak to strong. They are modified by **a little bit / a bit / quite / rather / fairly / pretty / very / really / terribly / awfully / extremely:** e.g., It's **really hot** today.

Other adjectives, such as **ruined, exhausted, destroyed, wrong,** are not measured on a scale, but are considered "all or nothing." They can be modified by **totally / absolutely / completely / utterly:** e.g., That argument is **utterly wrong.**

Exercises

57.1 Write responses to these statements using words from A opposite.

Example: I was expecting a tax refund of $1000 this year, but I got only $10!
That's a tiny amount compared to what you were expecting.

1. Five billion dollars of government spending was wasted because of inefficiency.
2. Over fifty people came to Jeanne's lecture yesterday. She was pleasantly surprised.
3. We have 120 students most years; we'll probably have the same this year, too.
4. There was only five dollars in my purse when it was stolen.
5. We've spent over 100 hours in meetings and gotten nowhere.

57.2 Here are some more adjectives that can combine with *amount*. Divide them into two groups, *small* and *large*. Use a dictionary if necessary.

minuscule   enormous   minute *(note pronunciation in the Index)*
overwhelming   meager   excessive   insignificant   sizable

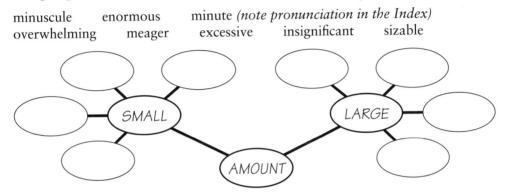

Now use them to fill in the blanks below. More than one answer may be possible.

1. Even a .... amount of sand can jam a camera.
2. I've had an absolutely .... amount of work lately.
3. Oh, you've given me an .... amount of food here!
4. It takes a .... amount of money to start a business.
5. An .... amount of fat in your diet is dangerous.

57.3 Fill in the blanks with *much/many, a lot of / lots of, plenty of, a number of, a good deal of / a great deal of.*

1. There's .... dust on these books. Get me a dust rag.
2. Please help yourself to more; there's .... food.
3. There wasn't .... we could do, so we went home.
4. We've put .... energy into this plan. I hope it works.
5. .... people seem unable to work with computers.

57.4 Using intensifiers from C opposite, say how you might feel in these situations.

Example: You hear that a friend is in trouble with the police.   *pretty anxious*

1. You've been working nonstop for 18 hours.
2. Three people give you different directions to get to the same place.
3. You pass an exam you had expected to fail.
4. Your best friend is going abroad for two years.

UNIT 58 Time

A Periods of time

the Ice Age   **the Stone Age**   **the Middle Ages**   the **age** of the computer
[major historical/geological periods]

After the war, a new **era** of peace and stability began. [long period, perhaps decades]

The doctor said I needed a **period** of rest and relaxation, so I'm taking three months' unpaid leave. [very general word]

We've had a **spell** of hot weather. [indefinite but short]

During the 1980s I lived in Hong Kong **for a time.** [vague, indefinite]

Do you want to borrow this book **for a while?** [indefinite but not very long]

B Useful phrases with time

It's **about time** you got here! We've been waiting for hours.

The doctor says you should stay in bed **for the time being.** [not specific]

He can get a little bit moody **at times.**

By the time we get home this pizza will be cold!

I've told you **time and again** not to call me at the office!

One at a time, please! I can't serve you all together.

We got there **just in time** for dinner.

I expected you to be late; the trains are never **on time.**

C Verbs associated with time passing

1987 ——→ 1997   Ten years had **passed/elapsed** before I heard from her again. Don't worry. The time will **pass** quickly. Time **passes** slowly when you're bored.

Elapse is more formal and is normally used in the perfect or past, without adverbs. **Pass** can be used in any tense and with adverbs.

San Francisco ——  —→ Tokyo   It **takes** ten hours to fly to Tokyo.

 The batteries in this radio should **last** three or four months.

This videotape **lasts/runs** for three hours.

The meeting **dragged on** for two hours. [longer than expected or desired, making it tedious]

Note also: **Take your time;** you don't need to hurry.

Exercises

58.1   Fill in the blanks as appropriate with *age, era, period, spell,* or *time.*

1. During the tax amnesty, there will be a .... of six months when people can pay their back taxes without a penalty.
2. The twentieth century will be seen by historians as the .... of the automobile.
3. These factories mark the beginning of a new .... of industrial development for the country.
4. For a .... I thought I would never find a job, but then I got lucky.
5. We had a very cold .... in February: All the pipes froze up.

58.2   Match the sentences on the left with the responses on the right.

1. Was your train on time?	Just in time to catch the last train!
2. When did you arrive at the station?	At times.
3. The train is finally leaving the station.	No, by the time I left work, it was too late.
4. Did you go to the movies last night?	No, it wasn't. In fact, it's almost always late.
5. Do you ever miss your country?	It's about time!

58.3   Which phrases from B opposite could you use in the following situations? Write exactly what you might say, as in the example.

Example: To a child who repeatedly leaves the refrigerator door open despite being told not to many times.   *I've told you time and again not to leave that refrigerator door open!*

1. To someone you're happy to see who arrives just as you are serving tea/coffee.
2. On a postcard you expect will arrive at someone's house after you do.
3. A large group of people want to talk to you, but you'd prefer to see them individually.
4. Ask someone to use an old photocopier while the new one is being repaired.
5. Explain to someone that the weather occasionally gets very cold in your country.
6. Tell someone you'll do your best to arrive punctually at a meeting.
7. Your friend just got a job. You think she should have gotten one long ago.

58.4   Complete the sentences using verbs from C opposite.

1. The ferry crossing . . .
2. Use this cassette to record. It will . . .
3. These shoes have been great; they've . . .
4. Everyone got bored because the speeches . . .
5. The disaster occurred in 1932. Many years . . .
6. I'll miss you terribly. I only hope the weeks . . .
7. There's no hurry at all; just . . .
8. It was a long movie. It . . .

Distances and dimensions

A Wide, broad, tall, high, deep, shallow

Wide is more common than **broad**, e.g., It's a very **wide** road/aisle/doorway.

Make a note of typical collocations for **broad** as you meet them, e.g., This book covers a **broad** range of subjects; We came to a **broad** expanse of grassland. [big area]

Note the word order for talking about dimensions, e.g., The room is **five meters long** and **four wide.**

Tall is used for people, but it can be used for things like buildings and trees when they are **high** and **thin** in some way. Otherwise, use **high** for things.

She's very **tall** for a five-year-old.
His office is in that **tall** building on the square.
There are some **high** mountains in the North.

deep ≠ **shallow**
the **deep** and **shallow** ends of a swimming pool

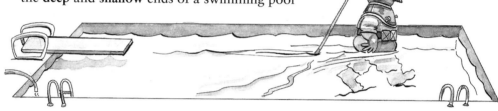

B Derived words, phrases, and compounds

long: Let's measure the **length** of this rope.
I swam twenty **lengths** (of the swimming pool).
I've **lengthened** her skirt for her. [**shorten,** see below]
Getting a visa can be a **lengthy** process. [usually refers to time]
Can I make a **long-distance** phone call?

short: The new road will **shorten** our trip by ten minutes.
There's a **shortcut** to the station. [quick way]

wide: Let's measure the **width** of the room.   They're **widening** the road.

broad: I want to **broaden** my experience. [usually abstract contexts]
She's very **broad-minded** and tolerant of others.

high: The **height** of the ceiling is nine feet.
The fog **heightened** the feeling of mystery.

low: You can **lower** the microphone if it is too high.

far: He loves traveling to **faraway** places.

deep: The **depth** of the river here is about ten feet.
His death so soon after hers **deepened** our sadness even further.

C Other verbs for dimensions and for changing them

Our property **stretches** all the way to the river, so we have plenty of room to **extend** the house if we want to.
The cities are **spreading** and the countryside is **shrinking.**

Exercises

59.1   Complete B's replies using a form of the dimension/distance words opposite.

1. A: These pants I bought are too long.
   B: Well, why don't you get . . .
2. A: He's a big boy, isn't he? Almost six feet!
   B: Yes, he's . . .
3. A: Why are we taking this side street?
   B: Just to get there a little bit quicker; it's . . .
4. A: We'll have to measure how high the room is.
   B: That's not necessary; we already know the . . .
5. A: The traffic seems to move faster on this road since I was last here.
   B: That's because they . . .
6. A: Why do they have to have music on TV news programs? It seems totally unnecessary!
   B: They want to create a feeling of drama, and the music is supposed to . . .
7. A: Do you think it's safe to dive here?
   B: I wouldn't. At this end of the pool, it's only three feet . . .

59.2   Give opposites.

1. the length of the room
2. to shorten
3. a broad range of goods
4. a local call
5. deep water
6. nearby places

59.3   Match the columns.

1. The city's spread a lot;   for miles along the river.
2. It takes ten weeks;   you should broaden it.
3. We extended the house   it's much bigger now.
4. You can choose;   there's a wide range.
5. Your experience is too narrow;   it's a lengthy procedure.
6. The forest stretches   to give us more room.

59.4   Prepositions with distance. Fill in the prepositions. If you are unsure, try looking up the word *distance* in a good dictionary.

1. The car was parked .... a distance .... about 150 yards from the scene of the robbery.
2. I saw you .... the distance yesterday, but I didn't call out because I could see you were with someone.
3. She's a great shot. She can hit an empty can .... a distance of about 100 feet, which I can't.
4. What's the total distance .... here .... Paris?
5. My office is .... walking distance .... my home.
6. Tom isn't very friendly. He likes to keep people .... a distance.

UNIT 60 Obligation, need, and probability

A   **Obligation**

Have to says that circumstances oblige you to do something, e.g., "I **have to** leave early." **Have got to** has the same meaning and is often used in spoken English and informal situations, e.g., "**I've got to** run." (informally spoken as "**I gotta run.**")

Must is an instruction or command; it is often found in signs, notices, and "official language," e.g., "All those entering **must** have a valid passport." It is sometimes used to show urgency, e.g., "It's an emergency; I **must** see the doctor right now."

I've **got to** get my hair cut. I have an interview tomorrow.

There's no bus service, so I **have to** walk to work.

The company **is required to / obliged to** refund your money if the tour is canceled.
You **are liable** for any damages when you rent a car. [formal/legalistic]
The bank robbers **forced** him at gunpoint to open the safe.
We **had no choice/alternative but** to sell our house; we owed the bank $100,000.
A prison sentence is **mandatory** for drug trafficking. [automatic; no alternative]
"Were sports **compulsory/obligatory** at your school?" "No, they were **optional.**" [optional: you can choose]
Nonprofit organizations are usually **exempt** from taxes. [free from obligation]

The negative of **must** and **have (got) to** are formed with **need to** and **have to** when we mean something is not necessary / not obligatory, e.g., "You **don't need to / don't have to** wash the dishes; we have a dishwasher."

Note: **Must not** shows prohibition, e.g., "Passengers **must not** stand in the aisles."

B   **Need**

The grass **needs** cutting.

This plant **is in need of** water. [more formal than **needs**]

C   **Scale of probability: from "cannot happen" to "will definitely happen"**

impossible → unlikely → possible → probable → certain → inevitable

It's highly **probable** that the Senator will run for President. In fact, it's **certain.**

120

Exercises

60.1   Complete the sentences using obligation words and phrases from A opposite, with the words in parentheses.

1. They were losing $10 million a year, so the company . . . (close down)
2. You can rent a video camera, but you . . . (put down a deposit)
3. In some countries, military service . . . (for young people)
4. This jacket has ketchup stains on it; I really . . . (the cleaners)
5. He didn't want to give them the money, but they had guns; they . . . (hand it over)
6. We'll have to sell the house. I'm afraid we have . . . Otherwise, we'll go bankrupt.
7. I didn't want to take math, but I had to. It's . . . (in high school)
8. How kind of you! But you really . . . (buy us a present).

60.2   List something in your world that . . .

1. regularly needs cutting.   *my hair, the lawn*
2. there is a lack of.
3. is compulsory once a year.
4. you are in need of.
5. is inevitable.
6. you no longer have to do.
7. was compulsory when you were in elementary school.
8. you were once forced to do.

60.3   Which combinations are typical? Circle the words that might be used with the *probability* word in the last column, e.g., quite possible, very possible, but *not* absolutely possible.

1. (quite)   (very)   absolutely   **possible**
2. very   absolutely   highly   **impossible**
3. absolutely   highly   quite   **probable**
4. highly   absolutely   extremely   **unlikely**
5. very   extremely   absolutely   **inevitable**
6. absolutely   highly   quite   **certain**

60.4   Use the combinations in 60.3 to say how probable these things are.

1. Most people will have videophones in their homes during the 21st century.
2. There will be rain in the Amazon forest within the next eight days.
3. A human being will live to be 250.
4. A flying saucer will land in Hong Kong.
5. There will be a third world war.
6. A man will become pregnant.
7. Your ability to use English will improve after you've finished using this book.

Follow-up: Make up at least three more sentences like the ones above, using probability words.

UNIT 61 Sound and light

A General words to describe sound

I could hear the **sound** of voices/music coming from the next room. [neutral]
The **noise** of the traffic here is pretty bad. [loud, unpleasant sounds]
I tried to hear her voice above the **din** of the machines. [very loud, irritating noise]
The children are making a terrible **racket** upstairs. Could you tell them to be quiet? [very loud, unbearable noise, often of human activity]

Noise and **sound** are both countable when they are of short duration or when they are different sounds/noises. They are uncountable when they are continual or continuous.

Their lawnmower makes **a lot of noise,** doesn't it? [uncountable]
The **sound** of the ocean is very soothing. [uncountable]
I heard **some** strange **noises/sounds** during the night. [countable]

B Types of sounds and things that typically make them

These words can be used as nouns or verbs:

I could hear the rain **pattering** on the roof. We heard the **patter** of a child's feet.

Verb/noun	Example of what makes the sound
bang	a door closing heavily in the wind, someone bursting a balloon
clang	a big bell ringing, a hollow metal object being struck
crash	a heavy object falling onto a hard floor or hitting something
creak	stepping on a wooden stair, sitting on a bed with springs
hiss	gas/steam escaping through a small hole
roar	noise of heavy traffic, noise of a huge waterfall
rumble	distant noise of thunder, noise of traffic far away
rustle	opening a paper/plastic bag, dry leaves underfoot
thud	a heavy object falling onto a carpeted floor

C Darkness and types of light

These brown walls are kind of **gloomy.** We should paint them white.
This flashlight gives a **dim** light. I think it needs new batteries.
It was a **somber** room, with dark, heavy curtains. [serious, dark, gloomy]

The sun **shines** and gives out **rays** of light.
A flashlight gives out a **beam** of light.
A flashbulb of a camera gives a **flash** of light.
Stars **twinkle.**
A flame **flickers** in the breeze.
White-hot coals in a fire **glow.**
A diamond necklace **sparkles,** and a gold object **glitters.**

(See Units 17, 28, and 64.)

Exercises

61.1 Choose *sound(s)*, *noise(s)*, *din*, or *racket* to fill in the blanks.

1. There was a terrible .... outside our apartment building last night; it was a fight involving about six people.
2. I could sit and listen to the .... of the river all day.
3. My car's been making some strange .... I'll have to have it checked.
4. I hold my hands over my ears when I walk by that construction site because of the ....!
5. I can't sleep if there's .... of any kind, so I use earplugs.

61.2 What sound do you think each of these might make? Use words from the table in B opposite.

1. a bottle of fizzy mineral water being opened
2. a typewriter being dropped down an iron staircase
3. a mouse moving among dead grass and leaves
4. an overweight person falling on the floor
5. a starting gun for a sporting event
6. a slow train passing, heard through the walls of a house
7. an engine starting up on a jumbo jet
8. an old, worn-out gate opening slowly

61.3 As in the table in B opposite, think of something that might make the sound.

Verb/noun	Typical source(s) of the sound
hum	....
crunch	....
screech	....
chime	....
whistle	....
pop	....
jingle	....

61.4 What do you think the *figurative* meanings of the underlined words are?

1. She beamed at him.
   a) smiled   b) shouted   c) attacked
2. After a day of skiing, our faces glowed.
   a) were frozen   b) were dried up   c) were full of color
3. He has a twinkle in his eyes.
   a) a piece of grit   b) a sign of humor   c) a sign of anger
4. He flashed a look of surprise.
   a) briefly showed   b) hid   c) repeatedly showed

Possession, giving, and lending

A   Possession

All his **possessions** were destroyed in the terrible fire. [everything he owned]
Don't leave any of your **belongings** here; we've had a few thefts recently.
    [smaller things, e.g., bag, camera, coat; always plural]

Estate in the singular can mean a big area of private land and the buildings on it,
or all of someone's wealth upon death.

She owns a huge **estate** in the country. [land, house, etc.]
After his death, his **estate** was calculated at $3 million. [all his wealth]

Property (uncountable) is used in a general sense for houses, land, etc.

They went bankrupt and lost all their **property.**
A property (countable) is a building, e.g., house, office building, etc.
This **property** would be ideal for developing a resort.

B   Words for people connected with ownership

The **proprietor** of this restaurant is a friend of mine. [used for stores,
    businesses, etc. **Owner** is less formal.]
The **landlord/landlady** is raising the rent. [owner of rented property]
Do you own this house? No, we're just **tenants/renters.**

C   Giving

It gives me pleasure to **present** you **with** this clock from us all.
Would you like to **contribute/donate** something to the children's hospital fund?
The river **provides** the village **with** water / **provides** water **for** the village.
Moo Moo Dairy **supplies** the supermarket **with** milk. [often for "selling"
    contexts]
When she died, she **donated** her books to the library. She also **left** $5000 **to** a
    dog!
You've been **assigned** (**to**) room 24. Here's your key.

D   Lending, borrowing, renting, etc.

Remember: When you **lend,** you give; when you **borrow,** you receive.
Remember that ladder you **lent** me last week – could I **borrow** it again?
I'm trying to get a **loan** from the bank to buy a boat.

We've decided to **rent** a car. Can you recommend a good **car rental** company?
We'd like to **rent** a house; we're not quite ready to buy one.

Exercises

62.1   **What questions do you think were asked to get these answers? Use words from the opposite page.**

1. Oh no, we own it. Most houses here are owner occupied.
2. I'm sorry, but I need it to take photos myself.
3. You'll be in room 44. It's a pretty big office.
4. No, you have to buy textbooks yourself.
5. Sorry, but I've already given at the office.
6. Compact cars start at $30 a day; bigger cars are more expensive.

62.2   **Check the meaning of these phrasal verbs in a dictionary and fill in the blanks.**

hand over   hand out   let go of   give away   hand down

1. That bed has been .... from one generation to the next. It was my great-grandmother's originally.
2. Would you help us .... some leaflets at the meeting?
3. I don't want to .... that old painting. It might be valuable someday.
4. When Tim got too big for his bike, we .... it .... ; it wasn't worth trying to sell it.
5. If a robber attacked me, I'd .... my wallet.

62.3   **Think of something that . . .**

1. you would hand over to a mugger if threatened.
2. has been handed down in your family.
3. you have given away at some time in your life.
4. is often handed out in classrooms.
5. you value and would not want to let go of.

62.4   **The rise and fall of Mr. Fatcat – a sad story. Fill in the blanks with appropriate words from the opposite page.**

Horatio Fatcat began his career by buying up old .... (1) in the city when prices were low. He got .... (2) from several banks to finance his deals, and soon he was one of the biggest .... (3) in the city, with some 50,000 .... (4) renting houses and apartments from him. He was also the .... (5) of many stores and businesses. He became very rich and bought himself a huge .... (6) in the country, but he .... (7) more and more money from the banks and soon the bubble burst. Recession came and he had to sell all his .... (8) and .... (9) – everything. He was left with just a few personal .... (10) and finally died penniless.

63 Movement and speed

A Types of movement

Cars, trucks, buses, etc., **travel/drive** along roads.
Trains **travel** along rails.
Boats/ships **sail** on rivers / across the ocean.
Rivers/streams **flow/run** through cities/towns/villages.

Things often have special verbs associated with their types of movement.

White clouds **drifted** across the sky.
The flag **fluttered** in the wind.
The leaves **stirred** in the light breeze.
The trees **swayed** back and forth as the gale grew fiercer.
The car **swerved** to avoid a dog running across the road.

B Some verbs to describe fast and slow movement

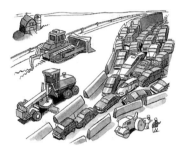

The traffic was **crawling** because of the construction.

Stop **dawdling!** We'll be late!

The car **tore** along the road at high speed.
Everyone was **hurrying/rushing** to get their shopping done.
The train was **creeping/plodding** along at 30 miles an hour. I knew we'd be late.

C Some verbs to describe walking

She **paced** up and down as she waited. [take regular steps back and forth]
I enjoy **strolling** in the park. [walk somewhat slowly and in a relaxed way]
He **tiptoed** around so he wouldn't wake anyone. [walk quietly as if on your toes]
The baby **toddled** unsteadily. [walk with short steps, trying to keep balanced]
Don't **shuffle** around like that! Pick up your feet! [walk slowly without lifting feet]
Since breaking her leg, she **limps / walks with a limp.** [walk slowly, with difficulty]

D Some nouns describing speed and their typical contexts

Speed is a general word used for vehicles, e.g., We drove at breakneck **speed.**
Rate is often used in statistics, e.g., The birth **rate** is declining/increasing.
Pace shows how you experience something as happening, fast or slow, e.g., The lesson was going at a very slow **pace.**
Velocity is used in technical/scientific contexts, e.g., the **velocity** of a bullet.

Exercises

63.1 What things are probably being described by these sentences?

1. It was swaying back and forth in the wind. In fact, I thought it might break.
2. It sails at dawn.
3. It flows through the capital city.
4. I had to swerve hard and nearly ended up in the river.
5. It was traveling at 80 miles per hour when it derailed.

63.2 What other things could be described by each verb? List as many as you can think of.

1. **sway:** a tree, *a person dancing, someone drunk, a boat*
2. **flow:** a river, ...
3. **crawl:** traffic, ...
4. **flutter:** a flag, ...
5. **drift:** a cloud, ...

63.3 In what situations might you . . .

1. tear out of the house?
2. deliberately dawdle?
3. plod along at a steady pace?
4. not even dare to stir?
5. walk with a limp?
6. tiptoe around the house?
7. pace up and down?
8. stroll (around) somewhere?

63.4 People and verbs of motion. What kinds of people do you think these are? Use a dictionary if necessary.

1. a slowpoke
2. a drifter
3. a plodder
4. a toddler

63.5 Fill in the blanks with *speed, rate, pace,* or *velocity.* Use the guidelines in D opposite to help you.

1. The increase in the .... of inflation is alarming.
2. I just couldn't stand the .... of life in the city, so I moved to a small town.
3. High-..................................... bullets are used in this rifle.
4. A: What .... were you doing at the time?
   B: Oh, about sixty miles an hour, I'd say.

Texture, brightness, density, and weight

Texture – how something feels when you touch it

Adjective	Typical examples
smooth	the cover of this book
polished	varnished wood / a shiny metal surface
silky	silk itself / fine, expensive stockings
sleek	the outside of a highly polished, streamlined new car
downy	newborn baby's hair
fluffy	a soft pillow
slippery	a fish just out of the water
furry	a thick sheepskin rug
rough	new, unwashed denim jeans / bark of a tree
coarse	sand
jagged	sharp, irregular edges of broken glass or metal
prickly	a thistle / a cactus / thorns on a rose
sticky	jam or glue left on a surface

Your hair has a silky **feel.** Have you just washed it?
The old table had a beautiful polished **surface.**
This cotton is very smooth **to the touch.**
The ground was rough **underfoot.**

Brightness – some adjectives

shiny shoes   a **dazzling** light   a **shady** corner of the garden

You wear such **dull** colors; why not get some **brighter** clothes?
The carnival costumes were all of **vivid** colors.
This flashlight is getting **dim;** it needs new batteries.
I wear sunglasses because of the **glare** of the sun.

Density and weight

a solid ≠ **hollow** object
an area with **dense** ≠ **sparse** vegetation
She has **thick** ≠ **thin/fine** hair.
These boxes are rather **weighty.** [heavier than expected]
Your bag's **as light as a feather!** Have you brought enough?
Your bag's **as heavy as lead!** What's in it, bricks?
This suitcase is very **bulky.** [large for its type; difficult to carry or store]

Exercises

64.1 **How would you expect these things to feel?**

1. honey on a bun
2. the feathers in a pillow or quilt
3. a wet bar of soap
4. the branches of a rosebush
5. a gravel pathway
6. the inside of a pair of sheepskin gloves
7. the edge of a piece of broken, rusty metal
8. heavy, stone-ground wholemeal flour
9. the surface of a mirror
10. the cover of a well-produced brochure

Look around your own home and find:

11. something sleek to the touch
12. something rough underfoot
13. something with a polished surface
14. something furry
15. something smooth

64.2 **Here are some common U.S. weights with their metric equivalents.**

Weight	Written as . . .	Metric equivalent
ounce	oz.	28.35 grams
pound (16 oz.)	lb.	453.6 grams (.454 kilogram)
fluid ounce	fl. oz.	29.57 milliliters
pint (16 fl. oz.)	pt.	.473 liter
quart (2 pts.)	qt.	.946 liter
gallon (4 qts.)	gal.	3.79 liters

1. A friend tells you her new baby weighed 7 pounds at birth. Is this a big, tiny, or more or less average baby?
2. If you drink a half liter of milk a day, is a gallon of milk enough for a week?
3. Make a (private!) note of your approximate weight both in pounds and kilograms.
4. Would 16 oz. of cheese be sufficient if you were making two cheese sandwiches?

64.3 **Quiz. Name the following.**

1. a creature with a sleek coat
2. a slippery creature
3. a creature with a furry coat
4. a prickly creature

64.4 **Pair puzzles. Each word has a letter in it that is part of a *related* word from the left-hand page. Fill in the letters, as in the example.**

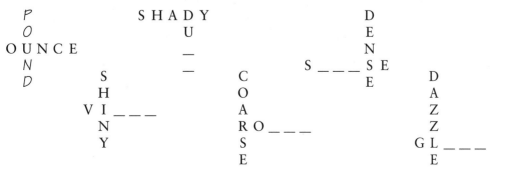

Success, failure, and difficulty

Succeeding

We **succeeded in** persuading a lot of people to vote. [**in** + **-ing**]
I **managed** to contact him just before he left his office.
We've **achieved/accomplished** a great deal in the past three years. [both can be
used with quantity phrases such as **a lot / a little**]
The company has **attained** all its **goals/aims/objectives** for this year.
We fully expect to **reach** our sales **targets/goals** in the next fiscal year.
She **fulfilled** a lifelong **ambition** when she learned to fly an airplane.
Your performance has not only **met**, but **surpassed/exceeded, expectations**.
We've finally **realized** our **dream** of buying our own home.

Failing

Plans and projects sometimes **misfire**. [don't turn out as intended]
Companies, clubs, and societies may **fold** because of lack of success. [close down]
A plan or project may **falter**, even if it finally succeeds. [go through a series of
ups and downs]
All your plans and hard work/efforts may **come to nothing**.
A plan can **go wrong**. [meet difficulties and fail]
I'm afraid I **missed** my **chance**; I'll have to try again.

> *Nothing succeeds
> like success.*

> *Success has a thousand parents.
> Failure is always an orphan.*

Difficulty

I have great **difficulty (in)** getting up in the morning.
I **find it difficult** to remember the names of everybody in the class. [**hard** can
be used here; it is more informal]
It's **hard/difficult** to hear what she's saying.
We've **had some trouble/problems with** the neighbors lately. [**trouble** is
uncountable; **problems** is countable.]
I **have trouble / a hard time** starting the car on cold mornings.
I have no money and my girlfriend left me. I need help; I just can't **cope** anymore.
I can't **cope with** our living situation: I'm leaving!

Word classes

Verb	Noun	Adjective	Adverb
succeed	success	successful	successfully
accomplish	accomplishment	accomplished	–
achieve	achievement	–	–
attain	attainment	attainable	–
fulfill	fulfillment	fulfilling	–
–	–	hard	hard

Exercises

65.1 Choose suitable verbs from the opposite page to fill in the blanks. There may be
more than one possible answer.

1. The charity drive failed to .... its goal of $100,000.
2. I never thought I would .... my ambition, but now I have.
3. Very few people .... all their hopes and dreams in life.
4. A: Did you .... to get there on time?
   B: Yes, just barely.
5. A: Did you .... in getting a loan from the bank?
   B: No, they turned me down. I'm still not sure what ....
   wrong.
6. Unfortunately, our marketing plans .... No one wanted to
   buy chocolate-covered pickles.
7. Our earnings increased by 20%. We .... our target of 10%!
8. Some people can't .... with a lot of stress.

65.2 Fill in the missing word forms where they exist. There may be more than one
possible form in some categories.

Verb	Noun	Adjective	Adverb
realize	....	....	....
....	difficulty	....	....
....	target	....	....
....	ambition	....	....
fail	....	....	....
....	trouble	....	....
....	expectation	....	....

65.3 Correct the mistakes in these sentences.

1. I find very difficult to understand English idioms.
2. She succeeded to rise to the highest rank in the company.
3. Do you ever have trouble to use this photocopier? I always seem to.
4. I've accomplished to get all my work done this week; I'm taking a long
   weekend!
5. I have hard time driving to work with all the traffic.
6. We've succeeded a great deal during this past year.

65.4 What might happen if . . . / What would you do if . . .

1. a plan misfired?   *I'd abandon it / look for an alternative.*
2. a club had only two members left out of fifty?
3. you were having a lot of trouble with your car?
4. you were running in a race but faltered halfway through?
5. you started a small business but it came to nothing?
6. you surpassed all your goals for English study?

(See also Unit 25 for words connected with problems.)

Containers and contents

Here are some common containers.

bag/shopping bag   barrel   basket   bottle   bowl   box

bucket   can   carton   crate   glass   jar   jug

mug   pack   package   pot   sack   six-pack   tube

Here is some additional information about each of these types of containers.

Container	Usually made of . . .	Typical contents
bag/shopping bag	cloth, paper, plastic	groceries, books, papers
barrel	wood and metal	wine, beer, rainwater
basket	cane, wicker	groceries, clothes, wastepaper
bottle	glass, plastic	milk, wine, other liquids
bowl	china, glass, wood	fruit, soup, sugar
box	cardboard, wood	matches, tools, cereal, chocolates
bucket	metal, plastic	sand, water
can	aluminum, tin	soda, beer, soup, vegetables
carton	cardboard, plastic	milk, eggs, 10 packs of cigarettes
crate	wood, plastic	bottles
glass	glass, plastic	milk, water, other liquids
jar	glass, pottery	jam, honey, olives, instant coffee
jug	pottery	milk, cream, water
mug	pottery	coffee, tea, cocoa
pack	cardboard, plastic	envelopes, gum, cards
package	paper, plastic	cookies, rolls
pot	metal, pottery	food, plant
sack	cloth, plastic	potatoes
six-pack	six cans	six cans of soda, beer, etc.
tube	soft metal, plastic	toothpaste, paint, ointment

Exercises

66.1   Complete the blanks in the shopping list without looking at the opposite page.

> 2 .... of milk
> 4 .... of soda
> a .... of tuna fish
> a .... of chocolate chip cookies
> a large .... of matches
> a .... of honey
> 2 .... of mineral water

66.2   Try the following quiz about the words on the opposite page.

1. Which container would most likely be holding flowers in a garden?
2. Which three are you most likely to find in a cellar?
3. Which five would you be likely to find in a liquor store?
4. Name at least five that you might see on the breakfast table.
5. Which two are often used for carrying groceries?
6. Which five might have juice in them?

66.3   Name the containers and their contents

66.4   Think of two words that are often used with the following containers.

Example: shopping, garbage bag

1. .... box
2. .... bottle
3. .... can
4. .... bowl
5. .... glass
6. .... pot

66.5   Look in a kitchen cupboard or a supermarket. Can you name everything that you
see there? (You will find more useful vocabulary in Units 30 and 43.)

UNIT 67 Belief and opinion

A Verbs connected with beliefs and opinions

You probably already know **think** and **believe;** here are more.

> I'm **convinced** we've met before. [very strong feeling that you're right]
> I've always **held** that compulsory education is a waste of time. [used for very firm beliefs; **maintain** could be used here]
> She **maintains** that we're related, but I'm not convinced. [insist on believing, often against the evidence; **hold** could not be used here]
> I **feel** she shouldn't be forced to do the job. [strong personal opinion]
> I **suppose** they'll get married sometime soon. [an opinion about what is true / likely to happen based on what is already known]
> I **doubt** we'll ever see total world peace. [don't believe]
> I **suspect** a lot of people never even think about pollution when they're driving their own car. [have a belief, especially about something negative]

B Phrases for expressing opinion

> **In my view / In my opinion,** we haven't made any progress.
> She's made a big mistake, **to my mind.**
> **If you ask me,** he ought to change his job. [informal]
> **From** a teacher's **point of view,** the new examinations are a disaster. [how teachers see things, or are affected]

C Prepositions used with belief and opinion words

> What are your **views on** divorce?   What do you **think of** the new boss?
> Do you **believe in** God?   I'm **in favor of / opposed to** long prison sentences.

D Beliefs, ideologies, philosophies, convictions

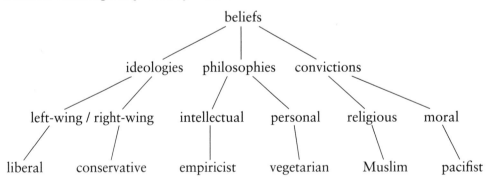

E

Some adjectives for describing people's beliefs and views, in pairs of similar – but not the same – meaning.

> fanatical/obsessive   eccentric/odd   conservative/traditional
> middle-of-the-road/moderate   radical/revolutionary   firm/strong

Exercises

67.1 Rewrite these sentences using the verbs in parentheses.

1. I've always suspected that she doesn't really love him. (doubt)
2. My view has always been that people should rely on themselves more. (hold)
3. Claudia is convinced that the teacher has been unfair to her. (maintain)
4. I felt a very strong feeling that I had been in that room before. (convince)
5. In his view, we should have tried again. (feel)
6. I expect that the government will raise taxes again soon. (suppose)

67.2 Connect the left and right columns, as in the example, adding the appropriate preposition.

Example: What do you think *of* the new teacher?

1. I have strong views   your opinion?
2. Some people believe   management's point of view.
3. I've always been opposed   raising children.
4. What do you think   wasteful government spending.
5. It's not a good contract   life after death, while others don't.
6. Is this the best strategy,   the proposed changes. Are you?
7. Well, that's just silly,   the new teacher?
8. I'm in favor   my mind.

67.3 Use adjectives from E opposite to describe the beliefs and views of these people, as in the example.

1. A person who insists that the earth is flat. (an *eccentric* belief)
2. Someone who believes absolutely in the power of love to solve world problems. (a .... believer in the power of love)
3. A politician neither on the left nor the right of the party. (a .... politician)
4. A vegetarian who refuses even to be in the same room as people who like meat. (a/an .... vegetarian)
5. A person who is somewhat old-fashioned. (a .... point of view)
6. Someone who holds that all taxes should be eliminated. (a .... thinker)

67.4 Complete the sentences below in any way you wish.

1. I believe in ....
2. I'm conservative about .... but liberal when it comes to
....
3. I doubt that ....
4. If you ask me, the best way to learn English is to ....
5. To my mind, the most important issue in the world today is
....
6. I'm in favor of .... but opposed to ....

UNIT 68 Pleasant and unpleasant feelings

A Happiness and unhappiness

You feel:

ecstatic when you experience an intense and overpowering feeling of delight.

content(ed) when you are peaceful and satisfied with what you have. Notice that **content** is not used before a noun. You can say "He is **content**" but you must say "a **contented** person."

cheerful when life is looking bright and positive.

grateful when someone has done something for you.

delighted when something has happened that gives you great pleasure – e.g., when you hear news of someone's good fortune.

miserable when everything seems wrong in your life.

discontented when your life is not giving you satisfaction.

fed up / sick and tired when you have had enough of something disagreeable. You could **be fed up with** someone's rudeness, or **sick (and tired) of** someone's behavior.

depressed when you are miserable over a long period of time. Depression is considered an illness in some severe cases.

frustrated when you are unable to do something that you want to do.

confused / mixed up when you cannot make sense of conflicting feelings or ideas; **mixed up** is more colloquial.

B Excitement, anger, and anxiety

You feel:

excited when you are expecting something special to happen, e.g., before a party.

inspired when you are stimulated to creative deeds or words. You might feel inspired after listening to some very powerful music or a moving speech.

enthusiastic when you have very positive feelings about something, e.g., a new project.

thrilled when something extremely exciting and pleasing happens. [informal]

furious/livid/seething when you are extremely angry; **in a rage/fury** are other ways of saying "furious" or "violently angry."

anxious when you are afraid and uncertain about the future. "I am so **anxious** about the results of my exams that I can't sleep."

nervous when you are afraid or anxious about something that is or may be about to happen. Feeling nervous is a little bit like feeling excited, except that excitement is usually positive and feeling nervous is negative.

apprehensive when you are nervous or anxious about something in the future.

worried when anxious thoughts are constantly going through your head.

upset when something unpleasant has happened to disturb you. It often combines feelings of sadness and anger.

Exercises

68.1   Complete the following table.

Adjective	Abstract noun	Adjective	Abstract noun
furious	....	frustrated	....
....	anxiety	....	cheerfulness
grateful	....	enthusiastic	....
....	ecstasy	....	apprehension
inspired	....	excited	....

68.2   Choose the best word to complete each of the sentences.

enthusiastic   confused   thrilled   depressed   sick and tired
upset   fed up   frustrated   discontented

1. I didn't know who was telling the truth. I felt totally ....
2. Some mothers are .... for several months after the birth of a baby.
3. I think she's bad tempered because she's .... She wanted to be an actress and not a schoolteacher.
4. Although he seems to have everything anyone could possibly want, he is still ....
5. He went skiing for the first time last month, but now he's so .... about it that he can't talk about anything else.
6. This rainy weather has lasted too long. I'm .... with it.
7. He was terribly .... when he heard the news of his friend's accident.
8. She was .... when she heard that she had won first prize.
9. I'm .... of your deception! Be honest for once!

68.3   Write sentences about when you (or someone you know) have experienced the following feelings.

Example: I felt anxious until we heard the results of my mother's medical tests.

1. anxious   3. grateful   5. miserable   7. enthusiastic
2. apprehensive 4. in a rage   6. inspired   8. nervous

68.4   Add the correct ending, either *-ed* or *-ing*.

Example: She was thrill*ed* by her present.

1. I found the movie very excit.................
2. The poet was inspir................. by the sunset.
3. This weather is terribly depress.................
4. I got worr................. when I didn't hear from you for a week.
5. She was confus................. by the ambiguous remarks he made to her.
6. It is very frustrat................. when the phones aren't working.

Likes, dislikes, and desires

A Words and expressions related to liking

I **really liked** Tom when we first met. However, I wasn't **attracted to** him at all, even though my friends thought he was handsome. He invited me out, but I must admit that I was more **tempted** by his sports car than by him at first. But it turns out that I really **enjoyed** spending time with him. He **fascinated** me with his stories of his travels around the world, and something mysterious about his past **attracted** me too. Soon I realized I had **fallen in love** with him. His sense of humor **appealed to** me, and I was also **enchanted by** his gift for poetry. Now, two years later, I'm **crazy about** him and can't understand why I didn't **fall for** him the moment we first set eyes on each other. He's a very **caring** person, **fond of** animals and children. He's always **affectionate** and **loving** toward me and **passionate about** the causes he believes in and the people he **cares for.**

B Words and expressions related to disliking

Loathe, detest, despise, hate, can't stand, and **can't bear** are all very strong ways of saying dislike, and they all can be followed by a noun or an **-ing** form.

I **loathe / detest / despise / hate / can't stand / can't bear** rude people.

Disgust, revolt, appall, and **repel** are all very strong words that describe the effect that something detested has on the person affected.

Those paintings **disgust** me. I was **revolted** by the way she acted. We were **appalled** by the conditions in the refugee camp. His behavior **repels** everyone.

C Words and expressions related to desiring

Desire is a formal word for **wish.**

I have a strong **desire** to see the Himalayas before I die.

Look forward to means think about something in the future with pleasant anticipation. The opposite of **look forward to** is **dread.**

I am **looking forward** to going to Fiji, but I'm **dreading** the flight. (*Note:* **to** is a preposition here, not part of the infinitive, so it is followed by a noun or an **-ing** form.)

Long for means to wish for something very much.

After this long, cold winter, I'm **longing for** spring.

Yearn for is a more poetic way of saying **long for.**

He will never stop **yearning for** his country, although he knows he can never return.

D Ways of addressing loved ones

honey	honeybun	sweetheart	
sweetie	darling	dear	baby

It's best to keep such words for people you have a close relationship with!

Exercises

69.1   Complete the following table.

Verb	Noun	Adjective	Adverb
–	passion	....	....
tempt	....	....	....
attract	....	....	....
appeal	....	....	....
disgust	....	....	....
hate	....	....	....
repel	....	....	....
–	affection	....	....

69.2   Complete the following sentences. Use a dictionary if necessary.

1. Misogynists hate ....
2. Ornithologists are fascinated by ....
3. People who suffer from arachnophobia find .... repulsive.
4. Kleptomaniacs are constantly tempted to ....
5. Masochists enjoy ....
6. Optimists look forward to ....

69.3   Reword the sentences using the word in parentheses.

Example: I really like reading thrillers. (enjoy)   *I enjoy reading thrillers.*

1. I strongly dislike jazz. (stand)
2. His art attracts me. (appeal)
3. Beer makes me feel sick. (revolt)
4. She has totally charmed him. (enchant)
5. I'm dreading the exam. (look)
6. I was attracted to him from the start. (fall for)

69.4   In each pair of sentences, which one probably expresses a stronger feeling?

1. a) Dear Ann, How are things?   b) Sweetheart, How are things?
2. a) They've fallen in love.   b) They're very fond of each other.
3. a) I dislike her poetry.   b) I loathe her poetry.
4. a) She's looking forward to seeing him.   b) She's longing to see him.
5. a) He's crazy about her.   b) He's attracted to her.

69.5   Complete the sentences or answer the questions in a way that is true for you.

1. What kind of food do you like? I like .... and I'm crazy about
   ...., but I can't stand ....
2. I'm fascinated by ....
3. What attracts you most in a loved one?
4. What do you enjoy most about your job or your studies?
5. If you were on a diet, what food or drink would tempt you most to break the diet?
6. What characteristics in people do you most despise?

Speaking

These verbs describe how loudly someone is speaking and may also indicate the person's mood. The verbs may be followed by clauses beginning with **that.**

Verb	Loudness	Most likely mood
whisper	soft	–
murmur	soft	romantic or complaining
mumble	soft (and unclear)	nervous or insecure
mutter	soft	irritated
shout, yell	loud	angry or excited
scream	loud (usually without words)	frightened or excited
shriek	loud (and shrill)	frightened or amused
stutter, stammer*	neutral	nervous or excited

*Note: Stuttering and stammering may also be the result of a speech impediment.

The following verbs indicate how the speaker feels. (*Note:* s.b. = somebody; s.t. = something.)

Verb	Patterns	Feeling	Verb	Patterns	Feeling
boast	to s.b. about s.t. / that...	proud of oneself	complain	to s.b. about s.t. / that...	displeased, annoyed
insist	on s.t. / that...	determined	maintain	that...	convinced
object	that... / to + -ing	unhappy, in conflict	confess	that... / to + -ing	repentant
threaten	that... / to do s.t.	aggressive	urge	s.b. to do s.t.	encouraging
argue	with s.b. about s.t. / that...	not in agreement	beg	s.b. to do s.t. / for s.t.	desperate
groan	that... / about s.t.	displeased, in pain	grumble	that... / about s.t.	displeased

C

To give an idea of the *way* someone speaks and their feelings, you can use an adverb ending in **-ly.** For example: He said **proudly.** She spoke **angrily.** (This is common in writing, but not in spoken English.)

If someone feels angry: angrily furiously bitterly
If someone feels unhappy: unhappily gloomily miserably sadly
If someone feels happy: happily cheerfully eagerly gladly hopefully
If someone feels worried: anxiously nervously desperately hopelessly

Other useful adverbs are boldly, excitedly, gratefully, impatiently, passionately, reluctantly, shyly, sincerely.

Exercises

70.1 Choose the verb that best fits the meaning of the sentences.

Example: "I love you," he *murmured.*

1. "I'm the one who broke the vase," he ....
2. "I'm the smartest person in the class," the little boy ....
3. "I'll cut off your allowance if you don't behave," she ....
4. "Please, please, help me," he ....
5. "This hotel is filthy," she ....
6. "Come on, Jim, try harder," he ....

70.2 Change the sentences above into reported speech using the same verbs.

Example: He murmured that he loved her.

70.3 The answers to these questions are all words with the same root as the verbs on the opposite page.

Example: How do you describe someone who boasts a lot? *boastful*

What's the word for . . .
1. what you make when you threaten?
2. what you make when you complain?
3. what you make when you object?
4. a person who asks for money on the street?

How do you describe . . .
5. someone who insists a lot?
6. someone who argues a lot?

70.4 Look at the verbs in the table in B opposite and do the following quiz.

1. Which verbs could replace **ask** in the sentence "She asked me to dance with her" without changing the grammar of the sentence?
2. Which prepositions usually follow (a) object, (b) insist, (c) complain?
3. Which two verbs can be used to mean "complain"?
4. Find a synonym for each of these verbs: boast, argue, confess, urge, beg.

70.5 Complete the following table.

Adverb	Adjective	Noun
angrily	....	....
furiously	....	....
bitterly	....	....
miserably	....	....
cheerfully	....	....
gratefully	....	....
anxiously	....	....
proudly	....	....

70.6 Write a sentence to match each of the eight adverbs listed at the end of C.

Example: excitedly *"Let's go right away," she said excitedly.*

The six senses

A The five senses are **sight, hearing, taste, touch,** and **smell.** What is sometimes called the "sixth sense" (or extrasensory perception) is a power to be aware of things independently of the five physical senses – a kind of supernatural sense.

The five verbs referring to the senses are modified by an adjective, not an adverb.

He **looks** awful.	The trip **sounds** marvelous.	This cake **tastes** good.
It **felt** strange.	The soup **smelled** delicious.	

B **Sight**

Yesterday I **glanced** out the window and **noticed** a man **observing** a house across from mine through a telescope. I thought I **glimpsed** a woman inside the house. Then I **saw** someone else **peering** into the window of the same house. I **gazed** at them through my window, wondering what they were doing. Suddenly the first man stopped **staring** through his telescope. He went and hit the other one on the head with the telescope, and I realized that I had **witnessed** a crime.

C **Hearing**

Scale of loudness: noiseless → silent → quiet → noisy → loud → deafening

D **Taste**

sweet (honey) **salty** (potato chips) **bitter** (strong coffee) **sour** (vinegar) **spicy** (salsa)

If you say something tastes **hot,** it may mean **spicy** rather than **not cold.** Food can be **tasty,** but **tasteful** refers to furnishings, architecture, or a style of dressing or behavior. The opposite of both is **tasteless.**

E **Touch**

She nervously **fingered** her collar.	He **stroked** the cat and **petted** the dog.
She **tapped** him on the shoulder.	He **grasped** my hand and we ran.
She **grabbed** her bag and ran.	It's rude to **snatch** things.
Please **handle** the goods with care.	**Press** the button.

F **Smell**

stinking   vile   smelly   aromatic   scented   fragrant
sweet-smelling   perfumed   musty

G **Sixth sense (ESP)**

Different phenomena that a person with a sixth sense may experience:

telepathy   ghosts   UFOs
premonitions   intuition   déjà vu

Exercises

71.1   Make a sentence about the situations using any of these verbs plus an adjective:
look, sound, taste, touch, smell.

   Example: You see a movie about the Rocky Mountains.   *They look magnificent.*

   1. You come downstairs in the morning and smell fresh coffee.
   2. A friend has just had her hair cut.
   3. A friend, an excellent cook, tries a new soup recipe.
   4. A little boy asks you to listen to his first attempts on the piano.
   5. You see a friend of yours with a very worried look on her face.
   6. Someone you are working with smells strongly of cigars.

71.2   Which of the verbs in B opposite suggests looking . . .

   1. on as a crime or accident occurs?
   2. closely, finding it hard to make things out?
   3. at something but getting only a very brief view?
   4. quickly?
   5. fixedly?
   6. in a scientific way?

71.3   Replace the underlined words with more precise verbs from the opposite page.

   1. I <u>became aware of</u> a leak in the roof.
   2. He <u>knocked</u> on the door <u>lightly</u>.
   3. She <u>took</u> my hand <u>firmly</u>.
   4. <u>Touch</u> the button to start.
   5. He <u>touched</u> the cat <u>affectionately</u>.
   6. We <u>looked</u> at the view for some time.
   7. The robber <u>took</u> the money and ran.
   8. She <u>picked up, carried, and set down</u> the boxes carefully.

71.4   Are the following best described as *sweet, salty, bitter, sour, spicy,* or *hot*?

   1. seawater
   2. chocolate cake
   3. chili powder
   4. lime
   5. curry
   6. strong, unsweetened coffee

71.5   Which of the adjectives in F best describe for you the smell of the following?

   1. herbs in a kitchen
   2. unwashed socks
   3. a beauty salon
   4. roses
   5. a room filled with cigar smoke
   6. an attic used for storage

71.6   Which of the phenomena mentioned in G have you experienced if you . . .

   1. see a flying saucer?
   2. suddenly think of someone an instant before they telephone you?
   3. see someone in white disappearing into a wall?
   4. feel certain someone can't be trusted, even though there's no real reason to
      believe so?
   5. walk into a strange room and feel you have been there before?
   6. refuse to travel on a plane because you feel something bad is going to happen?

71.7   Write a sentence about a remarkable experience each of your senses has had.

What your body does

Note: All the verbs on this page (except **shake** and **bite**) are regular verbs; almost all the words have an identical noun form: **to yawn / a yawn, to cough / a cough** (except **to breathe / a breath** and **to perspire / perspiration**).

A ## Verbs connected with the mouth and breathing

breathe: A nurse gave the old man artificial respiration and he started **breathing** again.
yawn: If one person **yawns,** everyone else seems to start too.
cough: It was so smoky in the room that he couldn't stop **coughing.**
sneeze: Dust often makes me **sneeze.**
sigh: She **sighed** with relief when she heard the plane had landed safely.
hiccup: Holding your breath and swallowing can help you stop **hiccupping.**
snore: She **snored** all night with her mouth wide open.

B ## Verbs connected with eating and digestion

burp: He patted the baby's back to make it **burp** after its feeding.
chew: My granny used to say you should **chew** every mouthful ten times.
rumble/growl: It's embarrassing if your stomach **rumbles/growls** during class.
swallow: Take a drink of water to help you **swallow** the pills.
suck: You're too old to **suck** your thumb!
lick: After having a meal, the cat **licked** herself clean.
bite: She always **bites** her nails when she's nervous.

C ## Verbs connected with the eyes and face

blink: She **blinked** several times to try to get the dust out of her eye.
wink: He **winked** at me across the room to try to make me laugh.
frown: Why are you **frowning?** What's the problem?
grin: She was so delighted with the present that she **grinned** from ear to ear.
blush: He **blushed** with embarrassment when she smiled at him.

D ## Verbs connected with the whole body

sweat/perspire   shiver   shake with anger

perspire/sweat: Exercise makes you **sweat/perspire.** [perspire is more formal]
tremble: My hands **tremble** when I've been drinking too much coffee.
shiver: Look at him! He's so cold that he's **shivering!**
shake: She laughed so hard that her whole body **shook.**

The pronunciation of some of the words in this unit is unusual. Check the Index.

Exercises

72.1 Find the word to match the definitions below.

Example: to draw the eyebrows together to express displeasure or puzzlement
to frown

1. to turn pink from embarrassment
2. to tremble, especially from cold or fear
3. to shut and open both eyes quickly
4. to deliberately shut and open one eye
5. to breathe out deeply, especially to express pleasure, relief, boredom, etc.

72.2 Say what could be happening in each of the situations below.

Example: (parent to child) Take your thumb out of your mouth!   *The child is sucking its thumb.*

1. Listen to that! I can't sleep in the same room as him.
2. Am I boring you?
3. If you take a drink of water, it might stop!
4. Are you hungry?
5. You shouldn't eat so much so quickly!

72.3 Which of the words on the opposite page do these pictures illustrate?

Example: 1. *sneeze*

72.4 Complete the puzzle. The central letters going downward will form a word from the opposite page if you add one more letter.

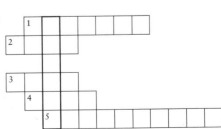

1. a type of gum
2. smile broadly
3. what you need to do to a stamp
4. what babies do after eating
5. a more formal word for sweating

72.5 Organize the words on the opposite page into one or more bubble networks. Add any other words that you wish to the network.

What animals do

A Noises animals make

Cats **meow** when they're hungry and **purr** when they're happy.
Dogs **bark**. They also **growl** when they're angry. Lions **roar**.
Sheep and goats **bleat**, horses **neigh**, pigs **grunt**, cows **moo**.
Frogs **croak** and ducks **quack**. Roosters/Cocks **crow,** hens **cluck**, birds **chirp**,
    owls **hoot**.

Note: All these verbs are regular.

B Movements animals make

Birds **fly** and fish **swim.**
Butterflies **flutter.**
Kangaroos **hop.**
Snakes **slither.**
Horses **trot, canter,** and **gallop.**
    (**Galloping** is the fastest.)
Lambs **romp** in the spring.

Note: All these verbs are regular except **fly** (flew, flown) and **swim** (swam, swum).

C Babies animals have

Cats have **kittens** and dogs have **puppies. Horses** have **foals. Pigs** have **piglets.**
Sheep have **lambs. Cows** have **calves. Bears, wolves,** and **lions** have **cubs.**
Ducks have **ducklings. Hens** lay eggs from which **chickens** hatch.
Tadpoles turn into **frogs. Caterpillars** turn into **butterflies.**

D People and animals

People are often compared to animals. These adjectives can be used about people.

catty: malicious
mousy: dull, uninteresting
sheepish: embarrassed, bashful

foxy: sly, cunning; attractive [informal]
dogged: stubborn; persistent
cocky: arrogant

Exercises

73.1   Match the verb with the sound.

1. chirp   baa-baa
2. bleat   tweet-tweet
3. bark   oink-oink
4. grunt   cock-a-doodle-doo
5. crow   woof-woof

73.2   Complete the following text, putting the appropriate missing verbs into the correct form.

It is not really all that peaceful out in the country. Yesterday I was awakened at dawn when the rooster started .... (1). The cows soon began .... (2) and this woke the dogs, who .... (3) until the horses started .... (4). Lots of hens .... (5) right outside my window, so I got up. I tripped over the cat, who was lying in the sun at the front door, but she didn't even stop .... (6).

73.3   Most of the verbs in A and all the verbs in B can also be used to describe sounds and movements made by humans. Mark the following statements true or false.

1. If someone growls at you, they are probably in a bad mood.
2. If someone croaks, they might have a sore throat.
3. If someone hoots, they are probably very unhappy.
4. If someone barks at you, they sound somewhat angry or abrupt.
5. If someone grunts when you ask something, they are showing a lot of interest in what you have said.

73.4   Illustrate the meaning of the words below by writing sentences (about people rather than animals).

Example: romp   *The children romped in the fields.*

1. fly   3. slither   5. trot
2. swim   4. hop   6. gallop

73.5   In the following notices, fill in the names of the appropriate young animal.

1. Newborn .... for sale. Pedigree spaniel.
2. Good home wanted for six .... All toms. Already house-trained. Part Siamese. Very intelligent.
3. Come and see the brand-new polar bear .... at the zoo.
4. Hadley Farm open this weekend. All children will enjoy the chance to hold the baby .... and stroke their soft wool.

73.6   Which of the adjectives in D would you be happy to be called?

Idioms and fixed expressions – general

Idioms are fixed expressions with meanings that are not always clear or obvious. For example, the expression **to feel under the weather,** which means "to feel unwell," is a typical idiom. The words do not tell us what it means, but the context usually helps.

A Tips for remembering idioms

Think of idioms as units, just like single words; always record the whole phrase in your notebook, along with information on grammar and collocation.

This can opener **has seen better days.** [it is fairly old and broken down; usually about things, always perfect tense form]

Idioms are often informal and include a personal comment on the situation. They are sometimes humorous or ironic. As with any informal word(s), be careful how you use them. Never use them just to sound "fluent" or "good at English," or you'll run the risk of being too intimate or informal when you don't mean to be.

Idioms can be grouped in a variety of ways. Use whichever way you find most useful to help you remember them. Here are some possible types of grouping.

By grammar

pull a fast one [trick/deceive somebody]
poke your nose in(to) [interfere] } verb + object

be in seventh heaven [extremely happy/elated]
feel down in the dumps [depressed/low] } verb + prepositional phrase

By meaning (e.g., idioms describing people's character/intellect)

He **takes the cake.** [is the extreme / the worst of all]
You're **a pain in the neck.** [a nuisance / difficult person]

By verb or other key word (e.g., idioms with **make**)

Don't **make a mountain out of a molehill.** [exaggerate the importance]
Since losing my job, I can barely **make ends meet.** [manage on my income]

B Grammar of idioms

It is important when using idioms to know just how flexible their grammar is. Some are more fixed than others. For instance, **barking up the wrong tree** [be mistaken] is always used in continuous, not simple, form: I think you're **barking up the wrong tree.**

A good dictionary may help, but it is best to observe the grammar in real examples.

(Note how Units 75–91 group idioms in different ways.)

Exercises

74.1 Complete the idioms with one of the key words below. If you are not sure, try looking up the key word in a good dictionary.

shot   bucket   plate   block   handle   pie

1. All the promises these politicians make! It's just ....*pie*............ in the sky. [big promises that will never materialize]
2. The tiny amount donated is just a drop in the .... compared with the huge amount needed. [tiny amount compared with a large amount]
3. I have enough on my .... as it is; I can't do that job too. [have more than enough work]
4. When I told her what I thought, she just flew off the .... and shouted at me. [lost her temper]
5. His father was a gambler too. He's a real chip off the old .... [just like one's parents/grandparents]
6. I wasn't really sure of the answer, so I guessed it; it was just a .... in the dark. [a wild guess]

74.2 Use a good dictionary or a dictionary of idioms to help you decide which version of these sentences is correct for the idiom concerned.

Example: You bark /(are barking) up the wrong tree if you think I did it.

1. Holland is springing / springs to mind as a good place for a bicycling trip; it's nice and flat.
2. That remark is flying / flies in the face of everything you've ever said before on the subject.
3. He was innocent after all. It just goes / is just going to show that you shouldn't believe what you read in the papers.
4. You sit / 're sitting pretty! Look at you – an easy job, a fantastic salary, a free car!
5. His attitude is leaving / leaves a lot to be desired. I wish he would try to be more responsible.

74.3 How would you organize these idioms into different groups? Use some of the ways suggested on the opposite page, plus any other ways you can think of.

be in a bind   child's play   rough and ready   be up to it
hold your tongue   be out of sorts   hold your horses   a fool's errand
odds and ends   keep mum   give or take

74.4 Without using a dictionary, guess the meaning of these idioms.

1. It's midnight. Time to hit the sack.
2. This is just kid's stuff. I want something challenging!
3. He was down and out for two years, but eventually he got a job and found a home for himself.

Everyday expressions

Spoken language is full of fixed expressions that are not necessarily difficult to understand but have a fixed form that does not change. These have to be learned as whole expressions. These expressions are sometimes hard to find in dictionaries, so it is important to be on the lookout for them.

A Conversation-building expressions

Here are some common expressions that help to modify or organize what we are saying. There are many more expressions like these. (See also Unit 100.)

Expression		*Meaning/function*
As I was saying, I haven't seen her for years.	⟶	takes the conversation back to an earlier point
Speaking of skiing, whatever happened to Bill Jakes?	⟶	starting a new topic but linking it to the current one
If you ask me, she's heading for trouble.	⟶	if you want my opinion (even if no one has asked for it)
That reminds me, I haven't called George yet.	⟶	something in the conversation brings something else to mind
Come to think of it, did he give me his number after all? I think he may have forgotten.	⟶	something in the conversation makes you realize there may be a problem/question about something

B Key words

This and **that** are examples of key words that occur in several expressions:

This is it. [this is an important point]

That's it. [that's the last thing, we've finished]

THIS/THAT

We talked about **this and that** or **this, that, and the other.** [various unimportant matters]

So, **that's that.** [it is agreed, settled, finalized]

C Common expressions for modifying statements

If worst comes to worst, we'll have to cancel the trip. [if the situation gets really bad]

If all else fails, we could fax them. [if nothing else succeeds]

What with one thing and another, I haven't had time to reply to her letter. [because of a lot of different circumstances]

When it comes to restaurants, this town's not that good. [in the matter of restaurants]

As far as I'm concerned, we can eat at any time. [as far as it affects me / from my point of view]

As luck would have it, she was out when I called. [by chance]

Exercises

75.1 Complete the fixed expressions in these sentences without looking at the opposite page, if possible.

1. Come ...., I don't remember giving her the key. I'd better call her and check, just in case.
2. If you ...., the economy's going to get much worse before it gets any better.
3. .... of vacations, what are you planning to do on yours?
4. That ...., I have a message for you from Maria.
5. As .... before the telephone interrupted us, we plan to take a long vacation next summer.

75.2 Which of the expressions with *this/that* opposite would be most suitable for the second parts of these mini-dialogues?

1. A: What were you and Mike talking about?
   B: Oh, ...
2. A: How many more?
   B: No more, actually. ....
3. A: Here comes the big announcement we've been waiting for.
   B: Yes, ...
4. A: Okay, I'll take our decisions to the committee.
   B: All right, so .... Thanks.

75.3 See if you can complete this network of everyday expressions with *now*, as with the *this/that* network opposite. Use a dictionary if necessary.

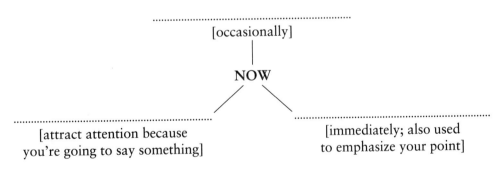

Use the expressions with *now* to rewrite these sentences.

1. Do you want me to do it right away, or can it wait?
2. So, everybody, listen carefully. I have news for you.
3. I bump into her in town occasionally, but not that often.

75.4 Which expressions contain the following key words?

1. come(s)   2. luck   3. fails   4. worst   5. far   6. thing

Similes – *as...as... / like...*

A

As ... as ... similes are easy to understand. If you see the phrase **as dead as a doornail,** you don't need to know what a **doornail** is, simply that the whole phrase means "completely dead." But, remember, fixed similes are usually informal/colloquial and often humorous, so use them with care.

Creating a picture in your mind can help you remember the simile:

as **blind** as a **bat**   as **strong** as an **ox**   as **quiet** as a **mouse**

Some can be remembered as pairs of opposites.

as **heavy** as **lead** ≠ as **light** as a **feather**
as **black** as **night** ≠ as **white** as **snow**

Some can be remembered by sound patterns.

as **b**usy as a **b**ee   as good as gold   as **c**ool as a **c**ucumber

Some other useful **as ... as ...** phrases:

When it comes to business, he's **as hard as nails.** [cold and cruel]
I'll give this plant some water. The soil's **as dry as a bone.**
He's **as mad as a hatter.** He crossed the Atlantic in a bathtub.
The fish must have been spoiled. After dinner, I was **as sick as a dog.** [vomiting]
Don't worry. Using the computer's **as easy as falling off a log.**
She gave the answer **as quick as a wink.**
When I told him, his face went **as red as a beet.**

Sometimes the second part can change the meaning of the first.

The new carpet was **as white as snow.** [beautifully white]
When he saw it, his face went **as white as a sheet.** [pale with fear/horror]

B

Like ...

My plan **worked like a charm,** and the problem was soon solved.
Be careful the boss doesn't see you; she has **eyes like a hawk.**
No wonder he's overweight. He **eats like a horse** and **drinks like a fish.**
Did you sleep well? Yes, **like a log.** [very well]
Oh, no! I forgot to call him again. I've got **a brain like a sieve!**
She goes around **like a bull in a china shop.** [very clumsy]
Instead of helping us out, she sat there **like a bump on a log.** [immobile, unresponsive]
Dick and Jane are so much alike; they're **like two peas in a pod.**

Exercises

76.1 Complete the *as ... as ...* similes.

1. Rose is as mad as a ....; you wouldn't believe the crazy things she does.
2. Jack always does the heavy lifting; he's as strong as an ....
3. He never says a thing; he's as quiet as a ....
4. After eating that bad cheese I was as sick as a ....
5. I'm afraid I can't read this small print; I'm as blind as a .... without my glasses.

76.2 Different similes contain the same word. Fill in the blanks.

1. I feel great now. I .... like a log.
2. It's as easy as .... off a log.
3. The old man's hair was as white as ....
4. Her face suddenly went as white as ....

76.3 Put the correct number in the right-hand boxes to complete the similes, as in the example. There are two that are not on the opposite page. Try and guess them.

	1 quick		☐ daisy
	2 busy		5 ox
as	3 flat	**as a(n)**	☐ wink
	4 fresh		☐ bee
	5 strong		☐ pancake

76.4 Simile word puzzle. Fill in the answers, as in the example.

Across   *Down*
1. red   1. blind
2. mad   2. nails
4. white   3. log
5. fresh   6. cold
7. quiet   8. cool
9. dry   10. light

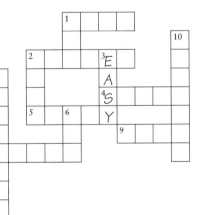

76.5 What can you say about . . .

1. a person who sees everything and never misses a thing?
2. a plan or course of action that worked very well?
3. someone who eats and drinks a great deal?
4. someone with a very bad memory?

Binomials

Binomials are expressions (often idiomatic) in which two words are joined by a conjunction (usually **and**). The order of the words is usually fixed. For example:

odds and ends: small, unimportant things, e.g., "Let's get the main things packed; we can do the **odds and ends** later."

give and take: a spirit of compromise, e.g., Every relationship needs some **give and take** to be successful.

A You can often tell something is a binomial because of the sound pattern.

Tears are **part and parcel** of growing up. [part of / belong to]
The boss was **ranting and raving** at us. [shouting / very angry]
He's so **prim and proper** at work. [rather formal and fussy]
She has to **wine and dine** important clients. [entertain]

B Other times, the clue is that the words are nearly synonyms.

You can **pick and choose**; it's up to you. [have a wide choice]
My English is progressing in **leaps and bounds**. [big jumps]
It's nice to have some **peace and quiet**. [peace/calm]
The doctor recommended some **rest and recreation / R&R.** [relaxation]
First and foremost, you have to work hard. [first / most importantly]
What we need to combat crime is **law and order.** [police enforcement of law]

C Many prepositions and adverbs combine to form binomials.

In this part of town you'll find cafés **here and there.** [scattered around]
We've had meetings **on and off.** [occasionally]
I've been running **back and forth** all day. [to and from somewhere]
To and fro can be used just like **back and forth.**
He's been **down and out** ever since he lost his job. [without a home or money]
She's recovered from the accident and is **out and about** again. [going out]
She ran **up and down** the street. [in both directions]

D There are binomials linked by words other than **and.**

He won't help her; she'll have to **sink or swim.** [survive or fail]
Slowly but surely, I realized the boat was sinking. [gradually]
Sooner or later, you'll learn your lesson. [sometime/someday]
She didn't want to be just friends; it had to be **all or nothing.**
Well, I'm sorry, that's all I can offer you; **take it or leave it.**
It's about the same distance as from here to Boston, **give or take** a few miles.
    [maybe a mile or two more, or a mile or two less]
This package weighs two pounds, **more or less.** [approximately]

Exercises

77.1 Here are some jumbled binomials (some are from the opposite page and some are new). Using similarities in sound, join them with *and*. Then check opposite or in a dictionary that you have the right word order and meaning.

prim	dine	high	give	sound
wine	take	dry	proper	safe

Now use them to fill in the blanks in these sentences.

1. I was left .... and .... with no one to help me.
2. I'm glad you're .... and .... after such a dangerous trip.
3. My hosts .... and .... me at the best restaurants.
4. The secretary is always so terribly .... and ....; the whole atmosphere always seems so very formal.
5. If we're ever going to reach a compromise, there must be some .... and ....

77.2 Match words from the left-hand box with words from the right-hand box to form binomials, as in the example *law and order*. There are more words on the right than you'll need. Look for words that are either near-synonyms or antonyms (opposites) of the left-hand word.

(law)		money	clean	drop
now		tired	soon	snow
neat		pay	bounds	terrible
pick	and	clocks	after	whisper
sick		(order)	then	dogs
leaps		scratch	heart	choose

Now rewrite these sentences using the binomials you formed above. The new sentences will often sound more informal than the original sentences.

1. The new mayor promised that efficient policing would be a priority.
2. The house looks orderly and spotless now for our visitors.
3. I have had enough of traffic jams. I'm going to start using the train.
4. My command of English vocabulary has improved rapidly since I've been using this book.
5. There are lots of courses. You can make your own selection.
6. I've seen her occasionally, taking her dog for a walk.

77.3 These binomials do not have *and* in the middle. What do they have? Check the opposite page or a dictionary if you are not sure.

1. sooner .... later
2. all .... nothing
3. head .... toe
4. sink .... swim
5. slowly .... surely
6. last .... not least

UNIT
78

Idioms describing people

 A Positive and negative qualities

Positive	Negative
She **has a heart of gold.** [very kind, generous]	He's **as hard as nails.** [no sympathy for others]
He's **as good as gold.** [generous, helpful, well-behaved; often used for children]	She's kind of **a cold fish.** [distant, unfriendly]

Note also:

He's **a pain in the neck.** Nobody likes him. [nuisance, difficult]
She **gets on everyone's nerves.** [irritates everybody]
I don't trust him. He's a real **back stabber.** [betrays trust]

 B People's "fast" and "slow" qualities

Fast	Slow
He's **a quick study.** He'll learn how to do the job in no time.	Come on! Hurry up! You're such **a slowpoke!**
You've asked him to marry you? You're **a fast worker!** You only met him three weeks ago!	She's a little **slow on the uptake.** It takes her a while to catch on.

 C How people relate to the social norm

Her ideas are **off the wall.** [informal: eccentric, bizarre]
He's a bit of **an oddball.** [peculiar, strange]
He's (gone) **around the bend,** if you ask me. [absolutely crazy/mad]
Sometimes she seems **as nutty as a fruitcake.** [very eccentric, odd in behavior]
My politics are **middle-of-the-road.** [moderate; neither left- nor right-wing]

 D Who's who in the class? Idioms for "people in the classroom"

teacher's pet   Mary's at the
head of the class.   a real
know-it-all   a big mouth   a lazybones

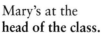

The last three idioms are said of people outside of the classroom too.

Exercises

78.1 Try to complete these idioms from memory if possible.

1. He'll give his last penny to charity; he has a heart . . .
2. Don't expect any sympathy from the boss; she's as hard . . .
3. I'm sure Jeanne will help you; she's as good . . .
4. She learned all the office procedures the first day at work. She's a quick . . .
5. You have to spell everything out for him. He's pretty slow . . .

78.2 How do we describe . . .

1. an irritating person who thinks he/she knows everything?
2. the person who is the teacher's favorite?
3. someone who can't keep a secret?
4. the one who gets the best marks?
5. a person who is very lazy?

78.3 You can also learn idioms by associating them with a key word or words. For example, two idioms on the opposite page have *gold* in them. Which are they? Here is a word fork based on *to have + heart*. Use the expressions to finish the sentences below.

to have ⎯
- a change of heart [change in attitude]
- your heart in the right place [good intentions, despite bad judgment]
- your heart set on something [wish for intensely]
- a heart [show compassion]
- a heart of stone [unsympathetic]

1. The boss isn't likely to give you a raise. He has . . .
2. Come on, . . . ! Make a donation to the children's fund.
3. Don't be angry with him. He has . . .
4. At first she didn't want to live in a big city, but she's had . . .
5. I really want to take a vacation next month. In fact, I . . .

Look for other sets of idioms based on key words.

78.4 Mini-quiz. Which part of the body might a difficult person (a) *get on,* (b) *be a pain in,* (c) *stab you in?*

78.5 Which idioms do these drawings represent?

1. 2. 3. 4.

Idioms describing feelings and mood

A Positive feelings, moods, and states

Mary seems to be **on cloud nine** these days. [extremely pleased/happy]
After he heard the good news, he was **walking on air.** [joyful, thrilled]
She seems to be **keeping her chin up.** [happy despite bad things]
Sandy's **a happy camper.** [content, in a good mood]

B Negative feelings, moods, and states

He really **looked down in the dumps.** [looked depressed/sad]
Kim is **in a bad/foul mood.** [a bad frame of mind/temper]
You **haven't been yourself** lately. Is anything wrong? [slightly ill or upset]

C Physical feelings and states

I could eat a horse! [very hungry]
I'm **feeling dead tired / dead on my feet.** [exhausted]
You're looking a little bit **under the weather.** [not very well / ill]
I was almost **at death's door** last week! [very sick or ill]

D Fear/fright

She was **scared stiff.** [very scared]
You **scared/frightened him to death.** [frightened him a lot]
We were all **shaking in our boots.** [trembling with fear]
The poor kid! You **frightened/scared him out of his wits.** [extremely scared]
I **jumped out of my skin** when I heard the bang. [gave a big jump]

Remember: There is an element of exaggeration in these idioms; they make comments on the situation and lighten the tone of what you are saying. So use them informally.

E

Horoscopes can be a good place to find idioms about moods and states, since the horoscope usually tries to tell you how you are going to feel during the coming day/week/month. Look at these horoscopes and note the idioms in italics. Collect more idioms from horoscopes if you can.

> **Capricorn** (Dec. 21–Jan. 19)
> Don't *get carried away* (1) by promises that won't be kept. *Keep a cool head* (2) and take everything as it comes. On the work front, things are looking better.
>
> **Taurus** (April 21–May 20)
> Someone will say something that will *make you swell with pride* (3) and you may *be on top of the world* (4) for a while, but the evening won't be so easy.

(1) get excited; lose control   (3) feel very proud
(2) stay calm   (4) extremely happy

Exercises

UNIT
79

79.1 Here are some more idioms that can be grouped as expressing either *positive* or *negative* feelings. Try to group them, using a dictionary if necessary.

to be in seventh heaven | to be in a snit
to feel/be a bit down | to feel/be as pleased as Punch

79.2 Using the idioms from 79.1 and from A opposite, say how you would probably feel if . . .

1. you were told you had just won a huge sum of money.   *on cloud nine*
2. your boss told you to redo a piece of work you'd already done three times.
3. you were told you'd gotten a very high mark on an exam.
4. you had a bad headache and your neighbor was making a lot of noise late at night.
5. nothing seems to have gone right for you today.
6. someone you were secretly in love with told you they were in love with you.

79.3 Complete the idioms in these sentences.

1. Don't creep up behind me like that! You scared me . . .
2. I don't need a doctor, I just feel a little bit under . . .
3. As long as he has his car to work on, he's a happy . . .
4. Last year, when I won that medal, I really was on . . .
5. I wasn't expecting such a loud bang; I nearly jumped . . .
6. I've had nothing since breakfast; I could . . .

79.4 Look for idioms about feelings, moods, and states in these horoscopes. Underline them, then check the meaning in a dictionary if necessary.

Scorpio (Oct. 23–Nov. 22)
You may be itching to travel today, but be patient; this is not a good time to take a trip. Events at work will keep you on the edge of your seat for most of the day. Altogether an anxious time for Scorpios.

Leo (July 21–Aug. 21)
You'll be up in arms over something someone close to you says rather thoughtlessly today, but don't let it spoil things. You may be of two minds over an invitation, but think positively.

Now use the idioms to rewrite these sentences.

1. I can't decide about that job in Brazil.
2. I've been in suspense all day. What happened? Tell me!
3. We enjoyed our vacation, but by the end of it, we were restless to go home.
4. Everyone protested loudly when they canceled the outing.

79.5 Which idioms on the opposite page include the words *wits*, *swell*, *foul*, and *carried*? Write a sentence using each one.

Idioms connected with problematic situations

A   **Problems and difficulties**

Idiom		*Literal phrase*
to be **in a fix**	=	be in difficulty
to be **in a bind**	=	be in a dilemma or predicament
to be **in a (tight) spot**	=	be in a situation that is hard to get out of

(these three all follow the pattern: **be + in + a**)

B   **Reacting in situations: more or less opposite idioms**

to **take a back seat** [not do anything; let others act instead]	≠	to **take the bull by the horns** [act positively to face and attack the problem]
to **stir things up** [do/say things that make matters worse]	≠	to **pour oil on troubled waters** [do/say things that calm the situation down]
to **play one's cards close to the vest** [hold back information]	≠	to **lay one's cards on the table** [be very open, state exactly what your position is]

C   **Idioms with *get***

This has to be done by next week; we'd better **get our act together** before it's too late. [organize ourselves to respond; informal]

We need a thorough investigation to **get to the bottom of** things. [find the true explanation or reason for the state of affairs]

It's difficult to **get** people **to sit up and take notice.** [make them pay attention to the situation]

I'm trying to **get a grasp of** what's happening; it's not easy. [understand]

(See Unit 87 for more idioms with **get**.)

D   **Changes and stages in situations**

The tide has turned against us; troubles are ahead.

We can see **light at the end of the tunnel** at last.

I'm afraid we've come to **a dead end** with our plans.

The tables are turned. Now we have the advantage.
I think I've reached **a turning point** in my career.

Exercises

80.1 When looking up words and idioms in the dictionary, look at what is just before and after the information you are looking for. In this way you can pick up some related words and expressions that you can record together.

For example, if you look up *take the bull by the horns* in a dictionary, you will probably also find these idioms:

   (to be/act) **like a bull in a china shop** [be very clumsy]
   (to talk) **a load of bull** [talk nonsense]

Look up these idioms using the underlined words as your key word and see what other idioms or useful phrases you can find near them in the dictionary.

1. come to a <u>dead</u> end
2. play your <u>cards</u> close to the vest
3. <u>pour</u> oil on troubled waters
4. <u>stir</u> things up

80.2 Choose suitable idioms from the opposite page to fill in the blanks.

1. I think I'll just .... and let the others work this out.
2. No, please, don't say anything; you'll only ....
3. It's been a long, hard struggle, but I think at last we can see ....
4. The police are trying their best to get to ...., but it's a real mystery at the moment.
5. We're in a tight .... financially; we probably won't be able to make our payments this month.
6. At last I've managed to get him to sit ....; he's done nothing at all for us so far.
7. I find it hard to get a .... global warming, don't you?
8. I'm going to lay .... so you'll know exactly what my intentions are.

80.3 Here are some more idioms connected with situations. Can you paraphrase their meaning, as in the example? Use a dictionary if necessary.

1. It's not working; we'll have to <u>go back to square one</u>.   *go back to the beginning again*
2. The teachers want one thing, the students want the exact opposite. I'm sure we can find <u>a happy medium</u>.
3. We were <u>on pins and needles</u> all night waiting for news from the hospital. They finally called us at 6:30 a.m.
4. Poverty and crime <u>go hand in hand</u> in this part of town.
5. You've been in a lot of trouble lately; you'd better <u>toe the line</u> from now on.
6. Things are improving, but problems remain. We're not <u>out of the woods</u> just yet.
7. We're desperate; this bank loan is our last hope. If it's not approved, we'll really be <u>up the creek</u>.

Idioms connected with praise and criticism

A **Praise**

Saying people are good at something

He's a really **first-rate / top-notch** administrator – the very best.
When it comes to grammar, she's really **on the ball.** [knows a lot]
Bill **has a way with** foreign students. The other teachers envy him. [good at establishing good relations / motivating them, etc.]
Sandra really **has a green thumb;** just look at those flowers! [good at gardening]

Saying people/things are better than the rest

Mary is **head and shoulders above** the rest of the girls in the class.
Our Olympic team is **the cream of the crop.** [the best or choicest; usually said of a group of people]
When it comes to electronics, our company is **miles / light years ahead** of the competition. [can be said of people or things]
That meal was just **out of this world.** [outstanding/superb; usually said of things]
Your garden **puts** the others in the neighborhood **to shame.** [surpasses, is far better]

B **Criticism**

Note: There are far more of these idioms in common use than idioms connected with praise!

This group could be learned in association with animals:

Don't be **chicken / a scaredy cat.** [easily frightened, cowardly]
He's always **crowing** about his accomplishments. [boasting]
I don't trust her; she's **a snake in the grass.** [devious]
Some people **worm their way** into good positions. [accomplish something dishonestly]

(See also Unit 73.)

This group could be learned in association with food words:

When it comes to unreliability, he really **takes the cake.** [is the epitome / most striking example of some negative quality]
Annemarie **wants to have her cake and eat it too!** [wants everything without any contribution from her side]
I think he's just trying to **butter me up.** [give false praise]

Note these idiomatic synonyms of the verb **to criticize:**

Must you always **put me down** in front of other people?
You shouldn't **run down / knock** your own country when you're abroad.
Why do you always **pick apart** everything I say?

Exercises

81.1 Using idioms from A opposite, rewrite these sentences without changing the meaning.

1. The hotel we were staying in was absolutely superb.
2. Joe is far ahead of the other kids when it comes to arithmetic.
3. This restaurant is much, much better than all the other restaurants in town.
4. You're way ahead of me in understanding all this technology; I'm impressed.
5. The very best graduates from our university went on to business school.

81.2 Which idioms opposite might these pictures help you to remember?

81.3 Which of the expressions in 81.2 is most appropriate for . . .

1. praising someone's knowledge/ability in their profession?
2. saying that someone is praising you too much in order to gain an advantage?
3. saying someone is scared for no good reason?
4. praising someone's gardening skills?

81.4 Express the *opposite* meaning to these sentences using idioms from the opposite page.

Example: She's a third-rate athlete.   *She's a first-rate (or top-notch) athlete.*

1. Al is extremely trustworthy.
2. Steve doesn't get along with the secretaries; just look at how they react when he wants something done.
3. He often says how wonderful his school is.
4. She praises everything I say.
5. She wants a promotion, a company car, and a raise, yet she can't even get to work on time. She doesn't ask for much.

81.5 Using a good dictionary or a dictionary of idioms, find more idioms that include the food words below for praising or criticizing people/things/actions. Make sentences with the expressions.

1. ham   2. tea   3. icing   4. nut   5. bacon

Idioms connected with using language

A Idioms connected with communication problems

...and that means...

Can...

...but if not, it could be...

uh...

...and another thing...

Why...

...not withstanding any other proviso not stated...

She **can't get a word in edgewise.**

I **can't make heads or tails of** what he's saying.

B Good talk, bad talk

The boss always **talks down** to us. [talks as if we were inferior]

My coworkers are always **talking behind my back.** [saying negative things about me when I'm not there]

It was just **small talk,** nothing more, honestly. [purely social talk, not on any serious matters]

It's gone too far this time. I'll just have to **give him a talking to.** [scold/warn him]

They always **talk shop** over lunch; they can't get enough of it! [talk about work]

Don't listen to her; she's **talking through her hat.** [talking ignorantly; telling lies]

OK, you **talked me into** it. I'll go to the movies with you. [persuaded]

Jim likes to **talk off the top of his head;** he doesn't always stop to think. [make statements without forethought/preparation]

C Talk in discussions, meetings, etc.

1. Who's going to **start the ball rolling?**

2. To put it **in a nutshell,** this is a waste of time.

3. I hope they **get to the point** soon.

4. I intend to **speak my mind.**

8. Jim is so **long-winded.**

7. Iris always **talks nonsense.**

6. I hope Bill **speaks up.** He always **makes sense.**

5. I hope we can **wrap up** the discussion by noon.

1. start the discussion
2. say it in few words
3. come to the important part of the matter
4. say exactly what I think

5. finish the discussion
6. say intelligent, reasonable things
7. say stupid things
8. say things in a long, tedious way

Exercises

82.1 Look at these dialogues and comment on them, as in the example.

Example: MARY: I don't expect someone with your intelligence to understand this
document.
ERIC: Gee, thanks.
It seems that *Mary is talking down to Eric.*

1. JOE: So that's what I'm going to do – take it all away.
   ANN: What about . . .
   JOE: And if they don't like it, they can just go and do what they like.
   ANN: But if they . . .
   JOE: Not that I have to consult them; after all, *I'm* in charge around here.
   ANN: I wonder if it . . .
   JOE: You see, I'm the kind of person who can make tough decisions.

   It seems that Ann can't get ....

2. MEG: So, area-wise the down-matching sales profile commitment would seem
   to be high-staked on double-par.
   DAN: Huh? Could you say that again? You've got me there.

   It seems that Dan can't make ....

3. SAM: So then George tells me that he never said it.
   LISA: You mean he actually denied saying it?
   SAM: That's right! Can you imagine – oh, George, I didn't see you standing there.

   It seems that Sam and Lisa are talking ....

82.2 What idioms on the opposite page do these drawings represent?

1. the discussion

3.
   start

2. (drawing)

4. ──────────────→ •
   get to / come to

82.3 Fill in the blanks to complete the idioms.

1. She is very direct and always .... her mind.
2. I get bored with small ....; let's get down to serious matters. I'm
   in love with you.
3. The boss gave me a real .... to after that stupid mistake I made. I
   admit it though, I was wrong.

UNIT 83 Idioms – miscellaneous

A Idioms connected with paying, buying, and selling

He did $600 worth of damage to the car, and his parents had to **foot the bill**.
[pay up, usually a large amount]

That restaurant was **a real rip-off**. *or* That taxi driver really **ripped us off**.
[made us pay much too much; very informal]

She **drives a hard bargain**. She knew I was desperate to buy an apartment, so
she charged as much as she could get. [ask a lot and resist lowering the
price]

If you go to that auto dealer, you'll pay **top dollar** for a new car. [a very high
price]

B Idioms based on parts of the body

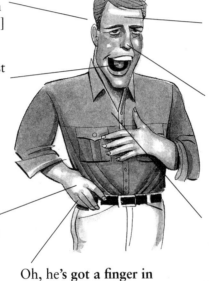

He's **made quite a bit of headway** with math lately. [make progress]

I know the name; I just can't remember it. It's **on the tip of my tongue**. [something that can't be remembered]

You've **got to hand it to** her; she's a great singer. [acknowledge/admit]

Oh, he's **got a finger in every pie**. [is involved in many different things]

If I seem preoccupied, it's because I've got a lot **on my mind** these days. [a lot to worry about]

We had to **pay through the nose** for those tickets. [pay a huge amount]

I hope you didn't mind me telling you. I just had to **get it off my chest**. [tell something that's been bothering you a lot]

C Idioms connected with daily routine

Come on! **Rise and shine!** [a command to someone to get up, often said to
someone who doesn't want to and at a very early hour] Time to leave! There's
no time for breakfast. We can **get a bite to eat** on the highway. [have a snack or
meal] I'll drive and you can **take a nap** in the back seat. [a short sleep] When
we get there, there'll just be time to **freshen up** before the meeting. [wash and
clean oneself up] It's going to be a long day; I'll be ready to **crash** pretty early.
[informal; be very tired/ready to sleep almost anywhere] Still, we can stay
home tomorrow and **put our feet up** [relax], and just watch TV like **couch
potatoes!** [people who lie around watching TV and aren't very active]

Exercises

83.1 Look at these mini-dialogues and answer the questions using idioms from the opposite page.

1. A: I'll give you $85.
   B: No, $100 or nothing.
   A: Oh, come on. Make it $90, OK?
   B: No, I said $100 and I mean $100.

   What's B doing?

2. A: I'm president of the tennis club, I'm on the parent-teacher committee, and I run three youth clubs.
   B: Really?
   A: And I'm on the board at the Social Center, and there's the YMCA . . .

   What kind of person could A be described as?

3. A: La-da-da-di . . .
   B: What's that song you're singing?
   A: Oh, it's . . . um, uh . . . I'm sure I know the title . . . It'll come to me . . .

   Does A know the name of the song or not?

83.2 Rewrite these sentences using an idiom instead of the underlined words.

1. Can I tell you about a problem I have? I just have to <u>tell somebody</u>. It's been <u>bothering me</u> for a while now.
2. They charged us $200 for a tiny room without a TV. They <u>robbed</u> us!
3. We'll have just enough time to <u>get a quick snack</u> before the show.
4. I <u>must admit</u>, Maria handled the situation admirably.
5. I <u>think</u> I'll just go upstairs and <u>sleep for a little while</u>, if nobody minds.
6. We had to <u>pay a very high price</u> for the apartment, but we had no choice.

83.3 Which idioms do these drawings suggest?

1.   2.   3.

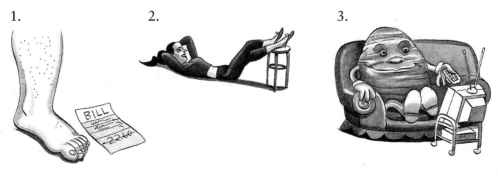

Follow-up: Look up idioms for other parts of the body, e.g., *tongue, heels, toe, back,* and make a note of examples.

Proverbs

Speakers tend to use proverbs, or old sayings, to comment on a situation, often at the end of a true story someone has told, or in response to some event. Like all idioms, they are useful and enjoyable to know and understand, but should be used with care.

A   Warnings/advice/morals – do*s* and don't*s*

Proverb		*Paraphrase*
Don't count your chickens before they're hatched.	⟶	Don't anticipate the future too much.
Don't put all your eggs in one basket.	⟶	Don't invest all your efforts or attention in just one thing.
Never judge a book by its cover.	⟶	Don't judge people/things by their outward appearance.
Never look a gift horse in the mouth.	⟶	Never refuse good fortune when it is there in front of you.

B   Key elements

Proverbs can be grouped by key elements, e.g., animals and birds.

When the **cat's** away, the **mice** will play. [people will take advantage of someone else's absence to behave more freely]

You can lead a **horse** to water, but you can't make it drink. [you can try to persuade someone, but you can't force him/her]

One **swallow** doesn't make a summer. [one positive sign doesn't mean all is well]

C   Visualizing

As with learning all vocabulary, visualizing some element often helps.

Where there's smoke, there's fire. [Rumors are usually based on some degree of truth.]

Too many cooks spoil the broth. [Too many people interfering is a bad way of doing things.]

People who live in glass houses shouldn't throw stones. [Don't criticize others' faults if you suffer from them yourself.]

Half a loaf is better than none. [Having less is better than having nothing at all.]

Exercises

84.1   **Find proverbs on the opposite page that fit these situations.**

Example: A friend says she has just been offered a free two-week vacation, but is hesitating about whether to accept the offer.   *Never look a gift horse in the mouth.*

1. You've been offered a good job, but the salary is less than you were expecting.
2. Your brother says he can't be bothered applying to different universities and will apply to just one.
3. Three different people have made different arrangements for the same meeting, so everyone comes at different times and the result is total confusion.

84.2   **Some proverbs are similar in meaning. Which proverbs on the left go with which on the right, and what do they have in common in terms of meaning?**

1. A bird in the hand is worth two in the bush.
2. Don't count your chickens before they're hatched.
3. All that glitters isn't gold.
4. Absence makes the heart grow fonder.

Never judge a book by its cover.

Familiarity breeds contempt.

Never look a gift horse in the mouth.

Don't cross your bridges before you come to them.

84.3   **People often refer to proverbs by saying only half and leaving the rest for the listener to "fill in." Complete the proverbs in these dialogues.**

1. A: Joe is always criticizing people who are stingy, yet he's terribly stingy himself.
   B: Yes, well, people who live in glass houses . . .
   C: Exactly.

2. A: The people in the office have been playing computer games all day since the boss left on vacation.
   B: Well, you know what they say: When the cat's away . . .
   A: Well, they're certainly doing that.

3. A: I didn't believe those rumors about Nick and Sue, but apparently they are seeing each other.
   B: You're too naive; you know what they say, where there's smoke . . .
   A: Mm, I suppose you're right.

Follow-up: **Try translating some proverbs from your language, word for word, into English. Then, if you can, ask native speakers of English if they recognize any English proverb as having the same or similar meaning.**

UNIT 85 Expressions with *do* and *make*

A The next seven units deal with phrasal verbs and other expressions based on common verbs. Phrasal verbs are verbs that can combine with different prepositions (or particles) to make verbs with completely new – and often unguessable – meanings. Phrasal verbs are used more in speaking than in writing.

B Some phrasal verbs with **do** and **make**. (*Note:* s.t. = something.)

Phrasal verb	Meaning	Example
do without	manage without	You'll have to do without a cigarette for a while. Smoking isn't allowed here.
do away with	abolish	Slavery was done away with in the U.S. in the 19th century.
do s.t. over	redo; redecorate	I'm doing my résumé over. It's full of mistakes.
make of	think (opinion)	What do you make of his remarks?
make off	leave hurriedly	She made off as soon as she heard their car turn into the driveway.
make up for	compensate for	The superb food at the hotel made up for the dingy rooms.

C Some phrasal verbs have many different meanings; **do up** can mean not only "fasten" but also "tie" and "put into a bundle." Similarly, **make out** can mean "pretend," "manage to see," "succeed or progress," and "understand" as well as "write" or "complete." **Make up** can mean "compose" or "invent"; it can also mean "constitute" or "form," "put cosmetics on," "prepare by mixing together various ingredients," and "make something complete."

D There are a lot of other common expressions based on **do** and **make**.

You **do:** the housework / the dishes / the laundry / the shopping / the cooking / some gardening / a good job / homework / your best / harm / business with . . . , and so on.

You **make:** arrangements / an agreement / a suggestion / a decision / a cup of coffee or tea / a meal / war / a promise / an attempt / a phone call / the best of . . . / the most of . . . / an effort / an excuse / a living / money / a mistake / a bed / a profit / love / (a) noise / a good or bad impression / a success of . . . / a point of . . . / allowances for . . . / believe . . . / a gesture / a face / fun of . . . / a fuss about . . . / trouble . . . , and so on.

Exercises

85.1 Here are some different ways in which *do up, make up,* and *make out* can be
used. What is the meaning of the phrasal verb in each case?

1. Can you make out that little house in the distance?
2. A human being is made up of many, often conflicting, desires.
3. Would you do up these buttons for me?
4. Those children are always making up silly stories.
5. How are you making out at your new job?
6. I like the way you've done up your hair.
7. I'll make out a check to you and you can cash it.

85.2 Add the necessary prepositions or particles to complete this story.

Last weekend we decided to start doing ...*over*............ (1) our cabin in the country.
We agreed that we could do .... (2) the old fireplace in the bedroom. As
we began to remove it from the wall, we found some old pictures done
.... (3) in a bundle behind a loose brick. At first we could not make
.... (4) what was in the pictures, but we wiped them clean and realized
they all depicted the same young man. We spent an enjoyable evening making
.... (5) stories to explain why the pictures had been hidden.

85.3 Correct the mistakes in the sentences below. Either the wrong preposition/particle
has been used or the word order is wrong.

1. I don't know what to make that statement of.
2. Try to make the most off a bad situation.
3. Your shoelaces are untied. Do up them or you'll trip on them.
4. They like to make away that they are terribly important.

85.4 Write word forks (see Unit 2) to help you learn the meanings of *make up, make
out,* and *do up.*

85.5 Divide the expressions in D opposite into any groups that will help you to learn
them.

85.6 Complete the following sentences using an appropriate expression from D.

1. Hippie posters in the 1960s used to say "MAKE LOVE NOT
   ....!"
2. It doesn't matter if you pass or not as long as you do ....
3. Companies that once made a huge .... are now going
   bankrupt.
4. His spelling isn't very good, but you should make .... the fact
   that he's only seven years old.
5. Dressing well for an interview helps you make ....
6. I don't like doing ...., but someone has to clean, wash, iron,
   and cook!

Expressions with *bring* and *take*

A Here are some common phrasal verbs with **bring**. A more formal equivalent is given in brackets.

I was **brought up** in the country. [raise, rear]
Please don't **bring up** the subject of taxes; you know it annoys me. [introduce]
Don't give up. I'm sure you'll **bring** it **off.** [succeed]
This bad cough was **brought on** by the wet weather. [cause to start]
Technology has **brought about** many changes in the way we live. [cause to happen]
I wish they'd **bring back** the old streetcars. [reintroduce]
This scandal will surely **bring down** the government. [destroy, remove from power]
Several companies are **bringing out** a new line of computers this year. [introduce]
Keep it up and you'll **bring** him **around** to your point of view. [persuade]
The seasoning really **brings out** the flavor of this dish. [reveal or expose]

B Here are some common phrasal verbs with **take**.

He **takes after** his father in more ways than one! [resemble or have similar traits]
I wish I could **take back** what I said to her. [withdraw]
She was completely **taken in** by him. [deceive]
Sales have really **taken off** now. [start to improve]
The plane **took off** right on time. [leave the ground]
We'll have to **take on** more staff if we're going to **take on** more work. [employ; undertake]
I'm **taking** my mother **out** for her birthday. [escort, invite to a restaurant, etc.]
When did you **take up** golf? [start a hobby, etc.]
Our company was **taken over** by a larger company. [take control]

C Here are some other common idioms with **bring** and **take**.

The new regulations will be **brought into force** in May. [become law]
Her research **brought** some very interesting facts **to light.** [reveal]
Matters were **brought to a head** when Pat was fired. [reach a point where changes have to be made]
It's best that everything be **brought out into the open.** [make public]
His new wife has **brought out the best/worst in** him. [be good/bad for him]
Don't let him **take advantage of** you. [use superiority unfairly]
Just because you're having a bad day, don't **take it out on** me! [cause somebody else to suffer because you are angry or unhappy]
I just **took it for granted** that you'd come. [assume]
His words **took my breath away.** [surprise, amaze]
She loves **taking care of** small children. [look after, care for]
We **took part in** a demonstration last Saturday. [participate]
The story **takes place** in Mexico. [happen]
He doesn't seem to **take pride in** his work. [draw satisfaction from]
Mother always **takes** everything **in her stride.** [deal with calmly]

Exercises

86.1 Complete these sentences with the appropriate preposition or particle.

1. They did away with capital punishment years ago, but now they're talking about bringing it ....
2. The long trip brought .... labor, and the baby was born on the bus.
3. Do you think our company will be taken .... by a corporate giant?
4. Maybe you're taking .... more work than you can handle.
5. If anyone can bring it ...., he can.
6. This time it's my treat: I'm taking *you* .... to dinner!
7. She brought .... six children all by herself.

86.2 The diagram below can be called a ripple diagram. Can you complete it?

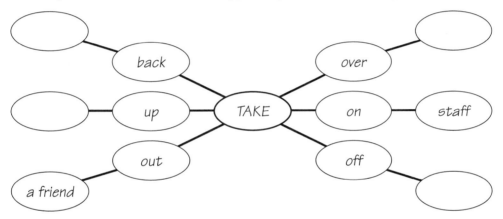

Now make a ripple diagram based on phrasal verbs with *bring*.

86.3 Reply to these questions using one of the phrasal verbs in A or B opposite.

1. What causes your rash?   *It seems to be brought on by strong sunlight.*
2. Who does your little girl resemble?
3. Do you have any special hobbies?
4. How's your new business doing?
5. Do you think you'll manage to persuade him to let you come?
6. Why do you suppose our plane is landing two hours late?
7. What do politicians often promise before an election?

86.4 Reword these sentences using expressions from C opposite.

1. The story of the movie happens in Casablanca during the war.
2. Today's newspaper reveals some fascinating information about the President.
3. How does he always manage to be so calm about things?
4. The view from the top of the hill was astonishing.
5. He capitalized on her weakness at the time and she sold it to him.
6. The main function of a nurse is to care for the sick.
7. Whenever you're upset, you always make the children suffer.

Expressions with *get*

A

Get is used frequently in spoken English. It has the following basic meanings:

- buy, receive, or obtain something, e.g., Please **get** me a newspaper when you're in town. I **got** a letter from John today. She **got** high marks on her exam.
- change one's position – move or be moved, e.g., How are you **getting** home tonight?
- change one's state – become or make, e.g., We are all **getting** older if not wiser.

B

Get also has many other specific meanings.

I don't **get** it. Why did he say that? [understand]
Her behavior really **gets** me sometimes. [annoy, irritate]
I'll **get the phone**. [answer]
Once we **got to know** each other, we were great friends. [gradually begin to know]

C

This table shows just some of the phrasal verbs based on **get**.

Phrasal verb	*Meaning*	*Example*
get along	have a good relationship with	He gets along well with his roommates.
get along	manage	How will we ever get along without you?
get at	reach, find	I hope the investigation will get at the truth.
get away with	do something wrong without being caught	The robbers got away with several thousand dollars.
get behind	fail to produce something at the right time	I've gotten terribly far behind with my work.
get by	manage (financially)	We couldn't get by on my salary alone.
get down	depress	This weather is really getting me down.
get down to	direct your attention to	It's about time we got down to work.
get out of	avoid a responsibility	I'll try to get out of that appointment.
get over	recover from	She's just getting over the flu.
get through	come to a successful end	What a relief that she got through all her exams!
get off	finish, leave	I get off work at 5:00 p.m.

D

Here are some other common expressions based on **get**.

You must have **gotten out of bed on the wrong side** today. [be in a bad mood]
The meeting **got off to a good/bad start** with JR's speech. [start well/badly]
I'm having a little **get-together**. I hope you can come. [informal social gathering]
When we moved, I **got rid of** half the things in the attic. [throw away, destroy]
I'm going to **get back** at her somehow. [take revenge]
After two days of meetings, we've **gotten nowhere**. [make no progress, waste time]

Exercises

87.1 There are a lot of expressions with *get* in the text below. Replace them all with other expressions that mean the same thing. Notice that you will be changing the text from informal to slightly more formal.

I don't get interesting advertising leaflets very often these days. However, an unusual one came this morning. It was headed "Are little things getting you down?" It went on, "If so, get some of our special tablets today. Taking just one in the morning will help you get along well at work, at home, or at school. It will stop the feeling that you're getting nowhere in life and will ensure that you get rich and successful with little effort on your part. Send just $25 today and you will get your tablets and your key to success within ten days."

87.2 Fill in the blanks with words from the opposite page.

1. She got .... all the interviews and was offered the job.
2. You're still sneezing! Haven't you gotten .... that cold yet?
3. We get .... only because we live very economically.
4. He doesn't get .... well with his coworkers. No one likes him very much.
5. It takes time to get to .... your teachers and classmates.

87.3 Match the situations in list A with the appropriate expressions in list B.

A. 1. Someone has been very impolite to one of your friends.
   2. Someone is about to throw something away.
   3. Someone is being negative about everything you suggest.
   4. Someone has done something very cruel to you.
   5. A good friend is leaving.

B. 1. I don't know how we'll get along without you!
   2. Just you wait! I'll get back at you one of these days!
   3. Don't get rid of that yet!
   4. You got out of bed on the wrong side this morning!
   5. Your rudeness really gets me!

87.4 Complete the sentences in any appropriate way.

1. I would hate to get rid of . . .
2. The dinner got off to a bad start when . . .
3. I find it very hard to get down to . . .
4. I wish I could get out of . . .
5. . . . is really getting me down.

87.5 There are many other common phrasal verbs and expressions based on *get* not listed on the opposite page. Write example sentences using any that you can think of.

Expressions with *set* and *put*

A Look at these examples of phrasal verbs based on **set**.

You should **set aside** some money for a rainy day. [reserve]
He tried to **set aside** their differences. [ignore, not think about]
Set back your clock one hour tonight. [fix at an earlier time]
The damage from the fire **set** us **back** more than $10,000. [cost]
The new law **set off** protests throughout the country. [cause, incite]
We should **set out** before dawn to get there on time. [depart, begin a trip]
She **set out** to climb Mount Everest. [begin work with a particular aim in mind]
The bank helps people who want to **set up** a business. [establish]

B Here are some of the many phrasal verbs with **put**.

She's good at **putting** her ideas **across**. [communicate to others]
Please **put away** your toys now. [pick up and put in the right place]
He is always **putting** her **down**. [criticize]
He **put** his own name **forward** to the committee. [propose]
We had a new air conditioning unit **put in** last year. [install]
I'm going to **put in** an application for that job. [submit]
You're **putting** me **on**! [informal: deceive or tease someone as a joke]
They've **put off** making their decision for another week. [postpone]
Your bad attitude really **puts** me **off**. [informal: discourage, irritate; also **turn off**]
He's good at **putting on** all kinds of accents. [pretend to have]
The firefighters quickly **put out** the fire. [extinguish]
Please don't let me **put** you **out**. [inconvenience]
You're not allowed to **put up** posters here. [hang, mount]
I can **put** you **up** for the weekend. [give accommodations to]
His friends **put** him **up** to jumping off the cliff. [instigate, incite]
Why do you **put up with** such rudeness? [tolerate]

C Here are some more expressions with **set**.

He has **set his heart/sights on** becoming a dancer. [longs to become]
Did someone **set fire to** the house / **set** the house **on fire** deliberately? [ignite]
Diane had never **set foot in** Italy before. [been to]
Jill is very **set in her ways**. [fixed in her habits]
Try to **set a good example**. [be a good model for others]

D Notice also the following common expressions with **put**.

to put your foot down: to be firm about something
to put all your eggs in one basket: to risk all you have on a single venture
to put your mind to: to direct all your thoughts toward
to put two and two together: to draw an obvious conclusion
to put in a good word for: to speak favorably on behalf of

Exercises

88.1 Put the following sentences into slightly more formal English by replacing the phrasal verbs with their formal equivalents.

1. They have recently set up a committee on neighborhood crime.
2. We try to set aside some money for our vacation every week.
3. Set aside all your negative feelings and listen with an open mind.
4. If we hadn't set out so late, we would have arrived on time.
5. The President's unpopular proposals set off a wave of protests.
6. When we cross the international date line, should we set our clocks back?

88.2 Write two nouns that could follow each verb. Remember that their meanings might be different depending on the noun that follows.

Example: put in *a good word / an entertainment system*

1. put out
2. put forward
3. put off
4. put across
5. put up
6. put on
7. put away
8. put up with

88.3 Write responses to the following statements or questions using any appropriate phrasal verb from A or B opposite.

Example: How should we publicize our play? *We could put up posters.*

1. That sports car must have cost a fortune.
2. This room is in a terrible mess.
3. Do you have room for one more guest this weekend?
4. Hey, guess what? I won the lottery! I'm rich!
5. What is George planning to do when he gets his business degree?
6. Was it her idea or did the other kids dare her to do it?

88.4 Using the expressions in C and D opposite, reword the following sentences without changing their meaning.

1. He never wants to do anything in a new or different way.
2. He's bound to draw the obvious conclusion if you keep on behaving like that.
3. Her aim is to become president of the company.
4. It's sound business advice not to risk everything at once.
5. Please concentrate on the problem at hand.
6. She threw lighter fluid on the trash and lit a match to it.
7. This is the first time I've ever been to the southern hemisphere.
8. You really should be firm with the children or there'll be trouble later.
9. If the teacher doesn't display good behavior, the children certainly won't behave.
10. Would you mind giving me a recommendation?

88.5 Choose ten of the phrasal verbs and other expressions with *set* and *put* that you particularly want to learn and write them down in example sentences of your own.

Expressions with *come* and *go*

A

Here are some phrasal verbs based on **come**.

I **came across** a beautiful old vase in that junk shop. [found by chance]
Nothing can **come between** him and soccer. [separate; be a barrier between]
How did you **come by** that bruise / that car? [receive, obtain]
Did the meeting you were planning ever **come off**? [take place]
When do the exam results **come out**? [be published, make public]
The stain on the carpet won't **come out**. [be removed]
She was knocked unconscious, but she **came to** quickly. [become conscious]
Your bill **comes to** $55. [amount to, total]
An important point **came up** at the meeting. [was raised]
The movie **comes on** at six. [start to be shown or broadcast]

B

Here are some expressions with **come to** (usually with an idea of arriving at) and **come into** (often with an idea of starting or acquiring).

come to: an agreement / a conclusion / a standstill [stop] / an end / a decision / mind [enter one's thoughts] / blows [start fighting] / terms with [acknowledge and accept psychologically] / one's senses [become sensible again after behaving foolishly]

come into: bloom / blossom / contact / a fortune / money / a legacy / operation [start working] / sight / view / power [a political party or a ruler] / existence / fashion / use

C

Some phrasal verbs based on **go**. Some of them have different meanings.

go on: What is **going on** next door? [happening] They **went on** working despite the noise. [continue] As the weeks **went on,** things improved. [pass] You **go on,** we'll catch up with you later. [go in advance / go ahead]

go through: I wouldn't like to **go through** that again. [experience, endure] Let's **go through** the plans again. [check] Unfortunately, the business deal we were hoping for did not **go through**. [be completed or approved] He **went through** a fortune in one weekend. [spend, use]

go for: He **goes for** older women. [be attracted by] Whichever job you **go for,** I'm sure you'll make the best of it. [choose]

Those shoes don't **go with** that dress. [suit, match]
The alarm **went off** when the burglars tried to open the door. [ring]
She would never **go back on** her word. [break a promise]

D

Here are some expressions based on **go**.

He's been **on the go** all day and he's exhausted. [very busy, on the move]
It **goes without saying** that we'll all support you. [be clear without being said]
Your work is good, **as far as it goes**. [but is limited or insufficient]
I'm sure she'll **go far**. [be very successful]
They **went to great lengths** to keep it a secret. [take a lot of trouble]
Unfortunately, the business **went bankrupt**. [be in a state of financial ruin]

Exercises

89.1 **Which meanings do these underlined verbs have?**

1. He <u>went on</u> composing music until he was in his eighties. *continued*
2. She <u>was so</u> suspicious that she used to <u>go through</u> his pockets every night.
3. She has a new book <u>coming out</u> in June.
4. I was sure he'd <u>go for</u> a sports car.
5. I <u>went through</u> three pairs of pantyhose this weekend.
6. After the surgery, it took the patient several hours to <u>come to</u>.

89.2 **Choose one of the expressions in B opposite to complete each sentence.**

1. I found it hard to make up my mind, but finally I came ....
2. No ideas come ...., but I'll tell you if I think of any.
3. I love it in spring when my cherry tree comes ....
4. Halfway up the hill, the bus came ....
5. All good things must come ....
6. The telephone first came .... in the 19th century.
7. They disagreed so fiercely that they actually came ....
8. As we rounded the corner the house came ....

89.3 **Replace each underlined expression with one of the expressions in D.**

1. <u>I don't need to say</u> that we wish you all the best in the future.
2. They <u>took great pains</u> to avoid meeting each other.
3. I've been <u>moving around</u> all day and now I'm ready to relax.
4. His teachers always said that he would <u>be a success in life</u>.
5. The book is good <u>up to a point</u>, but it doesn't tackle the problem deeply enough.

89.4 **Match the questions on the left with the answers on the right.**

1. Why is she looking so miserable?
2. Did anything new come up at the meeting?
3. When does your alarm clock usually go off?
4. How much does the hotel bill come to?
5. When does the game come on TV tonight?
6. What's going on over there?

Right after the news.
Over $1000!
It's a fight, I think.
Seven-thirty, normally.
The firm went bankrupt.
Only Jack's proposal.

89.5 **Complete the following sentences in any appropriate way.**

1. I came across not only some old letters in the attic . . .
2. Those shoes don't go with . . .
3. I never want to go through . . .
4. The jury came to the conclusion that . . .
5. It is not easy to come to terms with . . .
6. That stain won't come out unless you . . .

Expressions with *look*

A This diagram illustrates some of the most common phrasal verbs formed with **look.** The meaning of the phrasal verb is given in brackets.

look —
- **up to** — She has always **looked up to** her older sister. [respect]
- **into** — The police are **looking into** the case. [investigate]
- **for** — Could you help me **look for** my keys, please? [try to find]
- **back on** — I **look back on** my school days with nostalgia. [recall]
- **up** — **Look** it **up** in the dictionary. [find information in a book]
- **forward to** — I'm **looking forward to** starting work. [expect with pleasure]
- **out** — If you don't **look out,** he'll take your job away. [take care]

B Here are some more useful phrasal verbs based on **look.** They are illustrated below in a business context but they can also, of course, be used in other situations.

Please **look through** the proposal and let me know what you think. [examine]
I've **looked over** your proposal, but I haven't read the fine print. [examine quickly]
Business is **looking up** at last. [starting to improve]
When you're in New York, try to **look up** our representative there. [find and visit]
We are **looking to** the Far East for an increase in sales. [depending on]
The company is **looking ahead** to a bright future. [planning for the future]

C Here are some other useful expressions based on **look.**

Look on the bright side.   **Look me in the eye.**   **Look before you leap.**

Try to **look on the bright side** of things. [be cheerful in spite of difficulties]
He's beginning to **look his age.** [appear as old as he really is]
They're always **on the lookout for** new talent. [search for]
I **don't like the look of** those black clouds. [What I see suggests trouble ahead.]
I know she's hiding something when she won't **look me in the eye.** [look directly at someone without fear or guilt]
She **looks down on / looks down her nose at** anyone who is not good at sports. [regard as unimportant or socially inferior]
It's **not much to look at** but it's comfortable. [not attractive in appearance]
The office has **a new look.** [a fresh and more up-to-date appearance]
Look before you leap. [Think before you act boldly.]
The authorities sometimes **look the other way** when there's corruption. [ignore]
If you ask for a raise, you're just **looking for trouble.** [try to create problems]
He must have been angry. He **looked daggers at me.** [look at someone angrily]

Exercises

90.1 What words do you need to complete the sentences below?

1. I look .... that summer with some regrets.
2. He has great respect for his colleagues, but he doesn't really look ....
.... his boss.
3. You're going to Toronto? Look .... my brother while you're there.
4. A government investigation is looking .... the cause of the plane crash.
5. I'm sorry to hear you lost your job. I hope things will look .... for you
soon.
6. People shouldn't look .... the government to solve all their problems.
7. Look ....! You almost hit that car!

90.2 Match the statements or questions on the left with the responses on the right.

1. Try to look on the bright side.
2. Why don't you think she's honest?
3. I'm on the lookout for a new job.
4. You have a new look!
5. She certainly doesn't look her age.
6. I'm going to use my life savings to start a new company.
7. I think Nick painted graffiti on the walls.
8. Why do you think Mary is angry with you?

You'd better look before you leap.
She looked daggers at me just now.
Maybe. He's always looking for trouble.
It's pretty hard under the circumstances.
Good luck! It's not easy to find work.
She never looks you in the eye.
You'd never think she's a grandmother.
Yes, I've changed my hair style.

90.3 Complete the sentences below in any logical way.

Example: I have to look up   *their number in the phone book.*

1. I'm really looking forward to . . .
2. It's wrong to look down on . . .
3. The book looks back on . . .
4. When I look ahead . . .
5. If you have time, please look over . . .
6. Look us up when . . .

90.4 Replace the more formal underlined expressions with one of the phrasal verbs or other expressions from the opposite page.

1. The garden isn't <u>very attractive</u> now, but it's beautiful in the summer.
2. You'd better <u>be careful</u>, or someone might take advantage of you.
3. Try to <u>remain optimistic</u> if you possibly can.
4. Unfortunately, many people <u>regard</u> the homeless <u>as inferior</u>.
5. Have you had a chance to <u>examine</u> the job applications?
6. She didn't want to get involved, so she <u>ignored the situation</u>.

90.5 Write three nouns that might come after each of the phrasal verbs below.

1. look for   2. look up   3. look through   4. look up to

Miscellaneous expressions

This unit looks at more verbs that form the basis of idioms. Remember that these lists are not complete: English has many more phrasal verbs and expressions for each verb.

A   ## See

I'd better **see about/to** arrangements for the conference. [deal with, attend to]
They went to **see** Jim **off** at the airport. [say goodbye at an airport, station, etc.]
It's easy to **see through** his behavior. [not be deceived by]
I must be **seeing things.** [having hallucinations]
They **don't** always **see eye to eye.** [often disagree]
Pat has been **seeing someone** for a few months. [dating, having a romance]

B   ## Run

I **ran into** an old friend yesterday. [met unexpectedly]
Her patience has **run out.** [come to an end]
Let's **run over/through** the plans again. [review, rehearse]
Red hair **runs in my family.** [a characteristic that appears in many family members]
She **runs** the business. [manage / have overall responsibility for]

C   ## Turn

There was a very large **turnout** at the concert. [number of people who came]
She **turned down** the job offer. [refuse]
Who do you think **turned up** last night? [make an (unexpected) appearance]
I'm going to **turn over a new leaf** this year. [start again, with good intentions]
It's your turn to do the laundry. [It's your duty because I did it last time.]
It's late. I think I'll **turn in.** [go to bed]

D   ## Let

He has been **let down** so many times in the past. [disappointed]
He won't **let us in on** the plan. [tell something secret]
I hope the rain **lets up** soon. [becomes less strong]
Let go of the rope. [stop holding]
Please **let me be.** [stop bothering me]
She **let it slip** that she had been given a pay raise. [mentioned accidentally, casually]

E   ## Break

The car **broke down** again this morning. [stop working]
They have **broken off** their engagement, so there won't be a wedding. [end]
Burglars **broke into** our house while we were on vacation. [forcibly enter]
He has **broken her heart.** [make someone deeply unhappy]
The athlete **broke the record** for the 1000 meters. [be faster, higher, more successful, than anything before]

Exercises

91.1 Use the expressions on the opposite page to help you fill in the blanks in the text below. Use only one word in each blank.

Let's run .... (1) the plans for tomorrow's party one more time. First, I have to see .... (2) the food arrangements while you make sure that none of the equipment is likely to break .... (3). I don't suppose many people will turn .... (4) until later, but Nick and Jill promised to come early to help us. I'm sure they won't let us .... (5), even though Jill let it .... (6) the other day that they are thinking of breaking .... (7) their engagement.

91.2 Rewrite the following using the words in parentheses.

1. Why does she let herself be deceived by him? (see)
2. I met Jack by chance at the library yesterday. (run)
3. I cooked dinner yesterday. It's up to you to do it today. (turn)
4. I thought I was hallucinating when I saw a monkey in the garden. (see)
5. I wish you'd stop bothering me. (let)
6. When she left him, he was utterly miserable. (break)

91.3 Complete the sentences in an appropriate way.

1. If the snow doesn't let up soon, . . .
2. Halfway up the mountain, he let go . . .
3. Although the turnout for the meeting was not large, . . .
4. He felt terribly let down when . . .
5. She didn't turn up . . .
6. I'm afraid we've run out of . . .

91.4 Answer the questions.

1. Have you ever turned down an offer or invitation that you later regretted?
2. Have you ever had problems because of something (a vehicle or a piece of equipment, perhaps) breaking down at an inconvenient time? What happened?
3. Is there someone you don't see eye to eye with? Why not?
4. Is there a skill, quality, or physical trait that runs in your family?
5. Have you ever resolved to turn over a new leaf? In what way(s)?
6. Do you have any particular errands or chores to see to today? If so, what?
7. Has your home ever been broken into? What happened?
8. What time do you usually turn in?

91.5 The expressions opposite are only some of many expressions using these five verbs. Can you think of two other phrasal verbs or other idiomatic expressions using each of the five verbs? If you can't, try to find them in a dictionary.

Headline English

A

Newspaper headlines try to catch the reader's eye by using as few words as possible. The language headlines use is, consequently, unusual in a number of ways.

- Grammar words, such as articles or auxiliary verbs, are often left out, e.g.:
  EARLY CUT FORECAST IN INTEREST RATES
- A simple form of the verb is used, e.g.: MAYOR OPENS HOSPITAL
- The infinitive is used to describe something that is going to happen in the future, e.g.: PRESIDENT TO VISIT FLOOD AREA

B

Newspaper headlines use a lot of distinctive vocabulary. They usually prefer words that are shorter and sound more dramatic than ordinary English words. The words marked * can be used either as nouns or verbs.

Newspaper word	Meaning	Newspaper word	Meaning
aid*	help	key	essential, vital
ax*	cut, remove	link*	connection
back	support	loom	is likely to happen
bar*	exclude, forbid	move*	step toward a desired end
bid*	attempt	O.K.*	approve, endorse
blast*	explode, criticize	ordeal	painful experience
blaze*	fire	oust	push out
boost*	incentive, encourage	pact	agreement
boss* } head*	manager, director	plea	request
		pledge*	promise
clash*	dispute	poll*	election; public opinion survey
combat*	fight		
curb*	restraint, limit	probe*	investigation
cut*	reduction	quit	leave, resign
deny	contradict	seek	look for, pursue
drive*	campaign, effort	talks	discussions
go-ahead, nod	approval	threat	danger
		vow*	promise
hike*	increase	wed	marry

Newspaper headlines often use abbreviations, e.g., **Gov't** for Government, **House** for United States House of Representatives, **FDA** for Food and Drug Administration. (See Unit 98 for more abbreviations.)

C

Some newspapers enjoy making jokes in their headlines by playing with words or punning, as in this headline about a new treatment for colds:

> **CAN WE STOP SNIFFLES? GET ON YOUR SNEEZE AND SPRAY**

This is a play on the expression "Get on your knees and pray."

Exercises

92.1 Match the headlines on the left with the appropriate topics on the right.

1. FDA OKS HIV HOME SCREENING
2. STUDENTS BLAST MOVE TO OUST TEACHER
3. FAT LINKED TO HEART DISEASE
4. STAR WEDS SECRETLY
5. SPACE PROBE FAILS
6. MIDDAY NAPS GET THE NOD FROM RESEARCHERS, WORKERS

exploratory spacecraft is not launched
marriage of a famous person
new medical test for home use
work dispute at a school
study involving work and sleep
research about diet and health

92.2 Explain what the following headlines mean in ordinary English.

Example: STORE BLAZE – 5 DEAD   *Five people died in a fire in a store.*

1. MOVE TO CREATE MORE JOBS
2. GO-AHEAD FOR WATER CURBS
3. MAN QUITS AFTER JOB ORDEAL
4. POLL PROBES SPENDING HABITS
5. ELECTRIC COMPANY SEEKS RATE HIKE

92.3 The words marked * in B opposite can be either nouns or verbs. Note that the meaning given is sometimes in the form of a noun. The headlines below contain words from the table used as verbs. Look at the underlined verbs and explain what they mean. You may need to use more than one word.

Example: CITY TO CURB SPENDING   *limit*

1. GOV'T TO PROBE AIRLINE SAFETY
2. BOMB BLASTS BUILDING
3. MAYOR PLEDGES HOMELESS AID
4. PRESIDENT HEADS PEACE TALKS
5. TRADE PACT BOOSTS EXPORTS

92.4 Would you be interested in the stories under these headlines? Why (not)?

WOMEN BARRED FROM JOBS

New threat from vampire snakes

MAYOR DENIES DRUG USE

Bargain airfares boost tourism

Infectious disease crisis looms

Poll: Fewer single moms want to wed

92.5 Look through some English language newspapers and find some examples of headlines illustrating the points made on the opposite page. Beside each headline make a note of what the accompanying story is about. Try to find some examples of amusing headlines.

American English and British English

A

British English differs considerably from English in the U.S. Pronunciation is the most striking difference, but there are also a number of differences in vocabulary and spelling as well as slight differences in grammar. Yet on the whole, speakers of American and British English have little or no difficulty understanding each other.

B

British English words ending in **-our**, **-re**, and **-ise** usually end in **-or**, **-er**, and **-ize** in American English, e.g., colour/color, centre/center, criticise/criticize.

C

Here are some common American English words and their British English equivalents.

Travel and on the street		In the home	
American English	*British English*	*American English*	*British English*
gasoline	petrol	antenna	aerial
truck	lorry	elevator	lift
sidewalk	pavement	eraser	rubber
crosswalk	zebra crossing	apartment	flat
line	queue	apartment building	block of flats
vacation	holiday	closet	wardrobe
national holiday	bank holiday	to call (by telephone)	to ring
parking lot	car park	faucet	tap
trunk (of car)	boot	kerosene	paraffin
hood (of car)	bonnet	Scotch/adhesive tape	Sellotape
freeway/highway	motorway	cookie	biscuit
round trip	return	candy	sweets
one-way	single	garbage	rubbish
engineer (on train)	engine driver	diaper	nappy
subway	underground	pantyhose	tights
baby carriage	pram	flashlight	torch
shopping bag	carrier bag	bathroom	toilet, WC

D

Here are some words and phrases that can cause confusion because they mean something different in American English and British English.

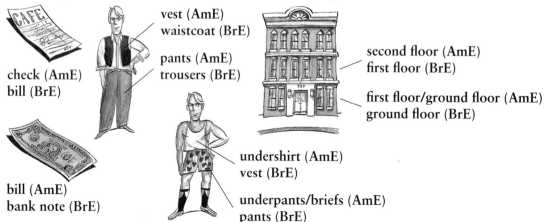

check (AmE)
bill (BrE)

vest (AmE)
waistcoat (BrE)

pants (AmE)
trousers (BrE)

second floor (AmE)
first floor (BrE)

first floor/ground floor (AmE)
ground floor (BrE)

undershirt (AmE)
vest (BrE)

bill (AmE)
bank note (BrE)

underpants/briefs (AmE)
pants (BrE)

Exercises

93.1 If you saw words spelled in the following way, would you expect the writer in each case to be a speaker of British English or American English? Why?

1. labor
2. centre
3. realize
4. movie theater
5. neighbour
6. industrialise

93.2 What are (a) the American and (b) the British words for the following things?

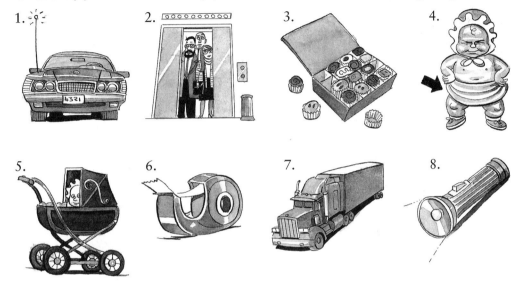

1.
2.
3.
4.
5.
6.
7.
8.

93.3 Translate the following into British English.

1. Let's take the subway.
2. Please pass the cookies.
3. It's in the closet.
4. We've run out of gas.
5. I'll call you tonight.
6. It's in the trunk.
7. I hate waiting in line.
8. One-way or round-trip?
9. He left the faucet on.
10. Excuse me, where's the bathroom?

93.4 Can you avoid some common confusions arising between British English and American English? Try the following quiz.

1. Which would surprise you more – an American or a British man telling you that he wanted to go and change his pants?
2. You have just walked into an office building. If the office you need is on the second floor, how many flights of stairs do you need to climb (a) in the U.K.? (b) in the U.S.?
3. If a British English speaker asks for a bill, is that person more likely to be in a bank or a cafe?
4. Would a man wear a vest over or under his shirt (a) in the U.S.? (b) in the U.K.?

93.5 Do you know any other examples of differences between American English and British English? Make a list in your vocabulary notebook or file.

(See also Unit 94 for English in different parts of the world.)

Varieties of English

Unit 93 explored some differences between American English and British English. This unit gives you just a small taste of some of the many other varieties of English used in different English-speaking regions. You may come across many of the words covered in this unit in your own reading, listening, or viewing.

A

In Canada, the two official languages are English and French. Canadian English has a great deal in common with American English, although it is sometimes similar to British English, especially in spelling. There are also many words and expressions that are unique to Canadian English.

Some distinctive Canadian words are **Mountie** for a member of the Royal Canadian Mounted Police, **chesterfield** for sofa or couch, **riding** for a political constituency, **reeve** for mayor, **first nations** for indigenous peoples, and **loonie** (informal) for the Canadian one-dollar coin with an image of a loon on one side. The terms **Anglophone/Francophone** (a person who speaks English/French), borrowed from French, are common. Canadian English spellings are sometimes the same as in American

English, e.g., **tire, radio program,** compared with the British **tyre, radio programme.** In other cases Canadian spellings are the same as in British English, e.g., **centre, colour,** compared with the American English **center, color.** However, there is variation among Canadians on such spellings.

B

Australian English is particularly interesting for its rich store of highly colloquial words and expressions. Australian colloquialisms often involve shortening a word. Sometimes the ending **-ie, -o,** or **-oh** is then added, e.g., a **truckie** is a truck driver, and a **milko** delivers the milk; **beaut,** short for *beautiful,* means "great," and **biggie** is "a big one." **Oz** is short for Australia, and an **Aussie** is an Australian. **G'day** (short for *Good day*) is a common greeting, pronounced guh-DAY /gəˈdeɪ/, with the first syllable said very quickly.

C

Indian English, on the other hand, is characterized by sounding more formal than other varieties of English. It has retained in everyday usage words that are found more in the classics of 19-century literature than in contemporary TV programs, e.g., The **bereaved** are **condoled** and the Prime Minister is **felicitated** on his or her birthday. An Indian might complain of a pain in his **bosom** (rather than his chest), and an Indian thief or bandit is referred to as a **miscreant.**

D

Scottish English uses a number of special dialect words.

aye: yes	**loch:** lake	**lassie:** girl
ben: mountain	**bonny:** beautiful	**kirk:** church
glen: valley	**wee:** small	**dram:** drink (usually whiskey)

Exercises

94.1   Make changes to these sentences so they are more typical of Canadian English.

1. We were driving down the Trans Canada when we saw a Royal Canadian Mounted Police officer in the rear view mirror.
2. Let's meet at the Eaton Center.
3. Most of the residents in this city are speakers of French.
4. All I've got is a one-dollar coin.

94.2   What do you think these examples of Australian colloquialisms mean? They are all formed by abbreviating an English word that you probably know.

1. She wants to be a <u>journo</u> when she leaves <u>uni</u>.
2. He's planning to do a bit of farming <u>bizzo</u> while he's in the States.
3. What are you doing this <u>arvo</u>?
4. We decided to have a party, as the <u>oldies</u> had gone away for the weekend.
5. Where did you go when you were in <u>Oz</u>?

94.3   Match the Indian English word on the left with its American English equivalent on the right.

1. undertrials	someone with extreme views
2. wearunders	have no children
3. issueless	underwear
4. Eve-teaser	the general public
5. the common man	people awaiting trial
6. ultra	man who annoys women

94.4   The statements below were made by a Scot. Answer the questions about them.

1. Mary had a bonny wee lassie last night.
   What happened to Mary yesterday?
2. They live next to the kirk.
   What would you look out for if you were trying to find their house?
3. "Are you coming, Jim?"   "Aye."
   Is Jim coming or isn't he?
4. They have a wonderful view of the loch from their window.
   What can they see from the window?

94.5   Which variety of English might each of these statements or questions represent? Write each one differently.

1. Would you like a wee dram?
2. We got terribly bitten by mozzies at yesterday's barbie.
3. That's a nice chesterfield.
4. The police nabbed the miscreant.

95 Computers and the Internet

Nowadays computers are everywhere. Even people who don't own or operate computers are exposed to computer terminology. This unit explores some of the most common words and expressions associated with computers and the Internet.

A   **Personal computers**

Review Unit 52, section B, which has an illustration of a personal computer. Here are some other words associated with personal computers.

personal computer / PC / desktop computer: a computer that fits on a desk, used by individuals at work or at home

laptop (computer): a lightweight portable computer that usually fits in a briefcase

computer hardware: computer equipment or machinery

computer software: programs that you put into a computer to make it run

floppy (disk) / diskette: a small plastic disk that stores (a limited amount of) information. A floppy can be inserted into a computer and taken out.

hard disk: a device inside a computer that stores large amounts of information

disk drive: an apparatus that allows information to be read from a disk or stored

modem: a piece of equipment that sends information from one computer along telephone lines to another computer

to download: to transfer data or software from a large computer to a smaller one

RAM / random access memory / memory: the memory available on a computer to store and use information temporarily, usually measured in **megabytes**

spreadsheet (program): a program or the grid you create with it to perform mathematical operations

computer graphics: pictures, images, and symbols that you can form on a computer

word processing: a program for writing and storing printed text on a computer

computer virus: hidden instructions in a program designed to destroy information

B   **The Internet**

The **Internet / "the net"** is a network connecting millions of computer users worldwide. You can **access** information on the Internet or send and receive **electronic mail / e-mail** from a computer, through a modem. Here is a small sampling of the many other words and expressions associated with the Internet.

to surf/cruise the net: to navigate around the Internet, sometimes aimlessly

World Wide Web / "the Web": a huge portion of the Internet containing linked documents, called **pages**

home page: a document on the Web giving information about a person or institution

newsgroup: a meeting place on the Internet for discussion of a particular topic

newbie: someone who is new to computers, to the Internet, or to a particular part of it

to flame: to post e-mail or other messages intended to insult or provoke another user

FAQ: "frequently asked questions," a list of common questions and helpful answers

IMHO: "in my humble opinion," a phrase used in e-mail and other postings

(See Unit 52 on technology, Unit 98 on abbreviations, and Unit 99 on new words.)

Exercises

95.1 Match the words to the pictures below.

floppy disk drive   modem   spreadsheet   laptop   desktop computer

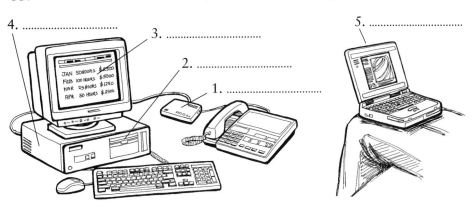

95.2 Fill in the blanks with appropriate words from the opposite page.

1. It's so easy to use a word .... program for writing letters and documents. But I still use a typewriter for envelopes and labels.
2. I've lost a lot of data on my computer. I wonder if my computer has a
   ....
3. I'm always amazed by people who carry their .... on airplanes and work on them during the flight.
4. Those .... disks don't store nearly enough information. You really need a .... disk for all the data you want to store.
5. If you need to look up statistics, you could try .... the Internet. You never know what you might find!
6. A: Can I ask you for some help getting on to the Internet? I'm a
   ....
   B: Sure, but why don't you look at this .... list first?
7. My sister is away at college, but we're constantly in touch by
   ....
8. You can contact the publisher of this book through their .... on the Web.

95.3 On the left are some common abbreviations used by people on the Internet. Try and match them with the phrases they stand for, on the right.

1. IMHO   Are you there?
2. BTW   rolling on the floor laughing
3. RU there?   in my humble opinion
4. LOL   laughing out loud
5. ROTFL   ta-ta for now (= goodbye)
6. TTFN   by the way

95.4 Do you use a computer regularly? If so, what are some advantages of using a PC? If you have access to the Internet, what do you use it for?

The language of signs and notices

Signs and notices in English often use words and expressions that are rarely seen in other contexts. Look at the signs and notices below with their "translations" into more everyday English.

No trespassing or soliciting. Violators will be prosecuted.

1. If you walk on this private property, ask for things (especially money), or try to sell things, you may be taken to court.

Feeding the animals strictly prohibited

2. You are not allowed to feed the animals.

Reduced speed ahead

3. Start driving more slowly soon.

Limit: 5 garments per customer

4. You may not take more than five pieces of clothing in (to the fitting room).

POST NO BILLS

5. You may not put up any posters or signs here.

PLEASE DEPOSIT REFUSE IN PROPER RECEPTACLES

6. Please put trash in the trash container or bin.

Valid ID required for the purchase of alcohol

7. To buy alcoholic drinks, you must have identification showing you are legally old enough.

MEMBERS MUST PRESENT MEMBERSHIP CARD AT RECEPTION

8. You must show your membership card at the reception desk.

RUMMAGING IN TRASH BINS STRICTLY PROHIBITED

9. You must not search through trash bins.

Reserved parking. Violators subject to tow away at vehicle owner's expense.

10. You may not park without permission. If you do, your car might be towed away and you must pay for the towing.

NO Bicycles Skateboards Rollerblades Playing ball
Monetary fine will be imposed.

11. You may not use bicycles, skateboards, or Rollerblades, or play ball here. If you do, you must pay money as a penalty.

Federal law prohibits tampering with, disabling, or destroying any smoke detector in any aircraft lavatory.

12. On an airplane, you may not touch the smoke detector in the bathroom/lavatory.

(See Unit 49 for examples of a specific kind of sign, road signs. See also Unit 7.)

Exercises

96.1 Where would you expect to see each of the notices on the opposite page?

Example: 1. *near private homes, apartments, or businesses*

96.2 Match the words on the left with their more everyday translations on the right.

1. to prosecute	money paid as a punishment
2. a receptacle	someone who disobeys the rules/law
3. a trespasser	to bring a legal case against
4. monetary fine	to damage, misuse, or alter something improperly
5. to solicit	a means of transportation, such as a car
6. to prohibit	to search through something, moving the contents about
7. a violator	a container, can, or bin
8. to tamper	to forbid something
9. a vehicle	someone who goes on private property without permission
10. to rummage	to ask for something (usually money) or try to do business

96.3 Explain these signs and notices in simpler language. Where would you expect to see each of them?

1.

NOTHING TO DECLARE

2.

Any spectator throwing objects onto the playing field will be ejected.

3.

Warning: Drinking alcoholic beverages during pregnancy can cause birth defects.

4.

All sales final

5.

UNLAWFUL TO LITTER CITY STREETS

6.

RIGHT LANE ENDS. MERGE LEFT.

7.

Shoplifters will be prosecuted to the full extent of the law.

8.

Spanish spoken here

9.

NO VACANCIES

96.4 What signs would a store manager put up in order to . . .

1. let customers know that the staff can speak Portuguese?
2. ask people not to put notices on the walls?
3. warn people not to come into the store to ask for money or do other business?

96.5 Sometimes signs have a humorous or ironic tone, rather than a formal one. What do these signs mean and where might you see them?

1. **If you break it, you've bought it.**

2. **Don't even think about parking here.**

Words and gender

In this unit we examine ways of avoiding sexist, or gender-biased, language.

A   ## Words and expressions with *-man*

Some words contain the generic **man** even though they refer to both sexes. Below are some suggestions for replacing such words.

Traditional word/expression	Possible substitute
man, mankind	human being(s), human(s), humanity, people, individuals
manpower	work force, staff
to man	to staff
man-made	synthetic, artificial, manufactured
workingman	worker, wage earner
man in the street	average/typical/ordinary person

B   ## *-man*, *-woman*, and *-person*

Here are some neutral words to replace traditional job titles and roles marked for gender by **-man, -woman,** or **-ess.** Sometimes, however, there is no neutral word (e.g., **fisherman**).

Neutral	Traditional male	Traditional female
chair(person)	chairman	chairwoman
police officer	policeman	policewoman
mail/letter carrier	mailman/postman	–
businessperson, executive	businessman	businesswoman
firefighter	fireman	–
flight attendant	steward	stewardess
salesperson, sales representative	salesman	saleswoman
worker	workman	–
camera operator	cameraman	–
crew member	crewman	–

C   ## Social marking of roles

Some words, particularly the names of jobs, are "socially marked" as belonging to one gender, even though the words are neutral in form. For example, **nurse** has been thought of as "female" for so long that if a nurse is a man, some people say **male nurse.** Try to avoid using **girl, woman, lady, male,** etc., before the names of jobs, e.g., **male nurse, woman doctor, female taxi driver, male secretary,** etc. In general, these modifiers give the impression that there is something strange about one gender having this particular job or role.

Exercises

97.1 Look at this rather sexist advertisement for an airline. Change the wording to make it more neutral.

> **Now Eagle Airlines offers even more to the businessman who needs comfort!**
>
> Let us fly you to your destination in first-class comfort, served by the best-trained stewardesses in the world. Successful businessmen know that they must arrive fresh and ready for work no matter how long the journey. With Eagle Diplomat-Class you can do just that. And, what's more, your wife can travel with you on all international flights for half the regular fare! Your secretary can book you on any of our flights 24 hours a day at 800-555-1234. All she has to do is pick up the phone.

97.2 Many people consider some of the words below sexist. Match these words with their neutral alternatives.

man hours	cleaner	unmanned
unstaffed	human beings	ancestors
forefathers	supervisor	person hours
cleaning lady	mankind	foreman

97.3 Change gender-marked words into neutral ones.

1. We'll have to elect a new chairman next month.
2. Several firemen and policemen were hurt in the riots.
3. The airline reports that its stewardesses are on strike.
4. I wonder what time the mailman comes every day.
5. Is this fabric natural or man-made?
6. Her brother's a male nurse, and she's a lady doctor.
7. TV news reporters and cameramen rushed to the scene of the accident.
8. The candidate appeals to big business, but what about the workingman?
9. A salesman for the company will stop by and leave samples.
10. This radio program likes to conduct man-in-the-street interviews.

97.4 Here are more names of occupations. Which ones are marked for gender by the word itself? Are any of them "socially marked" as typically male or female? How are they translated into your language: by neutral or by gender-marked words?

1. barber	7. detective
2. secretary	8. monk
3. farmer	9. waitress
4. dressmaker	10. burglar
5. hairdresser	11. butcher
6. weatherman	12. truck driver

UNIT 98 Abbreviations and acronyms

A Some abbreviations are read as individual letters, usually representing the initials, or first letters, of each word.

ID	identification
INS	Immigration & Naturalization Service
R&D	research & development
UN	United Nations
ATM	automated teller machine
IRS	Internal Revenue Service
VCR	videocassette recorder
CIA	Central Intelligence Agency

B Some abbreviations are read as words; we call them **acronyms.**

NATO	North Atlantic Treaty Organization
OPEC	Organization of Petroleum Exporting Countries
AIDS	Acquired Immune Deficiency Syndrome

Some acronyms have become so normal as words that people do not think of them as abbreviations any longer, and so they are not written all in capital letters.

radar [radio detecting and ranging]   **yuppie** [young urban professional]
laser [light wave amplification by simulated emission of radiation]

C Some abbreviations are written forms only; they are spoken as the full word.

Mr. (Mister)   Dr. (Doctor)   St. (Saint or Street)   Rd. (Road)

D Abbreviations are used in the organization of language.

etc. and so on [Latin: et cetera]   **i.e.** that is to say [Latin: id est]
N.B. please note [Latin: nota bene]   **e.g.** for example [Latin: exempli gratia]
RSVP please reply [French: répondez s'il vous plaît]   **FYI** for your information

E Clippings: Some words are normally used in a shortened form, especially in informal situations. (See also Unit 7.)

lab (laboratory)   **phone** (telephone)   **typo** (typographical error)
dorm (dormitory)   **memo** (memorandum)   **fax** (facsimile)
exam (examination)   **plane** (airplane)   **rep** (business representative)

F Some abbreviations you might see on a letter/fax/envelope

c/o care of [e.g., S. Park, c/o J. Brown; the letter goes to J. Brown's address]
P.S. postscript [extra message after the letter has been ended]
ASAP as soon as possible [e.g., call me ASAP]   **P.O. Box** [post office box]
cc carbon copy [shows that someone other than the addressee receives a copy]
enc. enclosed [e.g., enc. application form]
a.m. before noon [Latin: ante meridiem]

(See also Unit 95 for abbreviations used with computers and the Internet.)

Exercises

98.1 What things in these addresses are normally abbreviated? How is *Ms.* pronounced in the second address?

1.
```
Mister Henry Chen
Post Office Box 202X
Saint Louis, Missouri
United States of America
```

2.
*Ms. Maria Howard
care of T. Rivera
430 Yonge Street
Apartment 5
Toronto, Ontario
Canada*

3.
N. Lowe and Company
7, Bridge Road
Freeminster
United Kingdom

98.2 Match these abbreviations with their meanings and then put them into groups as in A to F opposite.

1. BA	extension
2. FBI	condominium
3. Prof.	Federal Bureau of Investigation
4. PIN	self-contained underwater breathing apparatus
5. TOEFL	United Nations Educational, Scientific, and Cultural Organization
6. TBA	Bachelor of Arts
7. ext.	personal identification number (on a bank card, for example)
8. UNESCO	Professor
9. condo	Test of English as a Foreign Language
10. scuba	to be announced

98.3 "Translate" this note from the boss to the workers in an office into full words.

```
Memo from: Mr. Braneless         Date: 3/24
To: all staff
cc: C. Hothead, Supply Dept.     Re: lab equipment

All new lab equipment should be registered with the Supply Dept.,
Rm. 354 (ext. 2683). N.B.: New items must be registered before
5 p.m. on the last day of the month of purchase, i.e., within
the current budgeting month. All a/c nos. must be recorded.
```

98.4 Explain 1–6 and match them with the contexts on the right.

1. Speed limit 50 mph	on an aerosol can
2. Size: XL	on an invitation
3. UFOs sighted in desert	on an airline schedule or ticket
4. Ozone-friendly: CFC-free	on a clothing label
5. Dep. 3:00 p.m. Arr. 5:42 p.m.	on a road sign
6. RSVP	in a newspaper headline

New words in English

No language stands still. New words and expressions are always being created, usually because something new is invented or sometimes just for fun. Below are some relatively new words and expressions and new uses of old words. Note that all of these words had been in use for at least a few years before publication of this book.

A Science and technology

cyberspace: the realm where electronic data are stored or transmitted by computers

information superhighway: a giant communications network of computers with interactive services, e-mail, text databases, audio, and video

voice mail: an interactive computerized telephone system that stores spoken messages and notifies users when they have messages to play back

sound bite: a brief excerpt from a speech or statement, used in broadcast news

caller ID: a telephone service that identifies the caller before the call is answered

ozone hole: a part of the ozone layer that becomes depleted by pollution, thereby allowing harmful radiation to enter the earth's atmosphere

DNA fingerprinting: the use of genetic material (DNA) to identify an individual

B Health and medicine

managed care: a plan providing comprehensive health services at reduced costs

repetitive strain injury (RSI): soreness, numbness, and pain (usually) in the hand, wrist, or arm caused by repeated movement, e.g., keyboarding

eating disorder: a serious disturbance in eating habits, often from emotional causes

safe sex: sexual activity with precautions to prevent contracting disease (e.g., AIDS)

attention deficit disorder (ADD): an illness characterized by inattention and hyperactivity

C Entertainment and sports

karaoke: singing pop songs solo to recorded music

Tejano: a style of Mexican-American popular music

shock jock: a radio announcer who uses controversial and/or vulgar language

audio book: an audio recording of a book read aloud, sometimes in shortened form

snowboarding: gliding on snow by standing upright on a large single ski

D Employment, fashion, and social trends

telecommuting: working from home, communicating with the office by computer

downsizing: reducing the size of a company/organization, usually by firing people

outsourcing: hiring nonunion, outside workers for performing labor away from the company site

family leave: time that an employee takes off in order to care for family members

drop-dead: inspiring admiration, e.g., drop-dead good looks

Generation X: people born in the U.S. from the mid-1960s to the mid-1970s

bad hair day: a day when everything goes wrong and when one feels unattractive

(See Unit 95 for words and expressions associated with computers and the Internet.)

Exercises

99.1 Here are some more words and expressions that are fairly new. Match them with their definitions. Note that some of these are informal.

1. wannabee *(infml)*   waiter or waitress
2. in-line skate   ordinary mail sent through the postal service
3. to channel-surf   to insult or show disrespect for someone
4. waitperson   a pill that's a tablet, but shaped like an oval capsule
5. to chill (out) *(infml)*   someone who aspires/wants to be something/someone else
6. snail mail   to switch TV channels/stations frequently, usually with
7. caplet   a remote control
8. to dis *(infml)*   a roller skate / Rollerblade with rubber wheels in a
        straight line
        to calm down

99.2 Fill in the blanks with words from the opposite page or from 99.1.

1. It is said that some cases of skin cancer are caused by ....
2. He lost his job of 20 years when the company began ....
3. .... sounds dangerous to me. I'll stick with regular skiing.
4. They say that in the next few years more and more people will start .... It should certainly ease traffic during the rush hours.
5. I can't stand listening to .... on the radio – they're so offensive.
6. Many politicians try to include some effective .... in their speeches.
7. She's a .... pilot. She would love to fly a plane herself.
8. There's no rush. I'll send you the report by .... rather than faxing it.
9. Using the computer so much at work has given me .... That's why I'm wearing this bandage on my wrist.
10. Thursday is .... night at the club. Everyone gets up and takes turns singing shamelessly! It's great fun.
11. Hey, you don't have to shout like that. Why don't you just .... ?
12. Here's a telephone number if you want to leave me a .... message.
13. Nick is taking a month off work for .... He's taking care of his father, who is very ill.
14. Sometimes soldiers killed in combat are identified through ....
15. I like to listen to an .... while I'm driving. It's almost like reading!

99.3 If you meet a new word, it may be possible to figure out its meaning from context. Practice by explaining what the underlined words might mean.

1. This area attracts quite a few ecotourists, who come to watch the wildlife.
2. They're a blended family. He has two children from a previous marriage, and she has one child from her first marriage.
3. When you're communicating on the Internet, it's considered bad netiquette to use all capital letters because it looks as if you're shouting.
4. You don't have to pay anything for this computer program. It's freeware.
5. She has cyberphobia. She refuses to go near a computer.

Discourse markers

A

Discourse markers are small words and phrases whose job is to organize, comment on, or in some way frame what we are saying or writing. A common everyday example is the use of **well** in speech:

A: So you live in Boston?
B: **Well,** near Boston.

Well here shows that A is not completely in agreement with B. In other words, **well** is a comment on what is being said.

B

Common markers to organize different stages of talk

Now, what should we do next?   **So,** what was it you wanted to talk about?
OK/Good, I'll call you on Sunday.   **Fine/Great,** let's leave it at that, OK?

C

In these mini-dialogues, the markers in bold modify or comment on what is being said.

A: So how do you like the new boss?
B: **To tell you the truth / To be honest,** I don't like her at all!
[softening a negative idea]

A: What's her number?
B: **Let me see / Let's see,** I have it here somewhere . . .
[a hesitation – gaining time]

A: It's cold, isn't it?
B: Yeah.
A: **Then again,** it *is* November, so it's not surprising.
[an afterthought – however]

A: And he said he was go-
B: **Well,** that's just like him!
A: **Hold on! / Wait a minute!** Let me tell you what he said!
[preventing an interruption]

D

Common markers in written English for organizing a formal text

First / First of all, we must consider . . . } for lists
Next, it is important to remember that . . .
Finally/Last, we should look at . . . [*Note:* not "At last"]
In summary, we can say that . . . [summing up the main points]
In conclusion, I would like to say that . . . [finishing the text]

E

Markers for explaining, rephrasing, etc., in speech and writing

Memorizing words requires reinforcement; **in other words / that is to say,** you have to study the same words over and over again.
Some words are hard to say, **for example / for instance,** "eighth."
She is, **as it were / so to speak,** living in a world of her own. [makes what you are saying sound less definite/precise]

Exercises

100.1 Underline the discourse markers in this monologue. Not all of them are on the opposite page.

> "Well, where shall I start? It was last summer and we were just sitting in the yard, not doing anything much. Anyway, I looked up and . . . see, we have this kind of long wall at the end of the yard, and it's . . . like . . . a highway for cats, for instance, that big fat black one you saw. Well, that one thinks it has a right of way over our vegetable patch, so . . . where was I? Oh, yeah, I was looking at that wall, you know, daydreaming as usual, and all of a sudden there was this new cat I'd never seen before, or rather, it wasn't an ordinary cat at all . . . I mean, you'll never believe what it was . . ."

100.2 Here are some small dialogues that use no markers at all, which would be unusual in actual informal talk. Add markers from the opposite page where you think the speakers might use them.

1. A: Are you a baseball fan?
   B: I like it, but I wouldn't say I'm exactly a fan.

2. A: He looks exhausted.
   B: Yes, he does.
   A: He has an awful lot of responsibility, so it's not surprising.

3. A: Which one is yours?
   B: *(pause)* . . . it's this one here, yes, this one.

4. A: Are you looking forward to your camping trip next month?
   B: I'm dreading it. I really hate camping.

100.3 Fill in the blanks with markers often found in written texts. You may need some markers that are not on the opposite page. The first letter of each phrase/word is given.

> ### *Crime and Punishment*
>
> F......... .... (1), it is important to understand why people commit crimes. I... .... (2), what are the motives that make people do things they would never normally do? F........ .... (3), a young man steals clothes from a shop; is it because he is unemployed? a drug addict? mentally disturbed? N............................... (4) it is essential to consider whether punishment makes any difference, or is it just, s...... .... (5), a kind of revenge? F............................... (6), how can we help the victims of crime? I...... .... (7), how can we get to the roots of the problem, rather than just attacking the symptoms?

Follow-up: If you can, make a recording of a natural conversation between English speakers (get their permission, but don't say why you need it). What markers do they use?

Pronunciation symbols

/ ... /	Pronunciations are shown between slashes in the International Phonetic Alphabet (IPA).
/ ' /	Primary stress: A raised stress mark appears before the syllable of a word with the strongest stress.
/ ˌ /	Secondary stress: A lowered stress mark appears before a stressed syllable with less than primary stress.
/ · /	A raised dot separates syllables as an aid to pronunciation.
/ (...) /	Parentheses enclose sounds that may or may not be heard in any given utterance of the word.

Vowel sounds

/ə/	*in unstressed syllables:* alone, sofa, label, habit, connect, suppose
	in stressed syllables: sun, glove, under
	In North American English the stressed and unstressed vowels in these words are similar in quality.
/ər/	*in unstressed syllables:* under, advisor, solar
	in stressed syllables: bird, fur, earn, sunburn
	An /r/ noticeably changes the sound of a preceding /ə/.
/i/	feet, sea, gladly
/ɪ/	fit, bid
/eɪ/	fate, bay
/e/	bet, bed
/æ/	bat, ban
/ɑ/	hot, bond, barn
/ɔ/	bought, saw, author
/oʊ/	go, boat, know
/ʊ/	put, good
/u/	blue, boot, shoe, lose
/aɪ/	bite, ride, height, sky
/aʊ/	house, now
/ɔɪ/	boy, join

Consonant sounds

/b/	bid, robe
/d/	did, ladder
/ð/	this, bother, breathe
/dʒ/	judge, gentle
/f/	foot, safe
/g/	go, rug
/h/	house, behind, whole
/j/	yes, onion
/k/	kick, cook
/l/	look, ball, feel, pool
/ᵊl/	settle, middle – *a syllabic consonant*
/m/	many, some
/n/	none, sunny, sent
/ᵊn/	kitten, button, botany – *a syllabic consonant*
/ŋ/	ring, think, longer
/p/	peel, soap, pepper
/r/	read, carry, far, card – *In some regions of North America, -r is not always pronounced at the end of words or before other consonants.*
/θ/	think, both
/s/	see, mouse, recent
/ʃ/	shoe, ash, nation
/t/	team, meet, sent
/t̬/	meeting, matter – *In North American speech, -t- or -tt- is usually voiced between vowels; the result is similar to /d/, but /t/ is also correct.*
/tʃ/	church, rich, catch
/v/	visit, save
/w/	watch, away, witch
/(h)w/	which, where – *Many North American speakers pronounce /hw/ in such words, and many pronounce /w/.*
/z/	zoo, has, these
/ʒ/	measure, beige, azure

Index

*The numbers in the index are **Unit** numbers, not page numbers.*

rep /rɛp/ 98
repair /rɪˈper/ 40
repel /rɪˈpɛl/ 35, 69
repetitive strain injury [RSI] 99
replace /rɪˈpleɪs/ 9 (~ment) 8, 11
reporter /rɪˈpɔrt̬·ər/ 29, 40
representation /ˌrɛp·rɪ·ˌzenˈteɪ·ʃən/ 54
representative /ˌrɛp·rɪˈzent·ət̬·ɪv/ 54
repress /rɪˈprɛs/ 10
reprint (v.) /riˈprɪnt/, (n.) /ˈriˌprɪnt/ 18
reptile /ˈrɛpˌtaɪl/ 1
republic /rɪˈpʌb·lɪk/ 44
repulsive /rɪˈpʌl·sɪv/ 69
require /rɪˈkwaɪr/ 60, 96 (~ment) 21
reread /riˈrid/ 9
rescue worker /ˈrɛsˌkju ˌwər·kər/ 29
research /rɪˈsərtʃ/ 26
research & development [R&D] 98
resentful /rɪˈzent·fəl/ 11
reservation /ˌrɛz·ər·ˈveɪ·ʃən/ 3, 50
reserved /rɪˈzərvd/ 96
residence /ˈrɛz·əd·ən(t)s/ 7
resign /rɪˈzaɪn/ 40
resolution /ˌrɛz·əˈlu·ʃən/ 25
resort /rɪˈzɔrt/ 50
respect /rɪˈspɛkt/ 10, 35
response /rɪˈspɑn(t)s/ 25
responsible /rɪˈspɑn(t)·sə·bəl/ 9
rest and recreation [R&R] 77
restaurant /ˈrɛs·t(ə·)rənt/ 45
result (in) /rɪˈzʌlt/ 22
résumé /ˈrɛz·əˌmeɪ/ 16
retirement /rɪˈtaɪr·mənt/ 11
return /rɪˈtərn/ 93
retype /riˈtaɪp/ 9
reverse /rɪˈvərs/ 23
revert /rɪˈvərt/ 10
review /rɪˈvju/ 2, 39, 42
revolt /rɪˈvoʊlt/ 69
revolution /ˌrɛv·əˈlu·ʃən/ (~ize) 54 (~ary) 54, 67
rewind /riˈwaɪnd/ 9
reword /riˈwərd/ 4
rheumatism /ˈru·məˌtɪz·əm/ 48
ribbon /ˈrɪb·ən/ 47
ribs /rɪbz/ 43
rice /raɪs/ 26, 43
ride /raɪd/ 2 (riding) 94
ridge /rɪdʒ/ 44
right /raɪt/ 19, 96
right angle /raɪt ˈæŋ·gəl/ (~d) 51
right-wing /raɪtˈwɪŋ/ 67
ring /rɪŋ/ 41, 93
rink /rɪŋk/ 41
rip /rɪp/ 37; expression with: ~ someone off 83

rip-off /ˈrɪpˌɔf/ 83
rise and shine 83
river /ˈrɪv·ər/ 44
road /roʊd/ 44, 49
Road [Rd.] /roʊd/ 98
roar /roʊr/ 61, 73
roast /roʊst/ 43
roast beef /roʊs(t) ˈbif/ 43
rob /rɑb/ (~ber, ~bery) 55
rocky /ˈrɑk·i/ 44
rod /rɑd/ 41
roll /roʊl/ 66
Rollerblade /ˈroʊ·lərˌbleɪd/ 96, 99
rolling on the floor laughing [ROTFL] 95
romance /roʊˈmæn(t)s/ 35
romantic /roʊˈmænt·ɪk/ 70
romp /rɑmp/ 73
roof /ruf/ 36
room /rum/ 50
roommate /ˈrumˌmeɪt/ 35
room service /ˈrum ˌsər·vəs/ 50
rooster /ˈru·stər/ 73
root /rut/ 4, 46
rosemary /ˈroʊzˌmer·i/ 43
rosy-cheeked /ˈroʊ·ziˈtʃikt/ 12
ROTFL 95
rough /ˈrəf/ 18, 64
rough and ready 74
round trip /raʊn(d) ˈtrɪp/ 93
round-faced /ˈraʊn(d)ˈfeɪst/ 33
route /rut/ 18
rowboat /ˈroʊˌboʊt/ 49
rowing /ˈroʊ·ɪŋ/ 41
royal /ˈrɔɪ·əl/ 1
RSI 99
RSVP 98
rub /ˈrəb/ 48
rubber /ˈrəb·ər/ 93
rubbish /ˈrəb·ɪʃ/ 93
rudder /ˈrəd·ər/ 49
rude /rud/ 34
ruined /ˈru·ənd/ 57
rumble /ˈrəm·bəl/ 30, 61, 72
rummage /ˈrəm·ɪdʒ/ 96
run /ˈrən/ 41, 49, 54, 58, 63, 91; expressions with: ~ in one's family 91; ~ into 91; ~ out 37, 91; ~ over 91; ~ through 91
run down (v.) /ˌrən ˈdaʊn/ 81; run-down (adj.) /ˈrənˌdaʊn/ 12
runner /ˈrən·ər/ 41
runway /ˈrənˌweɪ/ 49
rural /ˈrʊr·əl/ 3
rush /ˈrəʃ/ 63
rustle /ˈrəs·əl/ 61
RU there? 95
RV 49

sack /sæk/ 66
sadistic /səˈdɪs·tɪk/ 34
sadly /ˈsæd·li/ 70
sadness /ˈsæd·nəs/ 8
safe and sound 77
safe sex /ˈseɪf ˈsɛks/ 99
sage /seɪdʒ/ 43
sail /seɪl/ 19, 49, 63 (~or) 8
Saint [St.] /seɪnt/ 98
salad dressing /ˈsæl·əd ˈdres·ɪŋ/ 43
salary /ˈsæl·(ə·)ri/ 56
sale /seɪl/ 19, 96
sales /seɪlz/ (~man, ~person, ~woman) 97
sales representative /ˈseɪlz ˌrep·rɪˌzent·ət·ɪv/ 97
sales tax /ˈseɪlz ˌtæks/ 56
salmon /ˈsæm·ən/ 18, 43
salsa /ˈsɔl·sə/ 43
salt /sɔlt/ 28, 43 (~y) 43, 71
sand /sænd/ 18, 66 (~y) 44
sardines /sɑrˈdinz/ 43
satellite dish /ˈsæt̬·ᵊlˌaɪt ˈdɪʃ/ 53
satin /ˈsæt̬·ᵊn/ 15, 47
satisfaction /ˌsæt̬·əsˈfæk·ʃən/ 11
sauna /ˈsɔ·nə/ 16
sauté /sɔˈteɪ/ 16, 43
savings account /ˈseɪ·vɪŋz əˌkaʊnt/ 56
savings & loan 56
saxophone /ˈsæk·səˌfoʊn/ 15
scales /skeɪlz/ 46
scallops /ˈskɑl·əps/ 43
scalpel /ˈskæl·pəl/ 48
Scandinavia /ˌskæn·dəˈneɪ·vi·ə/ 31
scarcity /ˈsker·sət̬·i/ 8
scared stiff 79
scaredy cat /ˈskerd·i ˌkæt/ 81
scare out of one's wits 79
scene /sin/ 19, 42
scent /sent/ 19 (~ed) 71
schedule /ˈskedʒ·əl/ 49
scholarship /ˈskɑl·ərˌʃɪp/ 39
school /skul/ 2, 29, 39, 45
school bus /ˈskul ˌbəs/ 2
science /ˈsaɪ·ən(t)s/ 18, 52
science fiction /ˌsaɪ·ən(t)s ˈfɪk·ʃən/ 13
scientific /ˌsaɪ·ənˈtɪf·ɪk/ 52
scientist /ˈsaɪ·ən·təst/ 29
scissors /ˈsɪz·ərz/ 1, 27
scorching /ˈskɔr·tʃɪŋ/ 32
score /skoʊr/ 39
Scotch tape /ˈskɑtʃ ˈteɪp/ 93
scream /skrim/ 70
screech /skritʃ/ 61
screwdriver /ˈskruˌdraɪ·vər/ 2
scruffy /ˈskrəf·i/ 33

Proverbs

Absence makes the heart grow fonder. *84*
All that glitters isn't gold. *84*
Don't count your chickens before they're hatched. *84*
Don't cross your bridges before you come to them. *84*
Don't put all your eggs in one basket. *84*
Familiarity breeds contempt. *84*
Half a loaf is better than none. *84*
Never judge a book by its cover. *84*
Never look a gift horse in the mouth. *84*
Nothing succeeds like success. *65*
One swallow doesn't make a summer. *84*
People who live in glass houses shouldn't throw stones. *84*
Success has a thousand parents. Failure is always an orphan. *65*
Too many cooks spoil the broth. *84*
When the cat's away, the mice will play. *84*
Where there's smoke, there's fire. *84*
You can lead a horse to water, but you can't make it drink. *84*

Answer Key

Many of your answers will depend on your own particular interests and needs. In some cases the Answer Key can suggest answers only.

Unit 1

A 1. d   2. b   3. a

B 1. *Some possible answers:*

  a) a **chilly** day
  b) to **dissuade** someone from doing something
  c) **up to my neck** in work
  d) **independent** of someone / an **independent** country
  e) **get married** to someone

  2. a) **scissors** – used only in plural; if you want to count **scissors,** you have to say, e.g., **two pairs of scissors.**
  b) **weather** – uncountable
  c) **teach, taught, taught; teach** someone to do something; **teach** someone French.
  d) **advice** – uncountable; a piece of **advice;** verb = to advise (regular)
  e) **lose, lost, lost**
  f) **pants** – used only in plural; if you want to count **pants** you have to say, e.g., **three pairs of pants.**

  3. a) The **b** in **comb** is silent, as it is in **tomb** and **lamb** too.
  b) The final **e** in **catastrophe** is pronounced as a syllable, as it is in **apostrophe. Catastrophe** has four syllables. (See Index for pronunciation.)
  c) The stress is on the first syllable in **photograph,** and on the second syllable in **photography.** The "rule" is that the stress in long words in English frequently falls on the third syllable from the end of the word.
  d) The **w** in **answer** is silent, so the last syllable sounds like **sir.**

D The picture is a good clue to help you understand **tortoise.** You may recognize the word **shell** in **shelled** (as in **eggshell,** for example). Similarly, your knowledge of **life** and **long** together with the context should enable you to figure out what **life span** and **longevity** mean. The whole context of the sentence should help you to figure out the meaning of **tended.** Some of the underlined words may be similar to words in your own language, which can be another useful way of working out the meaning of a word you have not seen before.

Unit 2

A 1. *Possible words to add:* **purr, scratch, tail, claw,** and **whiskers**

  2. a) **Child, tooth,** and **foot** are all words with irregular plurals (**children, teeth, feet**). You could add more examples, e.g., **mouse (mice); goose (geese); ox (oxen or ox); deer (deer); phenomenon (phenomena).**
  b) **Cut, split,** and **put** are all irregular verbs whose three basic forms and pronunciations are identical to each other (i.e., **cut, cut, cut; split, split, split;** and **put, put, put**). You could add **burst, hurt,** and **set** to this group.
  c) **Information, furniture,** and **luggage** are all uncountable nouns. You could add **milk, money,** and **work** to this group.

  3. *Possible words and expressions to add:* **pricey, underpriced, price tag; to lend someone a hand, a handful, a handbag, underhanded.**

B *Possible pictures to help remember vocabulary:*

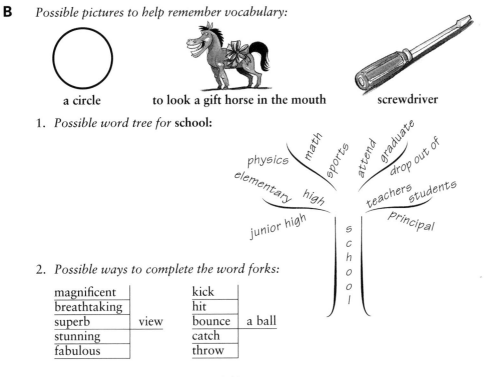

a circle   to look a gift horse in the mouth   screwdriver

1. *Possible word tree for* **school:**

physics · math · sports · attend · graduate · drop out of
elementary · high · teachers · students
junior high · principal
s c h o o l

2. *Possible ways to complete the word forks:*

magnificent			kick	
breathtaking			hit	
superb	view		bounce	a ball
stunning			catch	
fabulous			throw	

3. a) drove   b) flown   c) Riding

Unit 3

3.1 The list is probably connected to a lesson or text about time. A possible organization might include bringing the **clock** words together in a word map or bubble diagram (**clock, wristwatch, hands, minute hand**); other words could then be added later (**hour hand, face/dial, digital,** etc.).

Tell the time and What time is it? could form a separate list of time phrases, to which others could be added, e.g., **Do you have the time? My watch is fast/slow.** etc. **Drowsy** and **wide awake** could be treated as antonyms, and some notes about the usage of **beneath, under,** and **next to** would be useful. The list could have information about word classes (noun, preposition, etc.) too.

3.2 **Theater** seems to be the obvious word.

3.3 Other testing systems include reentering any word you have trouble remembering, so that it appears more than once in the notebook. Another useful discipline is to set yourself a small, fixed number of words to memorize each week (e.g., 15–20) and to check them off in the book as you memorize them. You could also take any ten words from your book and put them on individual slips of paper or Post-It notes that you attach to furniture around your room or house (e.g., on the refrigerator door), so that you look at them frequently.

3.4

Noun	Verb	Adjective	Person
production	produce	productive	producer
industry	industrialize	industrial	industrialist
export	export	export	exporter

Unit 4

4.1   *Possible answers:*

1. styles   slang   association
2. be   have   refer
3. informal   colloquial   suitable

4. extremely   mainly   frequently
5. of   for   in

4.2   Obviously your answers here depend on how you answered 4.1. If you chose the same words as we did, then your answers to 4.2 will be as follows:

styles *C*   slang *UC*   association *C*
be *IR, IT*   have *IR, T*   refer *R, T*

4.3

Verb	Infinitive	-ing form	Past participle
define	to define	defining	defined
mean	to mean	meaning	meant
write	to write	writing	written

4.4
1. root – *form*; prefix – *in*; suffix – *al*
2. formal
3. unofficial, relaxed, casual (e.g., casual clothes)
4. *possible answers:* form, formality, formalize, formless, deform, reform, reformation, etc.

4.5   syllable   colloquial   pejorative   collocation   period   comma   semicolon
apostrophe (note that there are four syllables)   hyphen   exclamation point
question mark   parentheses   quotation marks   capital letter

4.6   1. terrorist   2. skinny   3. wordy   4. stingy   5. cunning   6. smug

4.7   *Some possible answers:*

night and day   by chance; take a chance; given the chance; on the off chance
ladies and gentlemen   savings bank; savings account; savings bond; savings and loan

4.8   ( ) parentheses   ? question mark   ' apostrophe
; semicolon   – dash   - hyphen
, comma   " " quotation marks   ! exclamation point

Unit 5

5.2   2. slide (1)   5. piece of paper (4)
3. escape (7)   6. mistake (5)
4. get worse (3)

5.3   1. education; **ca,** the third syllable, is stressed
2. passport; **pass,** the first syllable, is stressed
3. length; only one syllable in the word
4. liberty; **lib,** the first syllable, is stressed
5. revision; **vi,** the second syllable, is stressed
6. brother; **bro,** the first syllable, is stressed

5.4   In the right-hand definition of **hairy**, synonyms are **frightening, dangerous,** and **exciting.**

There is no key for Unit 6.

Unit 7

7.1   1. **snooze** – a light sleep or nap / to sleep or to take a nap
2. **a guy** – a man
3. **a pal** – a friend
4. **a nerd** – someone who is boring and awkward, sometimes intelligent
5. **brainy** – smart/intelligent/intellectual
6. **a cop** – a police officer

7.2   *Suggested changes:*

JIM: Ann, can you lend me fifty **bucks?**
ANN: What for?
JIM: To pay the rent on my **apartment** (or **place**).

MOM: Where's today's **paper?**
DAD: Mary might have it. She was looking at the **ads.**
MOM: Well, where is she?
DAD: In her room, talking on the **phone.**

7.3   1. In this situation, **residence** is too formal. A classmate would probably say: "Should we go to your **place** or mine?"
2. **Offspring** would be too formal for this situation; **children** (neutral) or **kids** (informal) would be the normal words. **Offspring** would be suitable for legal contexts, religious language, serious history books, and scholarly books/articles.
3. Acceptable. People who work together or share an institutional context (such as universities and colleges) often develop a high degree of acceptable informality. In such institutional settings, clipped words and other short forms are widely used by everyone and operate as a sort of slang among the people involved, and are not heard as disrespectful.
4. The use of **kids** here sounds out of place compared with the formal tone of the rest of the letter, so it is too informal; **children** would be the preferred word. Over the phone, however, the same person might say, "Let me tell you about our new clothes for kids" in order to create a friendly relationship with the customer.

7.4   1. permitted
2. a) to regret   b) designated
3. Hi! Bye!

7.5   *Suggested answers:*
1. It's a way of saying "You must pay your bill today" or "Don't leave without paying." You might see this sign in a doctor's or dentist's office.
2. It means an airline (or carrier) can refuse to let a passenger get on a plane if the airline believes the passenger got the ticket illegally. This is a standard notice in the fine print of airline tickets.

Unit 8

8.1   1. windshield wiper(s)   3. professional photographer   5. hair dryer/drier
2. classical pianist   4. employee   6. organ donor

8.2   1. stapler   2. coffee grinder   3. can opener   4. calculator

8.4   1. **a typewriter** – a thing [machine for typing]; the person is a **typist**.
2. **a cleaner** – can be a person or a thing; e.g., a person who cleans in an office or a substance/instrument for cleaning ("This cleaner will get the grease off your oven").

3. **a CD player** – a thing [machine for playing compact discs].
4. **a dishwasher** – can be a person or a thing; a person who washes dishes, e.g., in a restaurant, or a machine that washes dishes.
5. **a singer** – a person who sings.

8.5 1. forgivable   2. admission   3. laziness   4. productive

8.7 1. **neighborhood** – it is a place (an area); all the others refer to human relationships.
2. **compliment** – all the others are verb + **ment,** e.g., **appoint** + **ment.** There is no verb *compli.*
3. **handful** – all the others are adjectives; **handful** is a noun, meaning a pile of something about as big as you can hold in one hand, e.g., a handful of sand.
4. **worship** – all the others are kinds of human relationships; **worship** refers to paying tribute to God, or, figuratively, as a verb, loving someone very very much, e.g., "He worships his parents." In addition, all the others are noun + **ship.** There is no noun *wor.*

Unit 9

9.1 1. indiscreet   3. unconvincing   5. inefficient   7. ungrateful
2. insensitive   4. irrelevant   6. irresponsible   8. disloyal

9.2 1. Inedible   2. Illiterate   3. Unemployed   4. Misspelled

9.3 1. disagree   2. disprove   3. unveiled   4. unload   5. disconnected

9.4 1. microwave   2. antibiotic   3. multinational   4. postgraduate   5. subway

9.5 1. are overworked and underpaid   4. rewrite it
2. postdated his check   5. misstated the facts
3. her ex-husband

9.6 There are many possibilities. Here are some examples:

Prefix	Examples
anti	antibusiness antiseptic
auto	autonomy automated
bi	biped bifocals
ex	ex-partner ex-employee
ex	express extort
micro	microchip microcosm
mis	mistrust mislead
mono	monorail monosyllabic
multi	multicultural multilateral
over	overrun overcharge
post	postcolonial postindustrial
pre	pre-Columbian prehistoric
pro	pro-life pronuclear
pseudo	pseudoclassic pseudoscientific
re	rephrase redefine
semi	semiliterate semiconscious
sub	sublet subterranean
under	underachieve underweight

Unit 10

10.1 The stress is on the underlined syllable in each of the words in the table.

Verb	Person noun	Adjective	Abstract noun
con<u>vert</u>	<u>con</u>vert	con<u>ver</u>ted	con<u>ver</u>sion
pro<u>duce</u>	pro<u>du</u>cer	pro<u>duc</u>tive	pro<u>duc</u>tion, <u>pro</u>duce, <u>prod</u>uct, produc<u>tiv</u>ity
<u>con</u>duct	con<u>duc</u>tor	con<u>du</u>cive	<u>con</u>duct, con<u>duc</u>tion
im<u>press</u>	–	im<u>pres</u>sive	im<u>pres</u>sion
sup<u>port</u>	sup<u>por</u>ter	sup<u>por</u>tive	sup<u>port</u>
im<u>pose</u>	–	im<u>pos</u>ing	impo<u>si</u>tion

10.2
1. was deported
2. advertisements
3. introduce
4. introductory
5. inspect
6. composed

10.3
1. It isn't easy to find synonyms for these words; the meaning is as follows: "She spends a lot of time thinking about her own thoughts and feelings; he's shy and quiet and not very talkative."
2. argue against
3. hold back
4. figure out based on the information available
5. made public
6. hold down, prevent

10.4 *Some possibilities:*

spect – circumspect behavior; a retrospective exhibition; a fresh perspective
vert – an extroverted person; covert operations; a perverted sense of humor
port – a hotel porter; reported speech; a portable television
duc, duct – to reduce taxes, to induce labor; induction into the hall of fame
press – blood pressure; compressed air; an original expression
pose, pone – to pose for a photograph; to suppose something to be true; exposure to sunlight

10.5
support – hold up
postpone – put off
oppose – go against
inspect – look at
deposit – put down
reduce – cut down
divert – turn away

The two-word verbs are more informal; you would expect to find them more in spoken English than in academic writing, for example.

Unit 11

11.1
1. kindness
2. security
3. sensitivity
4. friendliness
5. amusement
6. grace
7. originality
8. stupidity
9. attentiveness
10. excitement
11. popularity
12. weakness
13. equality
14. hope
15. resentment
16. wisdom

11.2
1. to collect
2. to empty
3. to satisfy
4. to intensify
5. to strengthen
6. to bore
7. to act
8. to excite
9. to produce
10. to own
11. to imagine
12. to adjust

11.3   *Some possible answers:*

There are many more possibilities for the B suffixes but not many for the C suffixes.

B **-ment** (un)employment entertainment involvement requirement
  -ion attraction direction diversion rejection
  -ness awkwardness foolishness loneliness madness
  -ity brutality familiarity productivity superiority
C **-ship** citizenship sponsorship championship
  -dom officialdom
  -th growth wealth stealth
  -hood falsehood nationhood

11.4
1. amazement
2. curiosity
3. brotherhood
4. chance
5. replacement
6. stardom
7. reduction
8. neighborhood
9. sight
10. freedom
11. rage (*or* anger)
12. prosperity

11.5
1. darkness
2. advice
3. injustice
4. Imitation
5. kingdom

11.6   How you answer this question is a matter of your own originality. Here are some quotations about these abstract nouns, however:
1. "Freedom is an indivisible word. If we want to enjoy it, and to fight for it, we must be prepared to extend it to everyone."
2. "Friendship is unnecessary, like philosophy, like art . . . It has no survival value; rather it is one of those things that gives value to survival."
3. "Life is a foreign language; all mispronounce it."
4. "Four be the things I'd be better without: Love, curiosity, freckles and doubt."
5. "Where there is no imagination, there is no horror."

Unit 12

When you are looking up compound adjectives in the dictionary, you may sometimes find the word listed under its second part rather than its first. Sometimes the word will not be listed at all if the meaning is absolutely clear from an understanding of the two parts.

If you are not sure whether a compound adjective is one word, two words, or hyphenated, check a dictionary. Be aware, however, that dictionaries sometimes differ, e.g., **absentminded** in one dictionary, but **absent-minded** in another.

Notice that the descriptions of Tom and Melissa on the left-hand page are lighthearted and far-fetched! They are not examples of good style – such long lists of adjectives would be inappropriate in a normal composition.

12.1   *Some possible answers:*

1. brown-eyed
   bright-eyed
   wide-eyed
2. foolproof
   waterproof
   fireproof
3. open-minded
   narrow-minded
   single-minded
4. blond-haired
   short-haired
   wavy-haired
5. custom-made
   ready-made
   factory-made
6. tax-free
   fat-free
   worry-free
7. hotheaded
   lightheaded
   baldheaded
8. coldhearted
   hardhearted
   brokenhearted

12.2   Here is one possible way of categorizing the words. There will be many other ways of categorizing them. What is important is not how you categorize them but the *process* of doing the exercise. The process should help you to learn the words.

Words connected with money: duty-free, interest-free

Words connected with comfort, safety, and convenience: air-conditioned, bulletproof, drip-dry, handmade, sugar-free

Words connected with time: last-minute, longstanding, off-peak, part-time, time-consuming

Words often connected with traveling: first-class, long-distance, off-peak

Odd ones out: so-called and top-secret!

12.3 *Some examples:*

self-assured *P*   self-confident *P*   self-conscious *N*   self-destructive *N*

self-effacing *N*   self-employed *neutral*   self-evident *neutral*   self-indulgent *N*

self-possessed *P*   self-satisfied *N*   self-seeking *N*   self-sufficient *P* or *neutral*

12.4 1. No, farsighted.   3. No, flat heeled / low heeled.
2. No, handmade.   4. No, loose-fitting.

12.5 *Some possible answers:*

air-conditioned car/movie	long-distance call/runner
bulletproof car/vest	longstanding arrangement/relationship
drip-dry shirt/sheets	off-peak travel/hours
duty-free perfume/liquor	part-time work/job
first-class ticket/letter	so-called expert/specialist
handmade clothes/jewelry	sugar-free diet/cola
interest-free credit/loan	time-consuming work/preparations
last-minute decision/arrival	top-secret information/file

12.6 1. up   2. on   3. back   4. of   5. out

Unit 13

13.1 Here are words that would fit appropriately into the networks.

Money	Health	Social issues
burglar alarm	headache	air-traffic control
credit card	heart attack	death penalty
bank account	blood donor	generation gap
income tax	birth control	greenhouse effect
mail order	family planning	labor force
pocket money	junk food	global warming
luxury goods	blood pressure	brain drain
	food poisoning	public works
	hay fever	race relations
		human rights
		birth control
		family planning
		grass roots
		mother tongue

13.2 Blood pressure and blood donor; air-traffic control and birth control.

Some possible answers:

1. junk mail   4. teapot   7. sales tax
2. computer program   5. identification card   8. food processor
3. blood test   6. word processing   9. checking account

13.3　1. answering machine *or* burglar alarm　5. death penalty
　　　2. greenhouse effect *or* global warming　6. credit card
　　　3. hay fever　7. handcuffs
　　　4. air-traffic control　8. mail order

13.4　*Suggested sentences:*
　　　1. "I get an enormous amount in the mail these days." (junk mail)
　　　2. "I use a lot of these to run my computer." (computer program)
　　　3. "It's usually required that couples take this before getting married." (blood test)
　　　4. "A nice big ceramic one brews nicely." (teapot)
　　　5. "You need to show one if you want to pay by check." (identification card)
　　　6. "It is so much more efficient than using a typewriter." (word processing)
　　　7. "Things are already so expensive, and then we have to add this on." (sales tax)
　　　8. "This is really convenient for chopping vegetables." (food processor)
　　　9. "There's usually not much money left in it by the end of the month." (checking account)

Unit 14

14.1　1. leaving the ground (of an aircraft)　4. test performance
　　　2. burglaries　5. robbery
　　　3. attempt to conceal information　6. escape

14.2　*Some possible answers:*
　　　1. nervous breakdown　4. retail outlets
　　　2. computer printout (*or* input, output)　5. positive feedback (*or* outlook)
　　　3. final outcome (*or* output)　6. drastic cutbacks (*or* layoffs, downturn)

14.3　1. takeover　3. checkout　5. BREAKOUT
　　　2. shakeup　4. feedback; input　6. pinups

14.4　1. write-off　3. workout; push-ups　5. holdup
　　　2. handouts　4. cleanup　6. turnout

14.5　1. **Outlook** means prospect or expectation; **lookout** is a person watching out for an enemy or danger.
　　　2. **Setup** means a plan or project; **upset** means disturbance.
　　　3. **Outbreak** means a sudden appearance (e.g., of war, disease); **breakout** means escape (e.g., from prison)
　　　4. **Outlay** means amount of money spent on something; **layout** means the way something is arranged, e.g., the **layout** of a page or a room.

Unit 15

15.2　*Possible answers:*
　　　inventions network:　Braille　saxophone　watt
　　　politics network:　boycott　Machiavellian　pamphlet　(**chauvinist** might fit here too)

15.3　1. saxophone　2. bedlam　3. boycott　4. cashmere　5. Spartan

15.4　*Some possible answers:*
　　　1. political, promotional　3. black, lycra
　　　2. trusted, great　4. male, ethnic

15.5　1. denim jeans/jacket　3. Spartan furnishings/atmosphere
　　　2. Machiavellian scheme/cunning　4. tweed jacket/pants

15.6   *Some possible endings for the sentences:*
1. . . . it was getting cooler.
2. . . . the company's products.
3. . . . is most addictive.
4. . . . by cowboys in the Southwestern U.S.
5. . . . ham.

15.7
1. A **Herculean** effort is a major effort, one that demands a lot of strength. The word **Herculean** comes from the name of the mythical Greek hero Hercules, who was famed for his strength.

2. A **platonic** friendship is one between a man and a woman based on affection but with no sexual element (from the name of the Greek philosopher Plato).

3. A **teddy bear,** the name given to the soft stuffed bear which is a popular child's toy, comes from Theodore Roosevelt, who was President of the U.S. from 1901 to 1909. A hunter of bears, Roosevelt was once said to have saved a young bear cub. The story was illustrated by a cartoon in the *Washington Post,* in which the toy bears were named Teddy, a nickname for Theodore.

4. A **jersey,** meaning sweater or close-fitting top, comes from the name of one of the Channel Islands, Jersey, well known for its knitting.

5. **Cesarean** section is a surgical operation in order to remove a baby from its mother's womb. The name originates from the name of the Roman Emperor Julius Caesar, who was reputedly born in this way.

6. **July,** the month, is also named after Julius Caesar.

7. A bottle of **champagne** is named after Champagne, the region of France where this particular type of sparkling wine is produced.

8. An **atlas,** or book of maps, is named after the Greek mythological Titan named Atlas, who as a punishment for attempting to overthrow Zeus was condemned to support the world on his shoulders. One of the first atlases, produced by Mercator in the late 16th century, had a picture of Atlas on its cover.

9. **Quixotic** comes from the hero of Cervantes' novel *Don Quixote de la Mancha.* Like Don Quixote, a quixotic person is overly romantic and foolishly impractical, especially when pursuing ideals.

Unit 16

16.3   *Some words that fit most obviously into the networks:*

Food	Politics	The arts	Sports
carafe	coup	avant-garde	judo
cuisine	embargo	ballerina	karate
delicatessen	guerrilla	drama	kayak
frankfurter	junta	easel	kung fu
hamburger	ombudsman	origami	lasso
kumquat	tsar	piano	ski
marmalade		soprano	slalom
molasses		waltz	snorkel
sauté			yacht
spaghetti			
tea			
yogurt			

16.4 *Other networks could include:*

Clothes: anorak shawl caftan pajamas dungarees boutique taffeta bazaar
Things in a house: futon mattress alcove carafe patio balcony
Animals: mosquito poodle dachshund mammoth lemming jackal
    hippopotamus cobra
Geographical features: fjord tundra steppe landscape

16.5
2. prima ballerina
3. strawberry yogurt
4. clinical psychology
5. Chinese cuisine
6. noisy kindergarten
7. total embargo
8. longstanding vendetta

16.6
1. guitar – Spanish
2. garage – French
3. guru – Indian
4. litchi – Chinese
5. intelligentsia – Russian
6. coffee – Turkish
7. haiku – Japanese
8. anonymous – Greek
9. taboo – Polynesian

Unit 17

17.2 *Some possible answers:*

cl: **clap** or **clatter;** both represent fairly sharp sounds. **To clap** is to applaud with your hands. **To clatter** is to make a long, continuous resounding noise, like hard metallic things falling on a hard surface.

gr: **gripe** and **grudge;** both have unpleasant meanings. **To gripe** is to complain, often accompanied by grumbling. **To grudge** is to be unwilling to give or do something.

sp: **spatter** or **spill;** both have an association with liquid or powder. **To spatter** means to splash or scatter in drips. **To spill** means to cause or allow a liquid to pour out of a container, so it goes beyond the edge, usually causing waste.

wh: **whirl** and **whisk;** both have associations with the movement of air. **To whirl** means to move quickly around and around. **To whisk** means move or sweep quickly through the air.

17.3
1. click
2. whirred *or* whizzed
3. mashed
4. clinked
5. crash
6. groaned *or* grumbled
7. splashing *or* to splash
8. drizzling *or* sprinkling

17.4
1. spit (spat, spat)
2. grumpy
3. spit [a long, thin metal spike on which meat is put for roasting]

17.5
1. a **gash** in someone's arm
2. a referee **whistling**
3. someone **spraying** her hair
4. someone **sprinkling** salt on his food
5. people **smashing** champagne glasses

17.6
2. a teakettle whistles
3. a bored child wriggles
4. a church bell clangs
5. the bell on a cat's collar tinkles
6. a fire crackles
7. a bad-tempered person growls
8. a prisoner's chain clanks
9. someone with asthma wheezes

Unit 18

18.1
1. They sang a psalm to honor the memory of the psychologist as she was laid to rest in the family tomb.
2. The psychiatrist was knifed in the knee as he was walking home.

3. You could have left me half the Christmas cake.
4. He should have whistled as he fastened the knot.

18.2   The odd one out appears first:

1. dome /oʊ/   come, some /ə/
2. plead /i/   head, tread /e/
3. wand /ɑ/   land, sand /æ/
4. boot /u/   took, foot /ʊ/
5. doubt /aʊ/   could, would /ʊ/
6. though /oʊ/   rough, tough /ə/

18.3   *Possible answers:*

2. allow   3. rough   4. go   5. flew   6. off

18.4
1. suspected; suspect
2. object; object
3. conflicting; conflict
4. upset; upset
5. increased; increase
6. permit; permit
7. progress; progress
8. conduct; conducting

18.5
1. muscle
2. catastrophe
3. handkerchief
4. chemical
5. subtle
6. receipt
7. height
8. recipe

18.6
1. photograph, photography, photographer, photographic
2. politics, political, politician
3. economy, economical, economics
4. psychology, psychologist, psychological
5. psychiatry, psychiatric, psychiatrist
6. mathematics, mathematician, mathematical

Unit 19

19.1
1. The woman I live (give) with knows a good club with live (five) music.
2. The main house (mouse) houses (browse) a collection of rare stamps.
3. You sow (show) the seeds while I feed the sow (cow).
4. The violinist in the bow (go) tie took a bow (now).
5. He's the lead (deed) singer in the heavy metal group "Lead (head) Bullets."
6. Does he still suffer from his war wound (mooned)?
7. I wound (round) the rope around the tree.
8. It's no use (juice)! I can't use (snooze) this gadget.

19.2
1. waste
2. sole
3. pane
4. allowed
5. through, faze
6. peel

19.3
1. You're too young to smoke.
   This is a play on words on the two meanings of **smoke** – to smoke a cigarette and a fire or chimney smokes [gives out smoke].

2. He wanted to draw the curtains.
   This is a play on words on two meanings of **draw**. One means make a picture and the other means pull (curtains) open or closed.

3. A nervous wreck.
   A **wreck** is a boat or ship that, for example, hits a rock and sinks to the bottom of the sea. A **nervous wreck,** however, is an expression commonly used to describe someone who is extremely nervous.

4. Because it's full of dates.
   This is a play on words on the two meanings of **dates.** One meaning refers to time (e.g., 1492, 2001) and the other to a sweet fruit that comes from a kind of palm tree.

5. A newspaper.

When we first hear the question, we assume the word **red** is a color, like black and white. But the word is really the verb **read** (same pronunciation as **red**) – the past participle of the verb **to read.** Of course, a newspaper is black and white and people read it all over. **All over** is another play on words: It could mean everywhere or all over the newspaper. (*Note:* Jokes and riddles like this one are usually spoken, not written, because the play on words is based on the sounds.)

19.4 1. (a) tea (b) tee   3. (a) right (b) write
2. (a) pear (b) pair   4. (a) waste (b) waist

Unit 20

20.1 2. Till then / Until then / Before that   6. As soon as
3. By the time   7. When/Once/After
4. While/When   8. The moment / The minute
5. Previously / Earlier / Before that

Other possible sentences:

While she was in Toronto, she missed home.
She went to a concert **after** going to Eaton Centre.
While she was driving home from Boston, she saw a bad accident on the highway.
Following her trip to Toronto, she went to Boston.

20.2 *Possible answers:*

2. . . . I usually feel bloated.
3. . . . look at the clock to see what time it is.
4. . . . lived in the same house.
5. . . . reading a book.
6. . . . go back home and look for a job.
7. . . . double-check that I have all my reservations made.
8. . . . upset.

Unit 21

21.1 1. **as long as / providing (that) / provided (that)** are all possible answers; **on condition that** is possible too, but it sounds a little stronger.
2. **In case of;** you can also say **In the event of,** which is sometimes seen in notices and regulations.
3. **Unless**
4. Since this is legal/official language, **on condition that** would be appropriate, or **providing (that) / provided that; as long as** is also possible but sounds a little too informal.
5. **Supposing / Suppose / What if**

21.2 *Suggested sentences:*

1. You cannot enter unless you have a visa. *or* You may enter providing (that) / provided (that) you have a visa.
2. You can't go in unless you're over 21. *or* You may enter providing (that) / provided (that) you are over 21.
3. Visitors may enter the mosque on condition that they remove their shoes. *or* You may go in as long as you take off your shoes. *or* You may not enter unless you remove your shoes.

21.3 1. No matter where she goes, she always takes that dog of hers.
2. If anyone calls, I don't want to speak to them, whoever it is.

3. Whatever I do, I always seem to do the wrong thing.
4. However I do it, that recipe never seems to work.

21.4   *Some possible answers:*

1. For the authors of this book, who are teachers, the prerequisites are a university degree and teaching qualifications.
2. Many people might move if they were offered a good job in another area. Others might not move under any circumstances.
3. In the United States, the normal admission requirements are a high school diploma and acceptable scores on the Scholastic Aptitude Tests (SATs).
4. Some people might say, "I would lend a friend my house/apartment on the condition that they promise to keep the place clean and pay the utility bills."

Unit 22

22.1   *Possible answers:*

1. The new law **brought about / led to / gave rise to** changes in the tax system.
2. The train crash was **caused by / due to** a faulty signal.
3. A violent storm **caused** widespread flooding. *or* **Owing to / Because of** a violent storm, there was widespread flooding.
4. Food shortages **sparked (off) / provoked / ignited** riots in several cities.
5. Declining profits **stemmed from / arose from** poor management of the company.

22.2   1. The reason I didn't call you was (because/that) I'd lost your phone number. *or* My reason for not calling you was . . . (acceptable, but sounds more formal)
2. I will not sign, on the grounds that this contract is illegal.
3. Lawmakers passed a new bill with the aim of balancing the budget. *or* The aim of the new bill passed by lawmakers was to balance the budget.
4. I wonder what her motives were in sending everyone flowers.
5. The high salary prompted her to apply for the job.

22.3   *Possible answers:*

1. The road was blocked due to a terrible snowstorm.
2. Owing to the cancellation of the performance, everyone got a refund.
3. The service was terribly slow. Consequently, the customers got angry.
4. We missed the last train. As a result, we had to take a taxi.

22.4   1. for   2. of   3. from   4. with; of   5. given; to

Unit 23

23.1   *Suggested answers:*

1. I agree (or more formal: I acknowledge) that you weren't entirely to blame, but you have to take *some* responsibility.
2. He conceded that we had tried our best, but he still wasn't content.
3. The company acknowledges that you have experienced some delay, but we do not accept liability. (**Acknowledge** is fairly formal and therefore appropriate in formal, legal situations like this one.)
4. Okay, I admit I was wrong and you were right; he *is* a nice guy.

23.2   *Possible answers:*

2. The apartment is a little small.
3. JIM: Isn't that hotel awfully expensive?
4. In the U.S., cars drive on the right side of the road.

23.3

Across	Down
1. all	1. apart
2. world	3. divide
4. in	5. hand
5. huge	

23.4 *Suggested answers:*

1. on the contrary
2. on the other hand
3. huge discrepancy
4. After all
5. despite all that (*or* in spite of it all)
6. world of difference
7. It's all very well
8. Admittedly

Unit 24

24.1 *Suggested answers:*

1. Pursuant to
2. In addition to / As well as / Apart from / Besides
3. etc. / and so on / and so forth
4. in addition to / as well as / apart from / besides
5. Furthermore / Moreover

Comments: In (2) and (4), the choice is wide, but the writer would probably choose different phrases to avoid repeating herself.

24.2

1. Physical labor can exhaust the body very quickly. Similarly, excessive study can rapidly reduce mental powers.
2. My cousin turned up, along with some classmates of his.
3. As well as owning a big chemical factory, he runs an enormous oil business. *or* He owns a big chemical factory as well as running an enormous oil business.
4. She was my teacher and a good friend to boot.
5. In addition to being the scientific adviser, I also act as consultant to the director.

24.3

1. I work part time as well as **being** a student, so I have a busy life.
2. Besides **having** a good job, my ambition is to meet someone nice to share my life with.
3. Apart from **having** many other responsibilities, I am now in charge of staff training.
4. In addition **to** a degree, she also has an advanced certificate. *or* In addition **to having** a degree, . . .
5. My father won't agree. **Likewise,** my mother's sure to find something to object to.
6. He said he'd first have to consider the organization, then the system, then the finance, **and so forth and so on.**

24.4   1. to boot   2. plus (+)   3. on top of (all) that *or* to top it off

Unit 25

25.1   2. issue   3. belief   4. problem   5. evaluation   6. view

25.2

1. issue (best here because it is something everyone is debating and disagreeing on; **question** is also okay)
2. problem/matter/situation (**crisis** or **dilemma** if it is really serious)
3. question (**mystery** would also be possible)
4. topic
5. approach/response/solution/answer

25.3 1. Situation in Sahel worsening daily
2. New argument over unemployment
3. Proposal to increase telephone rates draws fire
4. New approach to cancer treatment
5. Scientist rejects claims over fast food
6. Solution to age-old mystery in Kenya

Unit 26

C *Possible answers:*

cheese, meat, bread, cake, lettuce, yogurt, fish, milk, juice, etc.

26.1 1. no article   5. no article
2. no article   6. no article; a (*Note:* A quarter is a coin worth 25 cents, or a quarter
3. a   of a dollar, in both American and Canadian currency.)
4. no article

26.2 *Uncountables – Countables*
clothing – garment
advice – tip
baggage – suitcase
information – fact
work – job
travel – trip

26.3 *Some uncountable items you might pack in your suitcase:*
soap toothpaste shampoo makeup underwear clothing writing paper film
medicine

26.4 1. We had such terrible weather last night! The storm knocked out the electricity for
hours.
2. I love antique furniture, but I would need advice from a specialist before I bought any.
My knowledge in that area is very poor.
3. His research is definitely making great progress these days. He has done a lot of
original work recently.
4. If you have your hair cut at that salon, it will cost a lot of money.

26.5 *Possible answers:*

A soldier needs a lot of courage, discipline, determination, stamina, loyalty, and a lot of
training.

A nurse needs a lot of patience and goodwill. A little bit of charm also helps, and a lot of
commitment and training is needed.

A teacher needs great patience, a lot of energy, a little bit of creativity, intelligence, and
some training.

An actor needs a lot of determination, talent, creativity, discipline, and some training.

An athlete needs great determination, stamina, discipline, and a lot of commitment.

A writer needs a lot of creativity, talent, and a little bit of intelligence.

A receptionist needs charm, goodwill, reliability, and energy.

26.6 Could I have **some** vinegar?   Could I have **some** tape?
Could I have **a** broom?   Could I have **a** tea bag?
Could I have **a** needle?   Could I have **some** shoe polish?
Could I have **some** thread?

Unit 27

27.2   2. suspenders   4. tweezers   6. pliers
3. scissors   5. binoculars

27.3   shorts   overalls   underpants   pants/slacks

27.4   1. pajamas   3. whereabouts
2. proceeds   4. authorities; goods

27.5   1. pants   2. billiards   3. scissors   4. underpants

27.6   After teaching **gymnastics** for years, I decided that I wanted to be a pop star and moved to Los Angeles. I got a room, but it was on the **outskirts** of the city. The owner didn't live on the **premises,** so I could make as much noise as I liked. The **acoustics** in the bathroom **were** fantastic, so I practiced playing rock music and rhythm & **blues** there. I went to the **headquarters** of the musicians' union, but a guy there said I just didn't have good enough **looks** to be famous. Oh well, forget it!

Unit 28

28.1   1. Most people have **a cloth** somewhere in the kitchen to wipe the work surfaces and in case they spill something. People who like to make clothes might have **cloth** at home, usually in a room where a sewing machine is kept.

2. For those who like to use **peppers** in cooking (e.g., bell peppers, chili peppers, jalapeño peppers), they would be found in the kitchen. Most people have **pepper** (together with salt) in their kitchen or dining room.

3. You would have **a tape** if you have a tape recorder or a VCR (videocassette recorder), and you'd probably keep it near the machine. Most people keep Scotch **tape** in or near a desk, and some people keep a measuring **tape** in a sewing room or possibly in a desk.

4. Some people have **a fish** (or **several fish**) swimming around in a tank or fishbowl in their living room. Of course, for cooking, **fish** would usually be found in the kitchen.

5. Most people keep **glasses** (for drinking) in the kitchen, dining room, or other rooms. Most homes also have **glass** somewhere, usually in the windows.

28.2   *Suggested answers:*

1. Could I borrow an iron?   3. Could I have (or borrow) a glass?
2. Could I have some pepper?   4. Could I have some chicken?

28.3   *Possible answers:*

1. I drove over some glass. *or* There was glass on the road.
2. How about some pepper?
3. It's a very famous work of art, a painting.
4. Oh, it's a thread. I'll just cut it off.

28.4   1. **Painting** (uncountable) can be an occupation or a hobby. **A painting** or **paintings** are individual works of art, each created by someone.

2. **A noise / Noises** would mean one or more particular sounds. **So much noise** (uncountable) can mean many sounds (usually unpleasant) that might go on over a period of time.

3. **Light** (uncountable) usually means light to see by, e.g., electric light. In its countable form, as in the request "Can I have **a light**?", it usually refers to a match or lighter to light a cigarette or pipe.

Unit 29

29.1 1. swarms 2. school 3. gang 4. pack/deck 5. team/group

29.2 1. swimmers 2. a book 3. a hospital 4. cats

29.3 2. a herd of elephants 4. a swarm of bees
3. a gang of thugs 5. a pile of linen

29.4 1. There's a stack of tables in the next room.
2. There's a crowd of people waiting outside.
3. The staff is well paid.
4. He gave me a set of six sherry glasses.
5. She gave me a bunch of beautiful roses. (*or* a beautiful bunch of roses)

29.5 a whole **host** of questions a **string** of wild allegations
a **barrage** of complaints a **series** of short answers

Unit 30

30.1 1. a stroke of luck 5. a flash of lightning
2. a rumble of thunder 6. a blade of grass
3. a cloud of smoke 7. a drop of rain
4. an article of clothing 8. a means of transportation

30.2 1. My mother gave me a **piece of / bit of** advice that I have always remembered.
2. Suddenly a **gust of** wind almost blew him off his feet.
3. Would you like another **piece/slice of** toast?
4. Let's go to the park – I need a **breath of** fresh air.
5. I can give you an important **bit of / piece of** information about that.
6. I need to get some **pieces of** furniture for my apartment.

30.3 1. health 2. emergency 3. disrepair 4. uncertainty 5. poverty

30.5 *Possible sentences:*
1. We moved over a month ago, but we are still in a state of chaos.
2. The company has been going through a state of flux ever since the top executive resigned.
3. Everything seems to be in a state of confusion at the moment, but I'm sure it'll all be smoothed out before the wedding.
4. It's important for job applicants to be in a good state of mind before an interview.

Unit 31

31.1 1. Argentinean Venezuelan Costa Rican Panamanian Mexican Peruvian (note the *v*) Ecuadoran/-ean/-ian Bolivian Uruguayan Paraguayan Colombian Salvadoran/-ean/-ian Nicaraguan etc.
2. Ukrainian Yugoslavian Croatian Serbian Slovenian Bulgarian Bosnian Romanian Albanian Mongolian Moldavian Czechoslovakian Russian Georgian etc.
3. *Other groupings:* – *i* adjectives seem to be Muslim and/or Middle Eastern countries; four of the -*ese* adjectives are Asian.

31.2 1. Egypt → Egyptian 4. Vietnam → Vietnamese
2. Italy → Italian 5. Jordan → Jordanian
3. Canada → Canadian 6. China → Chinese

31.3
1. Madonna to marry a **Frenchman?** Hollywood sensation! (Note how *Frenchman* is normally written as one word. So is *Frenchwoman*.)
2. **Britons** have highest tax rate in EU
3. Elections in **Canada** today
4. Police arrest **Dane** on smuggling charge
5. **Iraqi** delegation meets **Pakistani** President

31.4
1. Languages most widely spoken, in order, are Chinese, English, Spanish, Hindi, Arabic.
2. China, India, the United States, Indonesia, Brazil (as of the publication of this book!)
3. If we take Scandinavia as strictly the geographical peninsula, then Sweden and Norway are the only countries completely in Scandinavia. If we consider it more as a language family, then Denmark and Iceland can be added, and if as a cultural family, then Finland can be added too.
4. A difficult question! However, most linguists seem to agree on around 5,000 mutually incomprehensible tongues. There are, of course, many many more dialects.
5. Inuit is an Eskimo language, and its speakers may be found in Northern Canada.
6. Malays, Chinese (or various ethnic subtypes), and Indians (many are Tamils and Sikhs).

Unit 32

32.1 Some of these combinations form one solid word and some remain as two words.
1. thunderstorm
2. torrential rain
3. downpour
4. heat wave
5. hailstones
6. snowdrift
7. gale warning

32.2
1. slush
2. sleet
3. frost
4. blizzards
5. snowdrifts
6. thaws
7. melts

32.3 *Possible answers:*
1. It was scorching/boiling/sweltering last month. *or* There was an awful heat wave last month.
2. It's stifling/muggy today.
3. We had terrible floods.
4. There was a blizzard that night.
5. Do you remember how mild it was that year?
6. There was a very bad drought.
7. Suddenly there was a very strong gust of wind.
8. After the hurricane/gale, the damage was unbelievable.

32.4
1. *bad:* too dry, a drought, or frost   *good:* mild weather just after a rain
2. *bad:* cold weather or windy weather or wet weather   *good:* warm, mild, or even cool (if it has been a very hot day) and preferably dry
3. *bad:* gales, high winds, hurricanes, storms, wet weather, mist/fog   *good:* clear, sunny, dry, breezy weather
4. *bad:* cold, wet, and windy weather or humid, muggy weather   *good:* clear, dry, but not too hot
5. *bad:* wet, windy, snowy weather   *good:* dry, no wind, warm nights
6. *bad:* fog/mist, rain   *good:* clear, dry, sunny weather

Unit 33

33.1   *Suggested answers:*

1. . . . the fair, bald guy (*or* straight-haired / curly-haired man).
2. . . . scruffy and messy (*or* sloppy) looking.
3. . . . the slim, dark-haired one.
4. . . . a teenager / in her twenties / twenty-something. (Another useful expression is "She's only a youngster," for a person who is a teenager or who is still very young.)

33.2   1. The author who wrote this exercise is tall, with brown hair that is going gray; he's white, in his forties, and thinks he's good looking! What about you?

33.3   *Suggested answers:*

Will Prowse: thin-faced; curly blond (*or* fair) hair; fair complexion.
Sandra King: dark wavy hair; stocky or heavy build, round-faced.
Jake "Dagger" Flagstone: bald, with beard and mustache; muscular build.
Louisa Yin: long, straight, dark hair.

Unit 34

34.1   *Opposites:*

1. bright – stupid
2. extroverted – introverted
3. rude – courteous
4. cruel – kindhearted
5. generous – tight-fisted
6. unsociable – gregarious

34.2   1. likes   3. likes   5. dislikes   7. dislikes
2. likes   4. dislikes   6. dislikes   8. likes

34.3   2. Nancy's usually blunt.
3. Jim's really stubborn.
4. Paul can be assertive.
5. Dick is awfully ambitious.
6. I find Annemarie self-assured.
7. Molly is somewhat inquiring.
8. Jack is kind of flaky.

34.4   1. sociable   3. assertive   5. extravagant   7. sensitive
2. pessimistic   4. inquiring   6. argumentative

34.5   *Possible questions:*

1. thrifty – Do you always try to buy things on sale rather than at full price?
2. blunt – If a friend asks you if you like her ugly new dress, would you say "No"?
3. sensible – If you won a lot of money, would you put it in savings rather than spend it on a luxury item you've always wanted?
4. naive – Do you always trust what people say or believe any promises they make?
5. even-tempered – If someone spills soup on your new clothes, do you just sigh and say "That's life"?
6. unconventional – Do you refuse to wear blue jeans because you don't want to look like everyone else?
7. obstinate – Do you become even more determined to do something if people try to persuade you not to?
8. confident – Would you feel calm and undisturbed if you had to make a speech in front of a group of people?

Unit 35

35.1 1. This is Jack. He's my roommate. *or* He and I are roommates.
2. My grandfather still writes to his old (*or* former) shipmates.
3. We were classmates at Lincoln High School, weren't we? *or* You were a classmate of mine . . .
4. She and I were teammates (on the softball team).

35.2 *Some possible answers:*

Josh Yates is Helen Cobb's ex-husband.
Helen Cobb is Josh Yates's ex-wife.
Helen Cobb and Bill Nash are old friends.
Bill Nash and John Silver are colleagues.
Bill Nash and Josh Yates are acquaintances.
Sue Watts is Bill Nash's ex-wife.
Bill Nash is Sue Watts's ex-husband.
Sue Watts and Nora Costa were Olympic teammates and classmates.
Ana Wood is Bill Nash's wife.
Bill Nash is Ana Wood's husband.
Fred Parks and Josh Yates are colleagues.
Fred Parks and Sue Watts were once acquaintances.
Laura Fine and Josh Yates are companions.

35.3 *Some possible answers:*

1. A teenage pop music fan might not see eye to eye with his/her parents, might worship or idolize a pop star, might dislike but might (secretly!) respect a strict teacher, and surely gets along with his/her best friend.

2. A secretary might like another secretary or might not get along well with her/him; might despise or hate the boss, or perhaps look up to him/her; and might be attracted to a very attractive coworker.

3. A 45-year-old might dislike teenagers or look down on them, or might like them; he/she might be repelled by an ex-companion, or the ex might still turn him/her on.

35.4 1. Dave and Phil don't see eye to eye. *or* . . . don't get along.
2. I had a falling out with my parents last night.
3. We had an argument but now we've made up.
4. Do you think those two are having an affair?
5. She should learn to respect her elders.

Unit 36

36.1 1. attic   4. master bedroom
2. landing   5. den *or* study
3. hall *or* hallway   6. driveway

36.2 1. basement   5. landing
2. (electrical) outlet   6. studio apartment (*or* studio)
3. attic   7. condominium (*or* condo)
4. patio/terrace/porch

36.3 1. a kitchen or dining room drawer
2. a bathroom cabinet [Dental floss is a kind of thread for cleaning between your teeth.]
3. a closet
4. the kitchen, probably in a drawer
5. a laundry room, kitchen, or basement

6. a living room, den, or basement, next to a TV set
7. a patio, terrace, or porch, or in a garden or yard
8. a den (study), living room, or bedroom
9. usually in every room of a home

Unit 37

37.1 *Suggested answers:*

1. My car broke down / wouldn't start. *or* My car battery was dead / had run out.
2. Our washing machine broke down / stopped working.
3. The doorknob came off.
4. I cut my finger.
5. The batteries in my radio / tape player have run out / are dead.
6. I seem to have misplaced my glasses / false teeth / contact lenses / etc.

37.2
1. break down – this means "fail mechanically"; **break** and **smash** both mean break physically.
2. stain – means "leave a mark"; **fall down** and **bump** both refer to ways you can injure yourself.
3. leak – refers to liquids; **come off** and **chip** can both refer to pieces falling off an object.
4. flood – refers to an excess of water; **cut** and **bruise** are both types of injury.

37.3 *Possible answers:*

1. Call the bank / credit agency and get them to cancel it immediately.
2. Offer the guest a new one.
3. Sew it back on.
4. Get it repaired or buy a new one if it were beyond repair.
5. Put ice on it immediately.
6. Reset it. *or* Get a new battery.

37.4
1. vase – cracked
2. sofa cushion – ripped
3. sink – stopped up
4. car – dented
5. elbow – banged
6. clock – stopped

37.5
1. . . . locked myself out.
2. . . . misplaced her phone number.
3. . . . broken. (It could also be **jammed,** which means mechanically stuck, e.g., by some broken film.)
4. . . . fell and twisted/sprained my ankle *or* cut my leg/knee, etc.

Unit 38

38.1
1. Drought; if the plants and trees are **withered,** they are probably dying because they have no water, and since the earth is **cracked** [hard, with a pattern of deep lines over it], it suggests it is very dry.
2. Earthquake; a **tremor** is a trembling movement of the earth. Note how disasters of various kinds can **strike,** e.g., The hurricane **struck** the coastline at noon.
3. A violent storm or wind, such as a hurricane/typhoon/tornado; if you **board up** your house you cover the windows and doors with wooden boards to protect them.
4. War, battle, or an attack of some kind; **shells** and **mortars** are projectiles that cause explosions when they strike.
5. Probably a plane crash; people who witness such crashes often describe the explosion as a **fireball,** or **ball of fire.**

38.2

Verb	Noun: thing or idea	Noun: person/people
explode	explosion	–
injure	injury	the injured
survive	survival	survivor
starve	starvation	the starving
erupt	eruption	–

38.3
1. getting worse (**spreads**)
2. getting worse / heading for a major disaster (a **time bomb** ticks like a clock and eventually explodes)
3. a disaster was avoided (the bomb was **defused** – made safe)
4. disaster avoided (**all survive** means no one died)
5. getting better (the oil is **receding** – going away from where it was heading, e.g., toward a beach)
6. disaster has happened / is happening (if you **heed** a warning, you take note, and do something; here the warning was ignored)

38.4
1. victims   2. refugees   3. casualties   4. survivors

38.5
1. malaria   2. cholera or typhoid   3. rabies

Unit 39

39.3
1. I can't go out. I'm studying. I'm **taking** a test tomorrow.
2. Congratulations! I hear you **passed / did well on / aced** your exams!
3. After she finished **college/university,** she went on to law school. *or* After she finished high school, she went on to **college/university.**
4. I got very good **marks/scores** on my tests this term.
5. **Private/Parochial** schools in the U.S. charge tuition.

39.4
1. nursery school / preschool
2. elementary school / primary school / kindergarten
3. elementary/primary
4. junior high / middle
5. private
6. marks/scores
7. college
8. major
9. bachelor's
10. graduate

39.5   *Possible questions:*
1. Did you get a scholarship or a grant to study?
2. Until what age do students have to attend school in the U.S.?
3. You look really tired. What've you been doing?
4. Did you pass / do well on / ace your exam?
5. Did your kids go to preschool / nursery school?

Unit 40

40.1
1. CEO, executive, director
2. union official
3. unskilled worker, entry-level employee
4. white-collar worker
5. supervisor, boss
6. accountant

40.2
1. construction / home improvement
2. health care
3. engineering
4. arts/entertainment
5. journalism
6. mechanics/repair

Possible answers:

health care: surgeon   arts/entertainment: costume designer
mechanics/repair: aircraft mechanic   construction / home improvement: painter
journalism: radio/TV announcer   engineering: mechanical engineer

40.4   *Suggested answers:*

1. This person was **laid off / made redundant.**
2. This person **works the night shift.**
3. She's **been promoted.** / She **got a promotion.**
4. This person **was fired.**
5. He is **unemployed.**
6. You are a **workaholic.**

40.5
1. get/have/find   3. work   5. offered
2. living   4. applied   6. moonlight

Unit 41

41.1   *Probable answers:*

1. bowling
2. in-line skating, windsurfing
3. auto racing
4. pool/billiards, but could, of course, apply to a number of other sports too, particularly target sports (golf, archery, bowling, etc.)
5. horseback riding

41.3   *Possible answers:*

2. volleyball, badminton   6. hockey, lacrosse
3. swimming, water-skiing   7. tennis, racquetball
4. horse racing, dog racing   8. auto racing, bicycle racing, in-line skating
5. wrestling, boxing

Other possible categories (there is likely to be overlap): handball games, football games, snow sports, ice sports, martial arts, jumping sports, land racing, water racing, air racing, equestrian sports, among others.

41.4   1. broken/set   2. beaten   3. win   4. holds   5. take up

41.5
2. a jockey, a rider   6. a hockey player
3. a race car driver   7. a long-distance runner
4. a discus/javelin thrower   8. a pole-vaulter
5. a gymnast

41.6   *Possible answers:*

1. tennis, squash, etc. Also basketball, volleyball.
2. golf (golf course) or horse racing (racecourse)
3. usually boxing or wrestling
4. baseball, football, soccer, field hockey, and many others
5. ice skating, ice hockey, roller skating
6. bowling
7. downhill skiing
8. running, jogging, racing (racetrack)

Unit 42

42.1 *Probable answers:*

1. sculpture (The verb **stand** is often associated with statues; it could also be architecture, if *Peace* is interpreted as the name of a building or huge monument.)
2. a performance of a play at a theater (Plays are divided into **acts** – major divisions – and **scenes** – smaller divisions.)
3. dance (**Movement** and **rhythm** are the clues.)
4. poetry (**Rhyme** – having the same sounds at the ends of lines – is sometimes thought of as a necessary quality of poetry.)
5. painting (**Oil**-based and **water**-based paints are two of the most popular types of paint used by artists.)
6. architecture (We talk of the **design** of a building.)
7. plays (Drama texts in written form.)
8. Probably a novel, but it could be any book divided into **chapters,** e.g., an academic textbook.
9. the movies (When a movie is shown at a theater, we sometimes say it's on the **big screen.**)
10. opera (**Performance** and **tenor** – an adult male singer in an opera – are the clues.)

42.2

1. What's the name of the **publisher** of that book you recommended? Was it Cambridge University Press? (An **editorial** is an article in a newspaper or magazine giving the opinions of the editor on matters of interest/concern.)
2. "Do I dare to eat a peach?" is my favorite **line** of poetry in English. (A **stanza** is a group of lines that make up the divisions of a poem or song.)
3. He's a very famous **sculptor;** he did that statue in the park, you know, the one with the soldiers. (**Sculpture** is the name of the art form; **sculptor** is the person who does it.)
4. Most of the **(short) stories** in this collection are only five or six pages long. They're great for reading on short trips. (A **novel** is a long work, usually more than 100 pages. Here **short story** or just **story** is clearly what the speaker is referring to.)
5. When will the President's biography be **published**? (A biography – a book – is published; a play, ballet, opera, etc., is **performed.**)
6. The cast wore beautiful **costumes** in the new production of the play. (**Costumes** are clothes worn by the actors; the **sets** are the scenery, furniture, etc., representing the location of the play.)

42.3 *Possible questions:*

1. Was the play (or movie) a success?
2. Would you like a ticket for the concert tonight?
3. What's the architecture like in your hometown?
4. Was it a good production/performance?
5. What's playing at the Arts Theater this week?
6. Do you like ballet?

42.4 *Follow-up:*

Unit 43

43.1 *Possible groupings:*

Found in salads: cucumbers spinach carrots green/red peppers lettuce cabbage
  radishes celery
"Onion-family" vegetables: leeks onions shallots
Grow underground: carrots potatoes turnips beets
Usually long-shaped: cucumbers zucchini corn eggplant

There are, of course, other possible groups too, e.g., green or yellow vegetables, leafy
vegetables, vegetables that are better raw/cooked, vegetables you like/hate.

43.2
1. hot, spicy
2. salty
3. sour
4. sugary
5. bitter, strong
6. bland, tasteless

43.3
1. These fries are greasy/oily.
2. This steak is overcooked/overdone.
3. This stew is too salty.
4. This is tasteless / very bland.
5. This roast beef is awfully fatty.

43.5
1. calf – veal; deer – venison; sheep – lamb (young animal), mutton (older animal);
   pig – pork, ham, bacon

Unit 44

44.1
1. waterfall
2. cliff
3. volcano
4. geyser
5. gorge
6. peak, summit of a mountain
7. mountain range

44.2 Brazil is **the** fifth largest country in **the** world. In **the** north, **the** densely forested basin of
the Amazon River covers half **the** country. In **the** east, **the** country is washed by **the**
Atlantic. **The** highest mountain range in South America, **the** Andes, does not lie in Brazil.
Brazil's most famous city is Rio de Janeiro, **the** former capital. **The** capital of Brazil is now
Brasilia.

44.3
2. steep gorge/hill
3. shallow brook/bay
4. rocky coast/mountain
5. turbulent river/sea
6. dangerous cliff/ridge

44.4 *Possible answers:*

1. Scotland
2. country
3. the north of Britain
4. agriculture
5. Scotland
6. the Clyde
7. the Western Highlands
8. Ben Nevis
9. Overfishing
10. Scotland

44.5 *Some possible answers:*

Unleaded gas causes less air pollution than leaded gas.

Recycling paper means that fewer trees need to be cut down.

Using recycled bottles and cans means that glass and metal are reused rather than thrown
  away. Thus there is less waste of resources and less waste dumped in landfills.

Environmentalists are also in favor of using solar or wind power, of using as little plastic
  as possible (because it is usually not biodegradable), and of developing energy-efficient
  technology, such as electrically powered automobiles that don't use gas. They also
  encourage people not to waste resources, such as water.

Unit 45

45.1
1. in New Mexico, a state in the Southwestern U.S.
2. more than 300 years (3 centuries) ago
3. There are many attractions, particularly those connected with the arts: museums, theaters, studios, and galleries, in addition to restaurants, nightclubs, churches, public buildings, and historic businesses. Most display the distinctive Santa Fe-style of architecture.
4. adobe (bricks or heavy clay made of sun-dried earth and straw)
5. walking
6. the Plaza
7. the Rio Grande and the Rocky Mountains
8. The climate is pleasant; there are four seasons.

45.4   *Some possible answers:*

1. natural history museum
   science museum
   modern art museum

2. sports center
   shopping center
   city center

3. higher education
   private education
   public education

4. basketball court
   squash court
   royal court

5. nightclub
   country club
   social club

6. employment agency
   travel agency
   real estate agency

Unit 46

46.1
1. mammal
2. pollen
3. *possible answers:* groundhog, tortoise, and bear
4. According to legend, the groundhog comes out of winter hibernation on February 2nd. If it sees its shadow, six more weeks of winter are predicted. If there's no shadow, then spring is "just around the corner."
5. cheetah
6. dove
7. breathing
8. An endangered species is any species that is in danger of dying out or becoming extinct, e.g., some breeds of tiger or whale.
9. The dinosaur is extinct; the emu is still in existence; the phoenix was a mythical bird, not a real creature.
10. *possible answers:* lily, daisy, and tulip; bluebird, robin, and seagull
11. Canada – maple leaf; U.S. – bald eagle; Scotland – thistle; England – rose; and New Zealand – kiwi bird
12. Your answer to this question depends, of course, on where you come from.

46.2   *Possible answers:*

prickly porcupine   sweet-smelling petals   noble eagle   sturdy oak
graceful willow   wriggly worm   rough bark

46.3
1. roots
2. claws; trunk/bark
3. hoof
4. bud
5. branches/twigs
6. bat; horse
7. bee; snail

Notice how people are compared to animals in sentences 6 and 7. These expressions (sometimes humorous) are common in English.

46.4 The words underlined below are worth learning. You can use them when talking about other animals too.

> **camel** A <u>mammal</u> of the <u>family</u> Camelidae (2 <u>species</u>): the **Bactrian,** from cold deserts in Central Asia and <u>domesticated</u> elsewhere, and the **dromedary;** <u>eats</u> any vegetation; <u>drinks</u> salt water if necessary; closes slit-like <u>nostrils</u> to exclude sand; humps are stores of energy-rich <u>fats</u>. The two <u>species</u> may <u>interbreed</u>: the <u>offspring</u> has one hump; the <u>males</u> are usually <u>sterile</u>, while the <u>females</u> are <u>fertile</u>.

46.5 The description of an elephant from the same encyclopedia is given below. While it is unlikely that you would need or want to write anything quite so technical, look at it carefully and pick out any vocabulary that could be useful for you to learn.

> **elephant** A large mammal of the family Elephantidae; almost naked gray skin; massive forehead; small eyes; upper incisor teeth form "tusks"; snout elongated as a muscular, grasping "trunk"; ears large and movable (used to radiate heat). There are two living species. The **African elephant** is the largest living land animal, with three subspecies. The **Asian elephant** has four subspecies. The African is larger with larger ears, a triangular tip on the top and bottom of the trunk tip (not just on the top), and obvious tusks in the female.

If you chose to write about another animal, compare your description if possible with one in an English-language encyclopedia.

Unit 47

47.1
1. heel; soles
2. laces (*or* shoelaces)
3. slippers
4. belt
5. hem; buttons

47.2
1. jeans
2. shorts
3. pairs (of underpants)
4. pair (of pantyhose)
5. ones

47.3
2. cashmere sweater
3. leather boots
4. corduroy pants
5. nylon jogging suit
6. cotton T-shirt

47.4 *Possible answers:*

The boy is wearing baggy jeans with a T-shirt. He's wearing high-top running shoes with the laces untied. He's also wearing a baseball cap backwards. He looks a little grungy.

The woman is wearing a long-sleeved, solid, turtleneck sweater and a knee-length striped skirt. She has high-heeled (*or* less formally: high-heel) shoes on and is carrying a large shoulder bag and a pair of gloves. She appears well-dressed.

Unit 48

48.1
1. hepatitis – fever, weakened condition, yellow color of skin
2. pneumonia – dry cough, high fever, chest pain, rapid breathing
3. rheumatism – swollen, painful joints or muscles, extreme stiffness
4. an ulcer – burning pain in abdomen, pain or nausea after eating
5. the flu – headache, aching muscles, fever, cough, sneezing

48.2
1. for taking someone's temperature
2. for giving injections (*or* shots)
3. for holding down the tongue while examining the throat
4. for making surgical cuts during operations

48.3
1. dermatologist
2. cardiologist
3. psychiatrist
4. allergist
5. obstetrician *or* gynecologist
6. osteopath *or* chiropractor
7. podiatrist
8. ophthalmologist

48.4

Noun	Adjective	Verb
breathlessness, breath	breathless	breathe
weakness	weak	weaken
shiver, the shivers	shivery	shiver
dislocation	dislocated	dislocate
ache	aching, achy	ache
treatment	treatable	treat
swelling	swollen	swell

48.5 *Possible answers:*
1. indigestion, a stomachache
2. bronchitis, lung cancer
3. bruises, broken bones, (eventually) arthritis
4. a broken leg
5. sunburn
6. rash, hives, get stuffed up, or other allergic reactions
7. breathlessness
8. an itch
9. indigestion, nausea, diarrhea
10. hypochondria

Unit 49

49.1

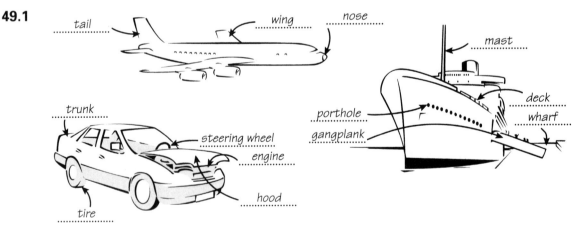

49.2   fender, rear view mirror – automotive, parts of vehicle
balloon, glider – types of air transportation
deck chair – water, associated facilities
sail, oar, rudder, funnel – water, parts of vehicle (boat or ship) (**rudder** can also be part of a plane)
gas pump, freeway – automotive, associated facilities
bus driver – automotive, people working with it
baggage claim, metal detector, check-in counter – air, associated facilities
canoe – water, kinds of vehicle

49.3
1. Construction / Road work ahead.
2. No left turn.
3. The road may be slippery when wet.
4. School crossing.

49.4
1. flight/plane
2. trunk
3. hood
4. garage
5. mechanic
6. out
7. departure lounge
8. delayed (*or* canceled)
9. train
10. dining

Unit 50

50.1 *Possible advantages and disadvantages:*

Vacation place	Advantage	Disadvantage
resort	lots of activities	expensive
motel	convenient	not many facilities
bed & breakfast	less impersonal than hotels	less freedom
campsite	cheap	uncomfortable
summer camp	kids: lots to do parents: kids are out of house!	kids: homesick parents: expensive
youth hostel	cheap	no privacy
time-share	can be very comfortable	same place every year

50.3
1. We like to jog around the lake.
2. I love sailing.
3. He spends too much time going fishing.
4. It's pretty expensive to go shopping in Rome.
5. I enjoy going horseback riding on weekends.

50.4 *Possible answers:*
1. Can I book a double room with a double / queen-size / king-size bed (*or* with two beds / twin beds), please?
2. Could I have a wake-up call at 6 a.m., please?
3. The television in my room isn't working. Could you send someone up, please?
4. What time does the pool open?
5. Can I have room service, please?

50.5

>   **campsite**
> The Wongs stayed at a <u>camping</u> last summer because all other
>   **vacation**
> kinds of <u>vacations</u> resorts were too expensive. Every day Mrs.
>
>   **sunbathed or went sunbathing**   **went sightseeing**
> Wong <u>took a sunbath</u>, Mr. Wong <u>made a sightseeing</u>, and the
>
>   **cycled or went cycling**
> children <u>did cycling</u> around the island.

Unit 51

51.1
1. 1, 3, 5, 7
2. 2, 4, 6, 8
3. Four to the third power (*or* four cubed) is (*or* equals) sixty-four.
4. 10.6 (ten point six)
5. *e* equals *m c* squared; it is Einstein's relativity equation in which *e* = energy, *m* = mass, and *c* = the speed of light.
6. two pi *r*; this is the formula for the circumference of a circle in which *r* = the radius of the circle. π (pi) is the mathematical symbol for 3.14159...

51.2
1. Seventy-nine percent of American women diet each year, yet ninety-five percent of those diets fail.
2. Zero degrees centigrade/Celsius equals thirty-two degrees Fahrenheit.
3. About fifteen percent of children under age ten are left-handed.
4. Two-thirds plus one-quarter (*or* one-fourth) times four squared equals fourteen and two-thirds.
5. Two million, seven hundred (and) sixty-nine thousand, four hundred (and) twenty-five people live here.
6. The inflation rate was three point five percent last year and point four percent (*or* zero point four percent) last month.

51.3   square   pentagonal   octagonal   rectangular   triangular   circular   oval
spherical   cubic   pyramidal   spiral

51.4
1. forty-six point six percent
2. nine hundred (and) seventy-nine meters
3. one thousand eight hundred (and) ninety-two cups *or* eighteen hundred (and) ninety-two cups
4. thirty-three years; nineteen sixty-one
5. (zero) point four square kilometers

51.5

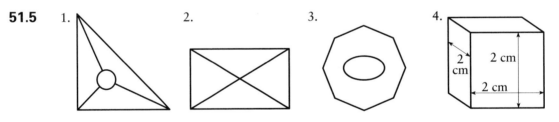

Unit 52

52.1   chemist
physicist
zoologist
geneticist
computer technician
civil engineer

Note: A **physician** is a doctor. Check in the Index for the pronunciation of these words, since they are frequently mispronounced.

52.2
1. VCR – a machine that records and plays back sound and pictures
2. photocopier – a machine that makes copies of documents
3. fax machine – a machine that makes copies of documents and sends them along telephone lines to another machine
4. tape recorder – a machine that records and plays back sound
5. modem – a piece of equipment that sends information along telephone lines from one computer to another computer
6. camcorder – a camera that records moving pictures and sound
7. word processor – a kind of sophisticated typewriter using a computer
8. food processor – a machine for chopping, slicing, mashing, blending, etc.

52.3 *Some possible definitions:*

1. A **personal stereo** (often called a **Walkman**) is a small, portable radio or cassette player that you listen to with lightweight earphones.

2. A **cellular phone** (or **cell phone**) is a portable telephone without an electric cord or a base, which uses a network of radio transmitters to operate.

3. An **automatic coffee maker** is an electric appliance that makes coffee quickly and conveniently.

4. A **clock radio** is a combination radio and alarm clock that you set to wake you up at a certain time with a radio broadcast.

52.4
1. discovery	4. conclusion	7. dissection
2. invention	5. patent	8. experiment/experimentation
3. combination	6. analysis	

Unit 53

53.1
1. detective show / movie	4. game show
2. documentary / nature show	5. current events show / news special
3. sports	6. talk show

53.3
1. A **foreign correspondent** is a journalist who sends news or commentary from abroad.
2. A **copy editor** is someone who edits the writing (or copy) submitted by newspaper reporters and decides on headlines to appear in the newspaper.
3. An **editor** is the person responsible for the publication of a book, newspaper (or section of a newspaper), or magazine.
4. A **librarian** is a person who works in a place (a library) that lends books.
5. A **bookseller** is someone who owns or works in a store that sells books.
6. A **publisher** is a person or company whose business is publishing (books, newspapers, magazines, etc.).
7. A **columnist** is a journalist who writes a regular column or feature for a newspaper/magazine.
8. A **critic** is a person who writes or broadcasts reviews of books, movies, plays, or music.

53.4
1. remote control	3. cut/edited	5. AM
2. camcorder	4. tabloid newspapers / tabloids	6. magazine

Unit 54

54.1
1. independence	2. overruled	3. running	4. elected	5. federation

54.2
1. branches	3. houses	5. election	7. Supreme Court
2. judiciary	4. elected	6. majority	8. appointed/nominated

54.3

Abstract noun	Person noun	Verb	Adjective
revolution	revolutionary	revolutionize	revolutionary
representation	representative	represent	representative
election	elector	elect	elective
dictatorship	dictator	dictate	dictatorial
presidency	president	preside	presidential
politics	politician	politicize	political

54.4 *Possible answers:*

1. U.K.   Sweden   Belgium
2. *presidential system:* Mexico, France; *parliamentary system:* Canada, Australia
3. Iceland

Unit 55

55.1

Crime	Criminal	Verb / Verb phrase	Definition
terrorism	terrorist	to terrorize, to commit acts of terrorism	using violence for political ends
blackmail	blackmailer	to blackmail	threatening to make someone's dark secret public in order to get money
drug trafficking	drug trafficker	to traffic in drugs, to peddle drugs, to deal in drugs	buying and selling drugs
forgery	forger	to forge	to try to pass off a copy (a fake) as the real thing
assault	attacker, assailant	to assault	physical attack on another person
pickpocketing	pickpocket	to pickpocket	stealing from someone's pocket or handbag
mugging	mugger	to mug	attacking someone, often on the street, generally to get money

55.2   1. robbed; stole   2. was stolen   3. are robbed

55.3
1. was convicted   4. sentenced
2. (had) defended   5. serve
3. felony   6. was acquitted

55.4   *Possible groupings:*

People connected with the law: lawyer   detective   member of a jury   judge   witness
Crimes: smuggling   hijacking   bribery   rape   drunken driving   theft
Punishments: prison   fine   death penalty   lethal injection   probation

Unit 56

56.1   1. Japan – yen; Australia – dollar; India – rupee; Russia – ruble
2. It is any currency that is reliable and stable.
3. MasterCard and Visa.
4. Alcohol and tobacco.
5. Rents from property; winnings from gambling; interest from banks.

56.2   1. interest – money chargeable on a loan or paid to savers
2. mortgage – a loan to purchase a home or property
3. an overdrawn account – a bank account with a negative balance
4. savings account – an account that is used mainly for keeping money
5. checking account – an account that checks are drawn on for day-to-day use
6. tuition – money paid for education
7. sales tax – tax paid at the time of a purchase
8. insufficient funds – the reason a check bounces

56.3   **Mortgage rates higher:** Most people who have a mortgage without fixed rates and anyone who wants to get a mortgage would not be happy.

Wages to be frozen: Most people who earn salaries would not be happy.

U.S. dollar falls: It depends. People living in the U.S. who don't buy a lot of imported goods wouldn't care one way or the other. Visitors to the U.S. would be happy because it means they spend less of their own currency and get more value for the money they exchange into dollars. Some people in countries whose currency is tied to the dollar would be unhappy because it would devalue their currency. Consumers who buy U.S. products in other countries would be happy if lower prices resulted.

Sales tax lowered: Most consumers would be happy to see this.

Interest rates down: People who want to borrow money or take out a loan, or those who regularly pay finance charges on credit cards, would be happy. However, those who live on fixed incomes from bank interest would not be happy.

56.4   1. inheritance tax   4. balance; finance charge
2. loan   5. fee
3. fare   6. penalty

Unit 57

57.1   *Suggested answers:*

1. That's a gigantic amount of money to waste!
2. That's a considerable number of people.
3. So it'll be about average again this year.
4. It's a good thing it was only a small amount of money.
5. That's a huge amount of time, considering the result.

57.2   *Suggested answers:*

small: minuscule   minute   meager   insignificant
large: enormous   overwhelming   excessive   sizable

1. minute/minuscule (Note the pronunciation of the adjective **minute**. The stress is on the second syllable, and the vowels are pronounced differently from those in the noun **minute**.)
2. overwhelming/excessive/enormous
3. excessive/enormous
4. sizable
5. excessive

57.3 1. a lot of   4. a good deal of / a great deal of / a lot of
       2. plenty of / lots of   5. Many / A lot of / A number of
       3. much

57.4 *Possible answers:*

1. utterly exhausted / extremely tired
2. rather/quite/pretty confused
3. utterly amazed / completely astounded / awfully surprised
4. a little bit / rather sad

Unit 58

58.1 1. period   2. age/era   3. era   4. time   5. spell

58.2 1. No, it wasn't. In fact, it's almost always late.
       2. Just in time to catch the last train!
       3. It's about time!
       4. No, by the time I left work, it was too late.
       5. At times.

58.3 *Possible answers:*

1. You're just in time for tea/coffee!
2. By the time you get this card, I'll probably already be there.
3. I'd rather talk to you one at a time, if you don't mind.
4. Could you use the old photocopier for the time being? The new one's being repaired.
5. It can get extremely cold at times in . . .
6. I'll do my best to be at the meeting on time.
7. It's about time (she got a job)!

58.4 *Possible answers:*

1. . . . **takes** about two hours.
2. . . . **run/last** for about an hour on each side.
3. . . . **lasted** three winters.
4. . . . **went on** for ages.
5. . . . have **elapsed/passed** since then, but people still remember that day.
6. . . . **pass** quickly.
7. . . . **take** your time.
8. . . . **lasted / ran / went on** for more than three hours.

Unit 59

59.1 1. . . . them shortened?   5. . . . widened it / . . . 've widened it.
       2. . . . very tall.   6. . . . heighten the feeling.
       3. . . . a shortcut.   7. . . . deep.
       4. . . . height.

59.2 1. the width of the room   4. a long-distance call
       2. to lengthen   5. shallow water
       3. a narrow range of goods   6. faraway/distant places

59.3 1. it's much bigger now.   4. there's a wide range.
       2. it's a lengthy procedure.   5. you should broaden it.
       3. to give us more room.   6. for miles along the river.

59.4 1. at; of
2. in
3. from (*or possibly* at)
4. from; to
5. within; of
6. at

Unit 60

60.1 1. . . . was forced to close down / had to close down / had no choice (*or* alternative) but to close down.
2. . . . have to / 'll have to / 're required to put down a deposit.
3. . . . is compulsory/obligatory/mandatory for young people.
4. . . . must / have to / 've got to take it to the cleaners.
5. . . . forced him to hand it over.
6. . . . no choice/alternative.
7. . . . compulsory/required/mandatory in high school.
8. . . . didn't have to buy us a present.

60.2 *Possible answers:*
2. Most people usually suffer from a lack of time or of money.
3. Filling out a tax return is obligatory once a year in many countries.
4. Most people feel they are in need of more time and money, and millions of people in the world are in need of food and shelter.
5. Death is certainly inevitable for all of us.
6. If you are an adult, you probably no longer have to wear diapers!
7. When I was in elementary school, math and English were compulsory subjects.
8. Maybe as a child you were forced to eat some foods you didn't like.

60.3 *Suggested answers:*
1. (quite)   (very)   absolutely   **possible**
2. very   (absolutely)   highly   **impossible**
3. absolutely   (highly)   (quite)   **probable**
4. (highly)   absolutely   (extremely)   **unlikely**
5. very   extremely   (absolutely)   **inevitable**
6. (absolutely) highly   (quite)   **certain**

Note: Some English speakers may have different opinions about the above collocations. These answers are provided as guidelines only.

60.4 *Suggested answers:*
1. A videophone in every home is quite possible at some point during the 21st century.
2. Rain in the Amazon forest within eight days is highly probable.
3. A human being living to 250 is absolutely impossible.
4. A flying saucer landing in Hong Kong is highly unlikely.
5. A third world war? Some say it's extremely unlikely; others say it's absolutely inevitable.
6. A man becoming pregnant is absolutely impossible!
7. We hope you'll say that it's absolutely certain (or at least highly probable) that your English will improve!

Unit 61

61.1 1. **Racket** would be an ideal word here.
2. **Sound** or **sounds** since it is obviously pleasant. The uncountable meaning (**sound**) describes continuous sound; the countable meaning (**sounds**) means *different* sounds.
3. **Noises/sounds** if you mean different sounds, but **noise/sound** is also possible here if you interpret "some" to mean not a plural number, but *one* sound of "a certain, unidentifiable type," e.g., "Some animal must have gotten into the garden last night; look at these footprints." (It's not clear what kind of animal.)
4. **Din** would fit best here; **racket** and **noise** are also possible.
5. **Noise/sound** (uncountable without **a**); **noise** is probably a better choice because the sentence implies something unpleasant.

61.2 *Suggested answers:*

1. hiss	3. rustle	5. bang	7. roar
2. crash *or* clang	4. thud	6. rumble	8. creak

61.3

Verb/noun	Typical source(s) of the sound
hum	an engine or electrical appliance switched on, e.g., computer, fan
crunch	someone biting into an apple
screech	a car's tires when the brakes are applied very suddenly
chime	an old-fashioned pendulum clock or a big public clock on a building when it is sounding the hour
whistle	a kettle boiling
pop	a cork coming off a bottle of champagne
jingle	a set of keys being handled

61.4 1. a   2. c   3. b   4. a

Unit 62

62.1 *Suggested questions:*
1. Do you rent this house?
2. Could I borrow your camera? / Would you lend me your camera?
3. Which room have I been assigned? / Which room am I assigned to?
4. Does the school provide/supply textbooks?
5. Would you like to contribute/donate something to the fund for the physically challenged?
6. What does it cost to rent a car?

62.2 1. handed down   2. hand out   3. let go of   4. gave; away   5. hand over

62.3 *Possible answers:*
1. your wallet/bag/money
2. furniture/jewelry
3. a book / used clothing / a photograph
4. handouts/tests
5. an antique / a set of books

62.4   1. properties
           2. loans
           3. landlords
           4. tenants
           5. owner/proprietor
           6. estate
           7. borrowed
           8. properties/property
           9. possessions
          10. belongings/possessions

Note that in (8), the answer could be **properties,** meaning many different buildings or parcels of land, or **property,** meaning all the holdings taken together.

Unit 63

63.1   *Possible answers:*

1. a tree; a flagpole, telephone pole, or other kind of pole
2. a ship or boat
3. a river
4. a car, motorcycle, or other vehicle
5. a train

63.2   *Possible answers:*

2. a stream; blood flows through the body (i.e., through the veins); ideas and words can flow
3. an insect, a baby
4. a bird's or butterfly's wings, an article of clothing on a clothesline in the wind, a person's eyelashes, a curtain in the wind
5. Anything moving slowly on water may be drifting if it's not being guided, e.g., a boat or a piece of wood; snow on the ground may drift; a person can drift through life (moving without any sense of purpose or direction); your thoughts can drift to something or someone (it happens unintentionally).

63.3   *Possible situations:*

1. If you were very late for something.
2. If you *wanted* to be late for something, e.g., something unpleasant.
3. If you weren't in a hurry or you weren't very interested or enthusiastic about something you were doing, e.g., if you plod along at your studies without making much progress.
4. If you were hiding from someone, e.g., under a bed or behind a door.
5. If you injured your leg or foot and had difficulty walking on it.
6. If you came home very late or got up very early and didn't want to wake anyone.
7. If you were nervous or anxious about something or awaiting some important news.
8. If you had some free time and wanted to relax; for example on a pleasant weekend you might stroll (around) in the park. (also: **go for a stroll**)

63.4   1. A **slowpoke** is a person who takes an unacceptably long time to do things.
           2. A **drifter** is someone who moves from one place or job to another frequently, never staying very long.
           3. A **plodder** is a person who does things slowly and usually with great effort, and who shows little imagination.
           4. A **toddler** is a small child who is just learning to walk.

63.5   1. rate   2. pace   3. velocity   4. speed

Unit 64

64.1   *Suggested answers:*

1. sticky
2. downy/fluffy
3. slippery
4. prickly
5. rough/coarse
6. fluffy/furry
7. jagged
8. coarse
9. polished/smooth/sleek
10. smooth/shiny

Examples of things you might find in your home:

11. the metal surface of a stereo or television
12. a heavy-duty carpet; a doormat; a basement floor
13. a highly varnished tabletop; a mirror; a brass object
14. a cat or dog; a fur coat
15. bed linen; the surface of a table

64.2
1. This is about average for a baby.
2. Yes, a half liter a day would be about 3.5 liters a week, just under a gallon.
3. The person writing this weighs about 160 lbs., or 72.5 kg.
4. 16 ounces is a pound, or about 454 grams. It's *more* than enough for two (normal) sandwiches.

64.3   *Possible answers:*

1. a big cat such as a panther or leopard
2. a fish; an eel
3. a bear; a panda
4. a porcupine

64.4

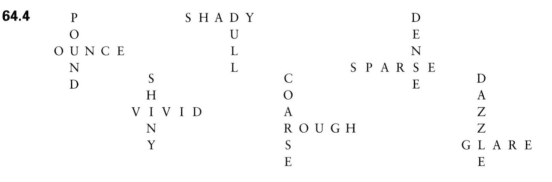

Unit 65

65.1
1. reach/attain/achieve/meet
2. fulfill/realize/achieve
3. realize/fulfill/accomplish
4. manage
5. succeed; went
6. misfired / came to nothing / failed
7. surpassed/exceeded
8. cope

65.2

Verb	Noun	Adjective	Adverb
realize	realization	realizable	–
–	difficulty	difficult	–
target	target	targeted	–
–	ambition	ambitious	ambitiously
fail	failure	failed, failing	–
trouble	trouble	troubling, troublesome, troubled	–
expect	expectation	expected, expecting	expectedly, expectingly

Comments:

difficult: has no adverb in English; we say "We did it **with difficulty.**"

targeted: "Our sales campaign is designed for a **targeted** group." [specifically chosen]

failed: "They have made three **failed** attempts to save the company."

failing: **failing** health

unfailingly: "failingly" doesn't exist, but **unfailingly** does, e.g., "She is **unfailingly** honest; you can trust her completely."

troubling: "We have seen some very **troubling** developments recently." [worrying]

troublesome: "They are a **troublesome** group of students." [cause trouble]

troubled: "I've been feeling rather **troubled** lately about my daughter." [worried with problems]

expecting: A woman who is pregnant is **expecting** (a baby). For this meaning, **expecting** is sometimes used without an object (informally).

65.3

1. I find **it** very difficult to understand English idioms.
2. She succeeded **in rising** to the highest rank in the company.
3. Do you ever have trouble **using** this photocopier? I always seem to.
4. I've **managed** to get all my work done this week; I'm taking a long weekend! (**accomplish** usually has a direct object, e.g., "I've accomplished a lot this week.")
5. I have **a** hard time driving to work with all the traffic.
6. We've **accomplished/achieved** a great deal during this past year.

65.4 *Possible answers:*

2. It would probably soon fold.
3. I'd have it checked.
4. Perhaps I'd rest and then continue the race, or stop if there were injuries.
5. Perhaps I'd try again, or abandon it and cut any losses.
6. I'd congratulate myself and then set new (and higher) goals!

Unit 66

66.1

2 cartons/bottles of milk
4 cans/bottles/six-packs of soda
a can of tuna fish
a package/box of chocolate chip cookies
a large box of matches
a jar of honey
2 bottles/cans of mineral water

66.2
1. pot
2. barrel, bottles, crate
3. bottles, cans, barrels, six-packs, crates
4. *any five of these:* bottle/carton (of milk or juice), jug (of milk or juice), mug (of coffee), box (of cereal), jar (of jam), glass (of milk or juice), bowl (of sugar), basket (of fruit)
5. (shopping) bag and basket
6. carton, bottle, can, glass, jug

66.3
1. a jar of peanut butter
2. a box of laundry detergent
3. a carton of orange juice
4. a tube of skin cream
5. a can of tomato sauce
6. a bag/sack of apples
7. a box of tissues
8. a jar of salsa
9. a carton of eggs
10. a bottle of dishwashing liquid

66.4 *Possible answers:*

1. tool, match
2. water, wine
3. beer, soda
4. fruit, fish
5. wine, hour
6. flower, tea

Unit 67

67.1
1. I've always doubted that she really loves him.
2. I have always held that people should rely on themselves more.
3. Claudia maintains that the teacher has been unfair to her.
4. I was convinced (that) I had been in that room before.
5. He feels/felt (that) we should have tried again.
6. I suppose (that) the government will raise taxes again soon.

67.2 *Suggested answers:*

1. I have strong views on raising children.
2. Some people believe in life after death, while others don't.
3. I've always been opposed to wasteful government spending.
4. What do you think of the new teacher?
5. It's not a good contract from management's point of view.
6. Is this the best strategy, in your opinion?
7. Well, that's just silly, to my mind.
8. I'm in favor of the proposed changes. Are you?

67.3 *Suggested answers:*

2. firm/strong
3. middle-of-the-road/moderate
4. fanatical/obsessive
5. conservative/traditional
6. radical/revolutionary

67.4 *Some possible sentences:*

1. I believe in God / the existence of God.
2. I'm conservative about finances but liberal when it comes to social policy.
3. I doubt that the weather will improve any time soon.
4. If you ask me, the best way to learn English is to practice it every chance you get.
5. To my mind, the most important issue in the world today is overpopulation.
6. I'm in favor of long prison sentences but opposed to capital punishment.

Unit 68

68.1

Adjective	Abstract noun	Adjective	Abstract noun
furious	fury	frustrated	frustration
anxious	anxiety	cheerful	cheerfulness
grateful	gratitude	enthusiastic	enthusiasm
ecstatic	ecstasy	apprehensive	apprehension
inspired	inspiration	excited	excitement

68.2
1. confused
2. depressed
3. frustrated
4. discontented
5. enthusiastic
6. fed up
7. upset
8. thrilled
9. sick and tired

68.3 *Possible answers:*

2. I felt slightly apprehensive before my first trip abroad.
3. I was very grateful to my friends for letting me stay at their home.
4. My father was in a terrible rage when he discovered a big dent in his parked car.
5. My friend was miserable for days when she broke up with her boyfriend.
6. I was so inspired by the book *The Story of San Michele* that I decided I would become a doctor.
7. I was initially very enthusiastic about skating, but I soon lost interest.
8. Most of my classmates are nervous right before an exam.

68.4
1. exciting
2. inspired
3. depressing
4. worried
5. confused
6. frustrating

Unit 69

69.1

Verb	Noun	Adjective	Adverb
–	passion	passionate	passionately
tempt	temptation	tempting	temptingly
attract	attraction	attractive	attractively
appeal	appeal	appealing	appealingly
disgust	disgust	disgusting/disgusted	disgustingly
hate	hatred	hateful/hated	hatefully
repel	repulsion	repulsive/repellent	repulsively
–	affection	affectionate	affectionately

69.2
1. women
2. birds
3. spiders
4. steal
5. pain/suffering
6. the future

69.3
1. I can't stand jazz.
2. His art appeals to me.
3. Beer revolts me. / I find beer revolting.
4. She has totally enchanted him.
5. I'm not looking forward to the exam.
6. I fell for him from the start.

69.4
1. b   2. a   3. b   4. b   5. a

69.5 *Possible answers:*

1. I like all kinds of fruit and I'm crazy about curry, but I can't stand liver.
2. language
3. sense of humor
4. I enjoy meeting people from all over the world.
5. chocolate
6. selfishness and a negative attitude toward life

Unit 70

70.1 *Suggested answers:*

1. confessed   3. threatened   5. complained/grumbled
2. boasted   4. begged   6. urged

70.2
1. He confessed to breaking the vase. (*or* He confessed that he had broken . . .)
2. The little boy boasted about being the smartest person in the class. (*or* He boasted that he was . . .)
3. She threatened to cut off my allowance if I didn't behave.
4. He begged me to help him. (*or* He begged for help.)
5. She complained/grumbled that the hotel was filthy. (*or* She complained/grumbled about the hotel being filthy.)
6. He urged Jim to try harder.

70.3
1. a threat   3. an objection   5. insistent
2. a complaint   4. a beggar   6. argumentative

70.4
1. urged/begged
2. (a) to   (b) on   (c) about
3. groan, grumble
4. boast – brag; argue – disagree; confess – admit; urge – encourage; beg – plead

70.5

Adverb	Adjective	Noun
angrily	angry	anger
furiously	furious	fury
bitterly	bitter	bitterness
miserably	miserable	misery
cheerfully	cheerful	cheerfulness
gratefully	grateful	gratitude
anxiously	anxious	anxiety
proudly	proud	pride

70.6 *Possible sentences:*
1. "We can easily break into the bank," she said **boldly.**
2. "Thank you so much," he said **gratefully.**
3. "I wish you'd hurry up," he said **impatiently.**
4. "I love you so much," she said **passionately.**
5. "I'll go if you really want me to," he said **reluctantly.**
6. "I don't know anyone here," she said **shyly.**
7. "Of course, I believe you," he said **sincerely.**

Unit 71

71.1 *Some possible answers:*

1. That smells wonderful.   4. That sounds terrific.
2. Your hair looks great.   5. You look upset/worried. What's the matter?
3. This tastes delicious.   6. He/She smells disgusting.

71.2
1. witness   3. glimpse   5. stare/gaze
2. peer   4. glance   6. observe

71.3   1. noticed   3. grasped   5. stroked/petted   7. grabbed/snatched
    2. tapped   4. Press   6. gazed   8. handled

Note: In (6) we would probably say **gaze**, rather than **stare**, at a view. You might gaze at something you admire or find interesting without knowing it.

71.4   1. salty   3. hot/spicy   5. spicy/hot
    2. sweet   4. sour   6. bitter

71.5   *Possible answers:*

    1. aromatic   3. scented/perfumed   5. vile/stinking
    2. smelly/stinking   4. fragrant   6. musty

71.6   1. UFOs   3. ghosts   5. déjà vu
    2. telepathy   4. intuition   6. premonition

71.7   *Possible answers:*

1. *sight:* I climbed up to the top of a mountain and was above the level of some low clouds. I could not see the ground but could see the tops of half a dozen other mountains rising out of the clouds.
2. *hearing:* I heard my newborn baby crying for the first time.
3. *taste:* I tasted some wonderful soup after a long day's walk in the hills.
4. *touch:* I touched the soft fur of a lion cub.
5. *smell:* I will always remember smelling the sea after a long time away from it.
6. *sixth sense:* I have often had the experience of not having written to an old friend for a long time, and then our letters to each other suddenly cross in the mail.

Unit 72

72.1   1. to blush   2. to shiver   3. to blink   4. to wink   5. to sigh

72.2   1. Someone is snoring.   4. Someone's stomach is rumbling.
    2. Someone is yawning.   5. Someone has burped.
    3. Someone is hiccupping.

72.3   2. frown   3. yawn   4. grin   5. wink   6. snore

72.4   1. chewing   2. grin   3. lick   4. burp   5. perspiring

The central word is **hiccup**.

72.5   It is possible to draw bubble networks in any way that seems logical to you and that helps you to learn. You could group together words associated with **illness** (sneeze, cough, shiver, etc.), or you could organize your networks around **parts of the body** (e.g., **yawn, lick, bite**, etc.) around the word **mouth**. Words that might be added to the networks include **hug, sip, wheeze**, and **stare**.

Unit 73

73.1   2. baa-baa   3. woof-woof   4. oink-oink   5. cock-a-doodle-doo

73.2   1. crowing   3. barked   5. were clucking
    2. mooing   4. neighing   6. purring

73.3   1. true
    2. true
    3. false – **hoot,** when used about people, is often followed by the phrase "with laughter."
    4. true
    5. false – **grunting** at someone suggests a lack of interest in that person.

73.4   *Possible sentences:*
    1. As soon as she heard the phone ring, she flew across the room to answer it.
    2. I learned to swim in the pond near my home.
    3. The hillside was covered with loose stones, and the hikers slithered uncertainly down the slope.
    4. He hopped across the room to avoid putting any weight on his painful ankle.
    5. The little children happily trotted off to school.
    6. I'll have to gallop through my work if I'm going to get it done on time.

73.5   1. puppy *or* puppies (a **spaniel** is a kind of dog)
    2. kittens (a **tom** is a male cat and a **Siamese** is a kind of cat)
    3. cub(s) (**polar bears,** like all other bears, have cubs)
    4. lambs (**wool** comes from sheep)

73.6   You probably wouldn't want to be called any of the adjectives in D except perhaps **dogged,** when it means persistent (in a good way), and **foxy,** when it means attractive.

Unit 74

74.1   2. bucket   3. plate   4. handle   5. block   6. shot

74.2   1. springs to mind   3. just goes to show   5. leaves a lot to be desired
    2. flies in the face of   4. 're sitting pretty

74.3   *Possible groupings:*

Be + prepositional phrase
be in a bind [be in a difficult situation or predicament], **be up to it** [be capable of something], **be out of sorts** [be unwell]

With 's
child's play [very easy] and **a fool's errand** [a wasted/pointless effort to get something] (see Unit 81 for more of these)

With hold
hold your tongue [be silent], **hold your horses** [wait before acting/speaking]. **Hold your tongue** could also go with **keep mum** [be silent] because they are very close in meaning. The difference is that **hold your tongue** is often used in aggressive commands, e.g., "Hold your tongue, you!" [Shut up!]

Binomials (phrases joined by and, but, or)
rough and ready [basic / lacking in comfort], **odds and ends** [small items difficult to group along with others], **give or take** [as in "It'll cost $700, give or take $50," meaning between $650 and $750 approximately] (see Unit 77)

74.4   1. go to bed
    2. a stronger, more informal version of **child's play** [simple, too easy]
    3. clearly means more than just "unemployed," since he didn't have a home; it means totally without money or property, living and sleeping on the streets

Unit 75

75.1   1. to think of it   3. Speaking   5. I was saying
2. ask me   4. reminds me

75.2   1. this and that *or* this, that, and the other   3. this is it
2. That's it.   4. that's that

75.3

now and then / every now and then
[occasionally]

|
NOW

Now then!   right now / here and now
[attract attention because   [immediately; also used
you're going to say something]   to emphasize your point]

1. Do you want me to do it here and now / right now, or can it wait?
2. Now then, everybody, listen carefully. I have news for you.
3. I bump into her in town (every) now and then, but not that often.

75.4   1. come to think of it . . .   3. if all else fails . . .
   if worst comes to worst . . .   4. if worst comes to worst . . .
   when it comes to . . .   5. as far as I'm concerned . . .
2. as luck would have it . . .   6. what with one thing and another . . .

Unit 76

76.1   1. hatter   2. ox   3. mouse   4. dog   5. bat

76.2   1. slept   2. falling   3. snow   4. a sheet

76.3   1. as quick as a wink   3. as flat as a pancake   5. as strong as an ox
2. as busy as a bee   4. as fresh as a daisy

76.4   *Across*
1. beet   2. hatter   4. sheet   5. daisy   7. mouse   9. bone

Down
1. bat   2. hard   3. easy   6. ice   8. cucumber   10. feather

76.5   1. He/She has eyes like a hawk.   3. She/He eats like a horse and drinks like a fish.
2. It worked like a charm.   4. He/She has a brain like a sieve.

Unit 77

77.1   1. high and dry   3. wined and dined   5. give and take
2. safe and sound   4. prim and proper

77.2   law and order   now and then   neat and clean
pick and choose   sick and tired   leaps and bounds

Suggested sentences:
1. The new mayor promised that law and order would be a priority.
2. The house looks neat and clean now for our visitors.
3. I'm sick and tired of traffic jams. I'm going to start using the train.

4. My command of English vocabulary has improved in leaps and bounds since I've been using this book.
5. There are lots of courses. You can pick and choose.
6. I've seen her now and then, taking her dog for a walk.

77.3   1. or   2. or   3. to   4. or   5. but   6. but

Unit 78

78.1   1. . . . of gold.   3. . . . as gold.   5. . . . on the uptake.
       2. . . . as nails.   4. . . . study.

78.2   1. a know-it-all   4. at the head of the class
       2. the teacher's pet   5. a lazybones (*note*: singular in form)
       3. a big mouth

78.3   *Idioms with gold:* to be as good as gold / to have a heart of gold

       1. . . . a heart of stone.   4. . . . a change of heart.
       2. . . . have a heart!   5. . . . have my heart set on it.
       3. . . . his heart in the right place.

Another example of a key-word family might be **eye**:
He only has **eyes for** Mary. [He never looks at other women.]
She has **an eye for** antiques. [She is good at spotting them.]
He has **eyes in the back of his head.** / He has **eyes like a hawk.** [said of someone who never misses anything, especially when other people are doing something wrong]

Look up **eye** in a dictionary and see how many more idioms there are using the word.

78.4   (a) your nerves (always with possessive: my, our, John's, etc.)
       (b) the neck (always used with **the**)
       (c) the back (always used with **the**)

78.5   1. a pain in the neck   2. a heart of gold   3. a cold fish   4. middle-of-the-road

Unit 79

79.1   *positive:*   to be in seventh heaven   to feel/be as pleased as Punch
       negative: to feel/be a bit down   to be in a snit

       Note: The expression "pleased as Punch" comes from the well-known puppet show "Punch and Judy." Punch is a quarrelsome, humpbacked, comic character who constantly fights with his wife, Judy. The phrase "pleased as Punch" describes Punch's pleasure and satisfaction when he escapes punishment for his behavior.

79.2   *Some possible answers:*

       1. on cloud nine, in seventh heaven, walking on air
       2. in a snit, or even in a foul mood
       3. as pleased as Punch, on cloud nine, walking on air, a happy camper
       4. in a snit *and* in a foul mood!
       5. down in the dumps, a bit down, not myself
       6. on cloud nine, in seventh heaven, walking on air

79.3   1. . . . to death.   4. . . . cloud nine.
       2. . . . the weather.   5. . . . out of my skin.
       3. . . . camper.   6. . . . eat a horse.

79.4   *Scorpio:*
itching to – have a great desire or longing to do something
(to be) on the edge of your seat – to be impatient, excited, in suspense, waiting for
   something to happen

Leo:
to be up in arms – to be very angry and protesting loudly
to be of two minds – unable to decide or make up your mind about something

1. I'm of two minds about that job in Brazil.
2. I've been on the edge of my seat all day. What happened? Tell me!
3 We enjoyed our vacation, but by the end of it, we were itching to go home.
4. Everyone was up in arms when they canceled the outing.

79.5   1. frighten/scare someone out of his/her wits   3. be in a foul mood
   2. swell with pride   4. be carried away

Example sentences:

1. That TV program about nuclear weapons frightened/scared me out of my wits.
2. Seeing him in the graduation procession made his parents swell with pride.
3. Careful! The boss is in a foul mood today.
4. I know I shouldn't have listened to her lies, but I got carried away by her charming
   personality.

Unit 80

80.1   You might find some of the following idioms and expressions, along with others,
   depending on your dictionary:

1. come to a **dead** end
   a **dead** duck [an idea, plan, or person that's doomed to fail; beyond hope]
   a **dead** ringer [someone who looks just like someone else]
   I wouldn't be caught **dead** . . . [something you would never do, wear, etc.]
   dead to the world [sleeping very deeply]

2. play your **cards** close to the vest
   in the **cards** [destined / very likely to happen]
   play your **cards** right [deal with situations skillfully]
   play your trump **card** [use your best advantage]
   hold all the **cards** [have all the power, control]

3. **pour** oil on troubled waters
   pour cold water on an idea / a plan [criticize something so that people don't want to
      do it anymore]
   pour your heart/troubles out to somebody [tell them all your troubles]
   it's **pouring** rain [raining very heavily]

4. **stir** things up
   cause a **stir** [cause great excitement or anger among everyone]
   stir-crazy [extremely restless because of feelings of being trapped]
   stir-fry [vegetables, meat, etc., fried quickly on high heat in a lightly oiled pan]

80.2   1. take a back seat   5. spot
   2. stir things up   6. up and take notice
   3. light at the end of the tunnel 7. grasp of
   4. the bottom of things / it / the matter   8. my cards on the table

2. a compromise
3. in great suspense
4. are found together in the same place and connected to one another
5. behave yourself / follow the rules
6. safe / out of danger
7. in an impossible or a hopeless situation

Unit 81

81.1   *Suggested answers:*

1. The hotel we were staying in was out of this world.
2. Joe is head and shoulders above the other kids when it comes to arithmetic.
3. This restaurant puts all the other restaurants in town to shame. / This restaurant is head and shoulders above all the other restaurants in town.
4. You're miles / light years ahead of me in understanding all this technology; I'm impressed.
5. The cream of the crop from our university went on to business school. *or* The top-notch graduates . . .

81.2
1. scaredy cat
2. to have a green thumb
3. to be on the ball
4. to butter someone up

81.3   1. (3)   2. (4)   3. (1)   4. (2)

81.4   *Suggested answers:*

1. Al is a snake in the grass.
2. Steve has a way with the secretaries; just look at how they react when he wants something done.
3. He often runs down / knocks his school.
4. She picks apart everything I say.
5. She wants a promotion, a company car, and a raise, yet she can't even get to work on time. She takes the cake! / She wants to have her cake and eat it too!

81.5   1. There is a verb **to ham it up,** which can be used to criticize an actor's performance if it is overdone and grossly exaggerated; we can call such an actor or actress **a ham.**

2. If you don't like something or somebody, you can say "It/He/She just **isn't my cup of tea,**" which means you do not feel attracted to it or to the person.

3. If you say something is **icing on the cake,** you are praising it as something extra good on top of something that is already good. "Flying first class was wonderful, and being met at the other end by a limousine was icing on the cake."

4. If you call a person **a nutcase, as nutty as a fruitcake,** or **nuts,** you mean they are mad/crazy or perhaps eccentric. Also, **a tough nut to crack** is a difficult problem or a person who is difficult to understand or convince.

5. If you say someone **brings home the bacon,** it means he/she earns a living and supports his/her family, which is usually seen as praise.

Unit 82

82.1   *Suggested answers:*

1. It seems that Ann can't get a word in edgewise.
2. It seems that Dan can't make heads or tails of what Meg is saying.
3. It seems that Sam and Lisa are talking behind George's back / are talking about George behind his back.

82.2   1. wrap up the discussion   3. start the ball rolling
          2. (put it) in a nutshell   4. get/come to the point

82.3   1. speaks   2. talk   3. talking

Unit 83

83.1   1. B is driving a hard bargain.
          2. A could be described as someone who has a finger in every pie.
          3. A knows the name of the song but just can't remember. It's on the tip of his/her tongue.

83.2   1. Can I tell you about a problem I have? I just have to **get it off my chest.** It's been **on my mind** for a while now.
          2. They charged us $200 for a tiny room without a TV. It was a **rip-off!** *or* They really **ripped us off!**
          3. We'll have just enough time **to get a bite to eat** before the show.
          4. **I've got to hand it to her,** Maria handled the situation admirably. *or* **I've got to hand it to Maria;** she handled . . .
          5. I think I'll just go upstairs and **take a nap,** if nobody minds.
          6. We had to **pay through the nose** for the apartment, but we had no choice. *or* We had to **pay top dollar** for the apartment . . .

83.3   1. foot the bill   2. put your feet up   3. couch potato

Follow-up:

to hold one's tongue: "I'm going to hold my tongue. The last time I said anything it only caused trouble, so this time, I'll say nothing."

to be head over heels in love (with someone): "Mike's head over heels in love. He talks about Jeanne all day long and blushes every time her name's mentioned."

to toe the line: "The boss gave him a very hard time yesterday about his lazy attitude and all his absences. He warned him he might lose his job. He's going to have to toe the line from now on."

to tiptoe / to walk on tiptoe: "We'll have to tiptoe past the children's bedroom. I don't want to wake them up."

to get someone's back up: "Sally won't get any sympathy from her coworkers; in fact, quite the contrary, she seems to get everyone's back up with her selfish attitude."

to back out (of): "We agreed to become business partners, but she backed out (of it) at the last minute."

to do something behind someone's back: "He's always talking about his friends behind their backs. That's why they don't stay friends."

Unit 84

84.1   1. Half a loaf is better than none.   3. Too many cooks spoil the broth.
          2. Don't put all your eggs in one basket.

84.2   1. Never look a gift horse in the mouth. [Both proverbs advise you to take advantage of good fortune when you have it in front of you.]

          2. Don't cross your bridges before you come to them. [Both proverbs warn you not to anticipate future events.]

          3. Never judge a book by its cover. [Both proverbs warn against trusting the external or superficial features of something.]

4. Familiarity breeds contempt. ["Absence makes the heart grow fonder" says that if you cannot be with someone or something, you will love the person / the thing more. "Familiarity breeds contempt" says that being with someone/something too much makes you come to hate the person / the thing.]

84.3   1. People who live in glass houses shouldn't throw stones.
2. When the cat's away, the mice will play.
3. Where there's smoke, there's fire.

Unit 85

85.1   1. manage to see
2. constitute (**make up** with this meaning is usually used in the passive)
3. fasten
4. invent
5. succeed *or* progress
6. tied and arranged
7. write

85.2   2. without   3. up   4. out   5. up

85.3   1. . . . make of that statement.   3. Do them up or . . .
2. . . . make the most of . . .   4. . . . make out that they . . .

85.4   *Possible word forks:*

	a story
make up	her face
	a prescription

	a check
make out	that he's rich
	some figures in the distance

	your buttons
do up	her hair
	your coat

85.5   *Possible groups:*

Work: **do** the housework / the laundry / some gardening / the dishes / the shopping / the cooking / homework / business with; **make** a living / a bed / a profit / a cup of coffee or tea / a meal.

Trying, succeeding, and failing: **do** your best / a good job / harm; **make** money / an attempt / an effort / a mistake / the most of / the best of / a success of / a good or bad impression / trouble / a point of / allowances for.

Things you say: **make** a promise / arrangements / an agreement / a phone call / a suggestion / a decision / an excuse / fun of / believe / a fuss about.

Physical things: **make** war / love / noise / a gesture / a face.

85.6   1. WAR   3. profit   5. a good impression
2. your best   4. allowances for   6. housework

Unit 86

86.1   1. back   3. over   5. off   7. up
2. on   4. on   6. out

86.2 *Here is one way of completing the diagram for* **take:**

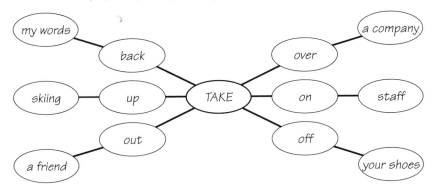

Here is a possible diagram for **bring:**

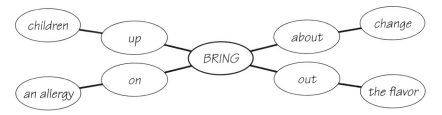

86.3 *Possible answers:*

2. She takes after her father.
3. I've taken up tennis recently.
4. It really seems to have taken off now.
5. I'll bring him around somehow.
6. Probably because it took off two hours late.
7. To bring about change.

86.4
1. The story of the movie takes place in Casablanca during the war.
2. Today's newspaper brings to light some fascinating information about the President.
3. How does he always manage to take things in his stride?
4. The view from the top of the hill took my breath away.
5. He took advantage of her weakness at the time and she sold it to him.
6. The main function of a nurse is to take care of the sick.
7. Whenever you're upset, you always take it out on the children.

Unit 87

87.1 *Suggested answers:*

I don't **receive** interesting advertising leaflets very often these days. However, an unusual one came this morning. It was headed "Are little things **depressing you?**" It went on, "If so, **purchase/buy** some of our special tablets today. Taking just one in the morning will help you **succeed/manage** at work, at home, or at school. It will stop the feeling that you're **making no progress** in life and will ensure that you **become rich** and successful with little effort on your part. Send just $25 today and you will **receive** your tablets and your key to success within ten days."

87.2   1. through   2. over   3. by   4. along   5. know

A1 – B5   A2 – B3   A3 – B4   A4 – B2   A5 – B1

87.4   *Possible answers:*

1. . . . my favorite coffee mug.
2. . . . Jack spilled soup on Jill's dress.
3. . . . work in nice weather like this.
4. . . . going to the meeting.
5. Living in such a small place . . .

87.5   *Some example sentences:*

She was the first to **get off** the plane. [disembark from]
I don't understand what you are **getting at.** [suggest, try to say]
They are due to **get back** at 6:00. [return]
You **get ahead** in that company only if you are related to the boss. [succeed, be promoted]
I'd like to **get in touch with** my old friends from school. [communicate with]
Get off my back, will you? [Stop nagging/criticizing me!]
Get lost! [very informal; Go away, stop bothering me!]
Get a life! [informal; often spoken in jest to tell someone to stop being boring or silly]

Unit 88

88.1
1. They have recently established a committee on neighborhood crime.
2. We try to reserve some money for our vacation every week.
3. Ignore all your negative feelings and listen with an open mind.
4. If we hadn't departed so late, we would have arrived on time.
5. The President's unpopular proposals caused a wave of protests.
6. When we cross the international date line, should we fix our clocks at an earlier time?

88.2   *Possible answers:*

1. put out a cigarette / your host
2. put forward an idea / a proposal
3. put off an appointment / customers
4. put across ideas / opinions
5. put up a guest / a sign
6. put on a fake smile / clothes
7. put away papers / tools
8. put up with someone's behavior / a bad situation

88.3   *Some possible answers:*

1. Yes, it set me back quite a bit.
2. I haven't had time to put things away yet.
3. Yes, of course, I can put you up.
4. You're putting me on!
5. He is hoping to set up a business of his own.
6. The other kids put her up to it; it wasn't her idea.

88.4   *Possible answers:*

1. He is very set in his ways.
2. He's bound to put two and two together if you keep on behaving like that.
3. She has set her sights/heart on becoming president of the company.
4. It's sound business advice not to put all your eggs in one basket.
5. Please put your mind to the problem at hand.
6. She threw lighter fluid on the trash and set fire to it / set it on fire.
7. This is the first time I've ever set foot in the southern hemisphere.
8. You really should put your foot down with the children or there'll be trouble later.
9. If the teacher doesn't set a good example, the children certainly won't behave.
10. Would you mind putting in a good word for me?

Unit 89

89.1 2. check   4. choose   6. become conscious
3. being published   5. used

89.2
1. . . . to a decision.
2. . . . to mind . . .
3. . . . into bloom/blossom.
4. . . . to a standstill.
5. . . . to an end.
6. . . . into operation/existence/use . . .
7. . . . to blows.
8. . . . into view/sight.

89.3
1. It goes without saying
2. went to great lengths
3. on the go
4. go far
5. as far as it goes

89.4
1. The firm went bankrupt.
2. Only Jack's proposal.
3. Seven-thirty, normally.
4. Over $1000!
5. Right after the news.
6. It's a fight, I think.

89.5 *Possible answers:*
1. . . . but also a box of photographs.
2. . . . that bag.
3. . . . such a terrible experience again.
4. . . . the defendant was guilty.
5. . . . the death of a loved one.
6. . . . put salt on it right away.

Unit 90

90.1 1. back on 2. up to 3. up 4. into 5. up 6. to 7. out

90.2
2. She never looks you in the eye.
3. Good luck! It's not easy to find work.
4. Yes, I've changed my hair style.
5. You'd never think she's a grandmother.
6. You'd better look before you leap.
7. Maybe. He's always looking for trouble.
8. She looked daggers at me just now.

90.3
1. . . . the party.
2. . . . anyone less fortunate than yourself.
3. . . . the author's childhood.
4. . . . I feel optimistic.
5. . . . the proposals at the end of the report.
6. . . . you're next in town.

90.4
1. much to look at
2. look out
3. look on the bright side of things
4. look down on / look down their noses at the homeless
5. look over/through
6 looked the other way

90.5 *Possible answers:*
1. look for your glasses / your keys / a new job / trouble / the meaning of life / love
2. look up a word / a date / a telephone number / an address / an old friend
3. look through a report / a document / a magazine / a stack of papers
4. look up to your parents / a friend / the boss / a leader

Unit 91

91.1   1. over/through   3. down   5. down   7. off
2. to/about   4. up   6. slip

91.2   1. Why doesn't she see through him?
2. I ran into Jack at the library yesterday.
3. I cooked dinner yesterday. It's your turn (to do it) today.
4. I thought I was seeing things when I saw a monkey in the garden.
5. I wish you'd let me be.
6. When she left him, it/she broke his heart.

91.3   *Possible answers:*

1. . . . the roads will be closed.
2. . . . of the rope and fell into a crevice.
3. . . . those who came were very enthusiastic.
4. . . . she refused to speak to him.
5. . . . until the party was nearly over.
6. . . . coffee.

91.4   *Some possible answers:*

1. I very much regret turning down an opportunity to work in Canada.
2. A train I was on once broke down, making me very late for an important interview.
3. When I was younger, I didn't see eye to eye with my parents very often. It was probably because different generations often see things differently.
4. Stubbornness and good looks both run in my family.
5. Every New Year I resolve to turn over a new leaf – I decide to reply to all my letters promptly and to be generally much more organized.
6. I have to see to the car, which has been making strange noises.
7. My own home has never been broken into, but a friend's house was once when I was staying with him.
8. I usually turn in by 11 p.m. on weekdays, later on weekends.

91.5   *Here are two possibilities for each verb:*

see
His parents have promised to **see** him **through** college.
It's hard to find your way around this building – I'll **see** you **out**.

run
Our dog was **run over** by a car.
She **ran up** an enormous bill at the department store.

turn
Please **turn down** your radio – I can't concentrate.
I **turned in** my homework a day late.

let
Let sleeping dogs **lie**.
This skirt is too tight – I'll have to **let** it **out**.

break
I'm **broke** – can you lend me ten dollars until payday?
Breaking in new shoes can be painful.

Unit 92

92.1 2. work dispute at a school
3. research about diet and health
4. marriage of a famous person
5. exploratory spacecraft is not launched
6. study involving work and sleep

92.2 *Suggested answers:*
1. Steps are being taken with the aim of providing more work for people.
2. Approval has been given to place restrictions on the use of water.
3. A man resigned from his job after undergoing some kind of unpleasant experience there.
4. A public opinion survey has investigated how people spend their money.
5. The electric company is trying to increase the rates people pay for electricity.

92.3 1. investigate
2. explodes (in)
3. promises
4. leads / is a major figure in
5. increases/encourages

92.5 Make sure that you note down not only the headline but also a brief indication of what the story was about so that the headline makes sense when you review your work later.

Unit 93

93.1 1. American English; British English is **labour.**
2. British English; American English is **center.**
3. American English; British English is **realise;** however, the ending **-ize** instead of **-ise** is becoming more common in British English these days.
4. American English; in British English it is spelled **theatre** (and a **movie theater** would be called a **cinema** in British English).
5. British English; American English is **neighbor.**
6. British English; American English is **industrialize.**

93.2 *The pictures represent:*

British English	American English
1. aerial	antenna
2. lift	elevator
3. sweets	candy
4. nappy	diaper
5. pram	baby carriage
6. Sellotape	adhesive tape / Scotch tape
7. lorry	truck
8. torch	flashlight

93.3 1. Let's take the underground.
2. Please pass the biscuits.
3. It's in the wardrobe.
4. We've run out of petrol.
5. I'll ring you tonight.
6. It's in the boot.
7. I hate standing in a queue.
8. Single or return?
9. He left the tap on.
10. Excuse me, where's the toilet/WC?

93.4 1. The British man, because people do not usually talk about needing to change their underclothes (**pants** in British English), although he might well express the desire to change outer clothes (**pants** in American English and **trousers** in British English).
2. (a) two flights in the U.K. and (b) one flight in the U.S.
3. A British English speaker would ask for a bill in a cafe.
4. (a) over his shirt in the U.S. and (b) under his shirt in the U.K. (*Note:* These are two different articles of clothing.)

93.5 There are many other words you could add. Some might be:

American English	British English
eggplant	aubergine
zucchini	courgette
french fries	chips
potato chips	potato crisps
roast (of meat)	joint
can opener	tin opener
trash can	rubbish bin
dishcloth	tea towel
counterclockwise	anticlockwise
unlisted (telephone number)	ex-directory
slowpoke	slowcoach
talk show	chat show
swimsuit	swimming costume
run (in a stocking)	ladder
suspenders (clothing)	braces
to like	to fancy
intermission	interval
orchestra seats (in a theater)	stalls
news clipping	news cutting
realtor / real estate agent	estate agent
checking account	current account
windshield (of car)	windscreen
license plate (of car)	numberplate
fast lane (highway)	outside lane
wrench	spanner
football	American football
soccer	football/soccer

Unit 94

94.1
1. We were driving down the Trans Canada when we saw a **Mountie** in the rear view mirror.
2. Let's meet at the Eaton **Centre.**
3. Most of the residents in this city are **Francophones.**
4. All I've got is a **loonie.**

94.2
1. journalist; university
2. business
3. afternoon
4. adults/parents
5. Australia

94.3
1. people awaiting trial
2. underwear
3. have no children
4. man who annoys women
5. the general public
6. someone with extreme views

94.4
1. She gave birth to a baby girl.
2. A church.
3. Yes, he is.
4. A lake.

94.5
1. Scottish English: Would you like a small glass of whiskey?
2. Australian English: We got terribly bitten by mosquitoes at yesterday's barbecue.
3. Canadian English: That's a nice sofa.
4. Indian English: The police caught the bandit/thief.

Unit 95

95.1
1. modem
2. floppy disk drive
3. spreadsheet
4. desktop computer
5. laptop

95.2
1. processing
2. virus
3. laptops / laptop computers
4. floppy; hard
5. surfing/cruising
6. newbie; FAQ
7. electronic mail / e-mail
8. home page

95.3
2. by the way
3. Are you there?
4. laughing out loud
5. rolling on the floor laughing
6. ta-ta for now (= goodbye)

Unit 96

96.1
2. at a zoo
3. on a road or highway
4. outside a fitting room in a store
5. on a wall
6. on a city street or other public place where there are trash cans/bins
7. in a store, bar, or other place where alcoholic drinks are sold
8. in a club, such as a health or sports club
9. near a trash bin or garbage dump
10. in a parking lot or garage
11. outdoors, possibly in a residential or business area, or in a park
12. on an airplane

96.2
1. to bring a legal case against
2. a container, can, or bin
3. someone who goes on private property without permission
4. money paid as a punishment
5. to ask for something (usually money) or try to do business
6. to forbid something
7. someone who disobeys the rules/law
8. to damage, misuse, or alter something improperly
9. a means of transportation, such as a car
10. to search through something, moving the contents about

96.3
1. You would see this sign at Customs (e.g., at an airport). It lets people know that this is the way to go if they do not have any goods to pay duty on.

2. You would see this at a sports stadium or playing field. It warns people who are watching the game that they must not throw anything onto the field or they will be forced to leave.

3. You might see this warning in a store, a bar, or any other place where alcoholic drinks are sold, as well as on bottles of beer and wine. It warns expectant mothers that it may be dangerous to drink alcohol while they are pregnant. (Notices like this are usually required by law.)

4. You would see this sign in a store. It lets customers know that they can't return goods they have bought there for a refund.

5. This would be an outdoor sign on a city street. It warns people that they would be breaking the law by throwing trash (papers, food, etc.) into the street.

6. You would see this sign on a road or highway. It lets drivers know that two lanes will become one very soon, and if they are driving in the right lane, they should try to move into the left lane.

7. You would see this sign in a store. It warns people that if they steal things from the store while pretending to shop, they will be arrested and taken to court.

8. You would see this in a store or other place of business. It lets people know that some (or all) members of the staff speak Spanish as well as English.

9. This might be a neon (electric) sign outside a hotel or motel. It tells people that there are no rooms available right now.

96.4
1. Portuguese spoken here.
2. Post no bills.
3. No soliciting. / Soliciting prohibited.

96.5
1. This means that if you break an item (even accidentally), you must pay for it. You would probably see this sign in a store.
2. This is a street sign that means "absolutely no parking." It would be seen on a sidewalk near a curb, where people might want to park their cars. (This sign is often identified with New York City.)

Unit 97

97.1   *Suggested rewording:*

> **Now Eagle Airlines offers even more to the business traveler who needs comfort!**
>
> Let us fly you to your destination in first-class comfort, served by the best-trained flight attendants in the world. Successful business executives know that they must arrive fresh and ready for work no matter how long the journey. With Eagle Diplomat-Class you can do just that. And, what's more, your spouse can travel with you on all international flights for half the regular fare! Your secretary can book you on any of our flights 24 hours a day at 800-555-1234. All you have (or s/he has) to do is pick up the phone.

97.2
man hours – person hours	cleaning lady – cleaner
unmanned – unstaffed	mankind – human beings
forefathers – ancestors	foreman – supervisor

97.3   *Suggested answers:*
1. We'll have to elect a new chair / chairperson next month.
2. Several firefighters and police officers were hurt in the riots.
3. The airline reports that its flight attendants are on strike.
4. I wonder what time the mail / mail carrier / letter carrier comes every day.
5. Is this fabric natural or synthetic?
6. Her brother's a nurse, and she's a doctor.
7. TV news reporters and camera operators rushed to the scene of the accident.
8. The candidate appeals to big business, but what about wage earners?
9. A sales representative for the company will stop by and leave samples.
10. This radio program likes to conduct interviews of average/ordinary people.

97.4
1. **Barber** is often socially marked as male.
2. **Secretary** is often socially marked as female.
3. **Farmer** is often socially marked as male.
4. **Dressmaker** is often socially marked as female.
5. **Hairdresser** is often socially marked as female.
6. **Weatherman** is linguistically marked as male by the suffix **-man**. A more neutral term would be **weather forecaster** or **meteorologist.**
7. **Detective** is often socially marked as male.
8. **Monk** is linguistically marked as male (female = **nun**).
9. **Waitress** is linguistically marked as female by the suffix **-ess**. A more neutral word is **server.**
10. **Burglar** is often socially marked as male.
11. **Butcher** is often socially marked as male.
12. **Truck driver** is often socially marked as male.

Note: Even though these words seem to bring to mind one gender or the other, it is best not to assume that someone in any of these occupations belongs to either gender, unless you know for certain.

Unit 98

98.1
1. **Mr.** Henry Chen
   P.O. Box 202X
   St. Louis, Missouri (or **MO**)
   U.S.A.

2. **Ms.** Maria Howard
   c/o T. Rivera
   430 Yonge **St.**
   Apt. 5
   Toronto, **Ont.**
   Can.

3. N. Lowe **& Co.**
   7, Bridge **Rd.**
   Freeminster
   U.K.

The title **Ms.** sounds like "miz." It is unusual in that it resembles an abbreviation but has no full form.

Note: In U.S. addresses, there is a two-letter abbreviation for every state, such as **MO** for **Missouri,** but some people write out the full word in addresses. Similarly, the Canadian province of **Ontario** might be abbreviated or written as a full word.

98.2
1. Bachelor of Arts (A)
2. Federal Bureau of Investigation (A)
3. Professor (C, E, F)
4. personal identification number (e.g., on a bank card) (B)
5. Test of English as a Foreign Language (B)
6. to be announced (A, D)
7. extension (telephone) (E)
8. United Nations Educational, Scientific, and Cultural Organization (B)
9. condominium (E)
10. self-contained underwater breathing apparatus (B)

Note: In (3), **Prof.** can be a title (sections C, F), short for *Professor,* in which case it is pronounced as the full form. As a clipping (section E), **prof** is used informally and pronounced as a one-syllable word.

98.3

Memorandum from: Mister Braneless   Date: March 24th
To: all staff
Copy to: C. Hothead, Supply Department
Regarding: laboratory equipment

All new laboratory equipment should be registered with the Supply
Department, Room 354 (extension 2683). Please note: New items must
be registered before five o'clock in the afternoon on the last day of
the month of purchase, that is, within the current budgeting month.
All account numbers must be recorded.

98.4
1. **mph** = miles per hour; on a road sign
2. **XL** = extra large; on a clothing label
3. **UFOs** = unidentified flying objects; in a newspaper headline
4. **CFC** = chlorofluorocarbons: harmful chemicals found in sprays, which can damage the environment; on an aerosol can
5. **Dep.** = depart/departure; **Arr.** = arrive/arrival; on an airline schedule or ticket
6. **RSVP** = please reply; on an invitation

Unit 99

99.1
1. someone who aspires/wants to be something/someone else (from *want to be,* spoken quickly)
2. a roller skate with rubber wheels in a straight line (sometimes called a Rollerblade)
3. to switch TV channels/stations frequently, usually with a remote control
4. waiter or waitress
5. to calm down
6. ordinary mail sent through the postal service
7. a pill that's a tablet, but shaped like an oval capsule (a blended word: **capsule** + **tablet** = **caplet**)
8. to insult or show disrespect for someone

99.2
1. ozone holes
2. downsizing
3. Snowboarding
4. telecommuting
5. shock jocks
6. sound bites
7. wannabee
8. snail mail
9. RSI / repetitive strain injury
10. karaoke
11. chill (out)
12. voice mail
13. family leave
14. DNA fingerprinting
15. audio book

99.3
1. tourists who travel to places with unspoiled natural attractions, such as wildlife, wetlands (a blended word: **eco** for ecology or environment + **tourist** = **ecotourist**)
2. a family with two parents who bring with them children from their previous marriages
3. etiquette, or manners, on the Internet (a blended word: **net** + **etiquette** = **netiquette**)
4. software that is given away, or costs nothing (a blended word: **free** + **software** = **freeware**)
5. fear of computers (**cyber** for "computer" and **phobia** for "fear" = **cyberphobia**)

Unit 100

100.1

"Well, where shall I start? It was last summer and we were just sitting in the yard, not doing anything much. Anyway, I looked up and . . . see, we have this kind of long wall at the end of the yard, and it's . . . like . . . a highway for cats, for instance, that big fat black one you saw. Well, that one thinks it has a right of way over our vegetable patch, so . . . where was I? Oh yeah, I was looking at that wall, you know, daydreaming as usual, and all of a sudden there was this new cat I'd never seen before, or rather, it wasn't an ordinary cat at all . . . I mean, you'll never believe what it was . . ."

Comments:

Where/how shall I start/begin? This is a very common marker at the beginning of a story or monologue while the speaker is composing his/her thoughts.

Anyway is probably the most common marker in spoken storytelling to divide up the story into its different stages (introduction / main plot / resolution, etc.)

See is often used in informal talk instead of *you see*, when someone is clarifying or explaining something.

Kind of is an informal way of saying *approximate* or *more or less*. It can modify a noun or an adjective, e.g., **a kind of ladder** or **kind of dark.**

Like is often used when the speaker hesitates, or to make something less precise, a little more vague.

Where was I? is used when the speaker wants to come back to the main subject after an interruption or diversion into another point or topic.

Oh yeah or **Oh yes** is often used when the speaker resumes the story; it does not have to be an answer to a question from someone. **Anyway** or **anyhow** are used in the same way.

Or rather is used when the speaker changes to a different word or to a better / more accurate way of saying something.

I mean is used to explain something or expand or illustrate what the speaker is saying.

This extract is typical of the number of markers found in everyday informal talk. The speaker is not a "lazy" or "bad" speaker; everyone uses markers, even if they are not conscious of it or do not want to admit it! Informal conversation without markers sounds odd and strained, and a little too formal.

100.2 *Possible answers:*

1. A: Are you a baseball fan?
   B: **Well,** I like it, but I wouldn't say I'm exactly a fan.

2. A: He looks exhausted.
   B: Yes, he does.
   A: **Then again,** he has an awful lot of responsibility, so it's not surprising.

3. A: Which one is yours?
   B: **Let me see / Let's see . . .** it's this one here, yes, this one.

4. A: Are you looking forward to your camping trip next month?
   B: **To tell you the truth / To be honest,** I'm dreading it. I really hate camping.

100.3

1. First of all
2. In other words
3. For example / For instance
4. Next
5. so to speak
6. Finally
7. In summary ("In conclusion" would not be appropriate here, since it means "this is the end of the text," whereas this sentence provides a summing up of the arguments in the text.)